T0306045

State-Owned Enterprise's Ownership Reform

In reviewing the new round of state-owned enterprise (SOE) reforms characterized by mixed ownership since 2013 in China, this book systematically investigates the theoretical underpinnings, model options and approaches to implementation of SOE mixed-ownership reforms.

SOE reforms have functioned as an integral part of China's transformation to a market-oriented economy. Responding to the changing economic context and negative repercussions of earlier SOE reforms launched in the late 1990s, SOE mixed-ownership reforms encourage the participation of different types of capital and sounder management mechanisms. The author first reviews the impetus behind SOE mixed-ownership reforms and discusses how modern property rights theory and decentralized control theory perform as the theoretical underpinnings of the reforms. Based on cases of many completed SOE mixed-ownership reforms, the book summarizes and assesses the feasible models and implementation details of the reforms. It also examines how the reforms have impacted state-owned assets as well as executives' compensation and incentives, both of which run parallel to the core reforms surrounding ownership.

The book will appeal to professional readers studying entrepreneurial theory, corporate governance, China's SOE reforms and Chinese business and the economy, as well as investors and policy makers interested in the Chinese market and Chinese enterprise reform.

Zhigang Zheng is Professor of Finance at Renmin University of China. His research focuses on corporate governance and SOE reform in China, and he serves as a member of advisory boards in the field.

China Perspectives

The *China Perspectives* series focuses on translating and publishing works by leading Chinese scholars, writing about both global topics and China-related themes. It covers Humanities & Social Sciences, Education, Media and Psychology, as well as many interdisciplinary themes.

This is the first time any of these books have been published in English for international readers. The series aims to put forward a Chinese perspective, give insights into cutting-edge academic thinking in China, and inspire researchers globally.

To submit a book proposal, please contact the Taylor & Francis Publisher for the China Publishing Programme, Lian Sun (Lian.Sun@informa.com)

Titles in economics include:

Chinese Macroeconomy
Dynamic Models, Calibration and Analysis
Ninghua Sun

The Emission Reduction Effects of Spatial Agglomeration
Zhang Ke

China's Economic Development
Implications for the World
Cai Fang

State-Owned Enterprise's Ownership Reform
A Chinese Modernization Approach
Zhigang Zheng

The Supply-Side Revolution With Chinese Characteristics
Fang Fuqian

For more information about this series, please visit: www.routledge.com/China-Perspectives/book-series/CPH

State-Owned Enterprise's Ownership Reform

A Chinese Modernization Approach

Zhigang Zheng

Routledge
Taylor & Francis Group

LONDON AND NEW YORK

First published in English 2023
by Routledge
4 Park Square, Milton Park, Abingdon, Oxon OX14 4RN

and by Routledge
605 Third Avenue, New York, NY 10158

Routledge is an imprint of the Taylor & Francis Group, an informa business

© 2023 Zhigang Zheng

English version by permission of China Renmin University Press

British Library Cataloguing-in-Publication Data
A catalogue record for this book is available from the British Library

Library of Congress Cataloging-in-Publication Data
Names: Zheng, Zhigang, 1970– author.
Title: State–owned enterprise's ownership reform : a Chinese modernization approach / Zhigang Zheng. Other titles: Guo qi hun gai. English
Description: Abingdon, Oxon ; New York, NY : Routledge, 2023. | Series: China perspectives | Includes bibliographical references and index.
Identifiers: LCCN 2022035813 (print) | LCCN 2022035814 (ebook) | ISBN 9781032418766 (hardback) | ISBN 9781032421544 (paperback) | ISBN 9781003361404 (ebook)
Subjects: LCSH: Government business enterprises—China. | Government ownership—China. | Business enterprises—China.
Classification: LCC HD4318 .Z45813 2023 (print) | LCC HD4318 (ebook) | DDC 338.6/20951—dc23/eng/20220825
LC record available at https://lccn.loc.gov/2022035813
LC ebook record available at https://lccn.loc.gov/2022035814

ISBN: 978-1-032-41876-6 (hbk)
ISBN: 978-1-032-42154-4 (pbk)
ISBN: 978-1-003-36140-4 (ebk)

DOI: 10.4324/9781003361404

Typeset in Times New Roman
by Apex CoVantage, LLC

Contents

Figures

Tables

Preface

The reform of state-owned enterprises (SOEs) is undoubtedly the most important corporate governance issue in China today. As longtime observers and researchers of corporate governance theory and practice, my team members and I have attached close attention to SOEs and their reform as a very important research subject. In fact, the reform of SOEs has long been the principal concern of economic restructuring and has even epitomized the 40-year reform and opening-up in China in view of their historical position and unique role in maintaining the national economy and people's livelihood.

In 2013, a new round of SOE reform was launched against a special realistic background. SOEs had lost their dividend from reform carried out in the late 1990s and fell into a new development predicament, and many of them therefore became "zombie enterprises" or facing the economic decline caused by overcapacity. On the other hand, when the market-oriented economy entered a new stage, the public dissatisfaction with the continuing monopoly operation and unfair competition maintained by massive subsidies of the state capital was very high. The above facts show that the new round of reform features the introduction of strategic investors with private capital background to realize mixed ownership, which is known as the mixed-ownership reform of state-owned enterprises (or SOE mixed-ownership reform).

This new round of SOE mixed-ownership reform, in a way, can be interpreted as the continuation of the previous reform of the employee joint-stock and shareholding system that was conducted with the logic of capital socialization. However, the fact that the targets of capital socialization ranged from employees to ordinary outside investors and then to strategic investors with private capital stressed in the new round of reform shows that, after long-term practice, the practitioners of SOE reform began to realize that it was urgent to solve the problems of owner absence, the vagueness of managers' fiduciary duties, the soft budget constraints, the conflict in multi-objective incentive and Chinese-style insider control. Only by introducing strategic investors with a clear profit motive and possessed of professional operation and management ability and making them take the place of the absent owners could the governance structure fundamentally be improved and the management mechanism drastically changed in SOEs. The transformation of the state-owned assets management system from managing personnel, affairs and enterprises to managing capital would help promote the final formation of the mixed-ownership structure of introducing strategic investors. Therefore, after 40 years of arduous exploration, we are pleased to see that we have opened a relatively clear path for SOE reform. If we can forge ahead along this road, it is not only expected that the SOE mixed-ownership reform will become an important means to maintain and increase the value of state-owned assets under the institutional conditions based on the market mechanism for the resource allocation, but also the inclusion and acceptance of private capital and the realization of competition-neutral mixed-ownership reform will also help ease the public dissatisfaction with the monopoly operation and unfair competition of the state-owned assets and boost economic development in harmonious community.

This book first searches for theoretical underpinnings for the new round of SOE reform on the basis of a comprehensive analysis and summary of the consensus reached by people from circles of practice and theory as to why SOEs need reform. The modern property rights theory still underlies this new round of SOE reform, as it was intended to address the problems of the owner absence and then the long-term incentives of shareholders who apply and design incentives for managers by the introduction of private capital strategic investors with a clear profit motive. The modern property right theory proposed by Oliver Hart was to reveal how authority is distributed in enterprises and explain the mystery of the modern joint-stock company why investors are willing to buy shares issued by joint-stock companies; the theory is recognized by Chinese scholars as the theoretical basis of SOE restructuring. In the same way, the decentralized control theory applied to address excessive intervention is now the other theoretical basis for the new round of SOE reform. The decentralized control theory focuses on the establishment of an automatic error correction mechanism by introducing new shareholders to establish a competitive relationship between major shareholders.

In practice, on the one hand, it is necessary to introduce strategic investors with private capital into real economy, implement an employee stock ownership plan and decentralized control at the same time. On the other hand, it is required that the newly established or reorganized state-owned capital investment and operating companies manage capital instead of enterprises under the management system of state-owned assets. In the choice of mixed-ownership modes, this book summarizes and selects a few implementation modes and approaches based on our observation and survey of the enterprises which have finished mixed-ownership reform and the result evaluation of those whose reform is still underway. In terms of the implementation modes regarding the introduction of private capital strategic investors into mixed-ownership reform, we can not only choose the Unicom model, in which state-owned capital dominates in the equity structure and strategic investors dominate in the board organization in the area of basic and strategic industries, but also the Northern Trust model for the non-basic and strategic industries, in which strategic investors dominate in both the equity structure and the board organization. The key to the success of mixed-ownership reform is to solve the incentive compatibility problem of strategic investors with private capital backgrounds to effectively ensure their rights and interests. The essence of SOE mixed-ownership reform is to choose with which party to share uncertainty through equity financing. The experience of the steel industry shows that good strategic investors with private capital backgrounds are better cooperators to share uncertainty in the SOE mixed-ownership reform than are local and excellent practitioners of the same trade and bankers. The cooperation with them has enabled the SOE mixed-ownership reform to establish a brand-new incentive system, restore the original function of the board of directors and realize the separation of management and ownership from another aspect. In the choice of the implementation modes of SOE reform, we emphasize that it is the mixed ownership that can urge reform, and that it is better to mix than to merge, just like only opening-up can promote reform.

The book derives its structure and material from three sources. The first is a large amount of study that my team and I have carried out on SOE reform and the problems of SOEs' corporate governance. The second comes from a large number of articles I wrote for the *New Vision of Corporate Governance* – a column of FTChinese.com, *Caijing Magazine* and *the Economic Observer*. The third is keynote and brief speeches I made at high-end forums and closed-door discussions on SOE reform of various sizes and standards. During the course of writing this book, I adjusted, selected and supplemented relevant content around the above-mentioned structure so that a book of a systematic discussion of reasons, theoretical basis, approaches and routes concerning SOE mixed-ownership reform has come into publication.

I have benefited from discussions and exchanges with many entrepreneurs from SOEs, policy makers, experts and colleagues of SOE reform during the time I wrote the book. They include Song Zhiping (president of China Association for Public Companies, president of China Enterprise Reform and Development Society, and former chairman of China National Building Material Group); Chu Xuping (former director of the Research Center of the State-Owned Assets Supervision and Administration Commission [SASAC] of the State Council and president of the Branch-Board of Chinese State-Owned Property Exchanges Association); Xu Xuhong (deputy secretary general of the Branch-Board of Chinese State-Owned Property Exchanges Association); Li Jin (chief researcher of China Enterprise Research Institute); Lu Hanyang (researcher of the Research Center of SASAC of the State Council); Yu Xingxi (secretary general of the Listed Companies Association of Beijing); Ju Jinwen, Lu Tong and Zhong Jiyin (researchers of the Chinese Academy of Social Sciences); Li Weian, Ma Lianfu and Wu Lidong (professors of Nankai University); Gao Minghua (professor of Beijing Normal University); Wang Xian and Gao Hao of Tsinghua University; Wang Dupeng (reporter of Xinhua News Agency); Wu Si (editor of *China Policy Review*); Sun Bing (reporter of *China Economic Weekly* of *People's Daily*); Jiang Dan and Sun Linlin (reporters of *Securities Times*); Chen Xin, Gu Xueyu and Yan Xuefeng (editors of *Directors and Boards*); Feng Tao (editor of FTChinese.com); He Gang and Lu Ling (editors of *Caijing Magazine*); Mei Yanshi (secretary of the board of directors of the Bank of China); Qin Yongfa (secretary of the Discipline Inspection Commission of China Coal Technology & Engineering Group); Liu Qixian (secretary of the board of directors of Xinxing Cathay International Group Co., Ltd.); Wu Xiangjing (director of the Leadership Development Research Center of State Grid Corporation of China); Wang Zhen and Ding Quan of PetroChina; Liu Zhengang and Wu Lei of Baogang Mining Industry Co., Ltd.; and many others. I also want to offer a heartfelt thank you to all my colleagues who have helped and encouraged my research on SOE mixed-ownership reform.

This book presents some of my observations and thoughts on the ongoing SOE mixed-ownership reform, and it is certainly far from complete. Colleagues and readers are welcome to point out and correct my mistakes.

Zhigang Zheng

Introduction

Why Must SOEs Be Reformed?

The reform of state-owned enterprises is the microcosm of the opening-up and reform that we have been carrying out for the past 40 years. During this period, there have been several SOE reforms around the adjustment of ownership structure and relevant changes to the corporate governance system.

There are two facts from a realistic background that account for the new round of SOE reform with the typical characteristics of mixed-ownership launched in 2013. First, SOEs had lost their dividend from reform carried out in the late 1990s and fell again into the development predicament, and many of them had become zombie enterprises or suffered from benefit declines due to excessive production capacity. Let's review what happened to SOEs in 2014, a year after which the SOE mixed-ownership reform began. On the list of the top 500 enterprises jointly released by China Enterprise Confederation and China Enterprise Directors Association in 2014, there were 43 in the red, and among them, there was only one private enterprise while the rest SOEs generated losses in industries of coal, steel, nonferrous metals and chemicals, building materials and water transportation. As many as 14% of the 300 SOEs operated in the red. Forty-two of them lost as much as 72.66 billion yuan in total, and 10 central government-owned enterprises lost 38.57 billion yuan in total. In contrast, of the 200 private enterprises, only one lost 50 million yuan.

Second, the public expressed dissatisfaction with the state-owned assets, which have long operated on the strength of monopoly and heavy subsidies. Apart from those money-losing ones, the money-making SOEs had made a huge profit owing to their monopoly and massive subsidies from the government, which was unfair for the private enterprises in competition.

By a new round of SOE reform, private enterprises were expected to share profit from the SOE mixed-ownership reforms, which would start the structural reform in China and finally establish the principle of competitive neutrality and make the market play a fundamental role in allocating resources.

Under the above two aspects of the realistic background, the new round of SOE reform featuring mixed ownership, known as SOE mixed-ownership reform, was launched in 2013.

It is undeniable that the SOEs are less efficient than their private counterparts. The academic circle has developed the following theoretical consensus.

DOI: 10.4324/9781003361404-1

First, the owner absence prevalent in SOEs has blurred the original clear-cut fiduciary duties that the managers should have. According to the modern property rights theory, shareholders should undertake limited liabilities in proportion to the amounts of capital and responsibilities if they make wrong decisions. On the other hand, they exercise the owner's equity by voting at shareholders' meetings for final decisions on major issues. Shareholders consequently become the authority of the corporate governance; directors, managers included, shall legally hold to the shareholders fiduciary duties, including loyalty and diligence, so that they will work hard to maximize the shareholders' value. The governance structure described above shows that the fiduciary duty the directors hold to shareholders is relatively clear and the clear fiduciary duty defined as the judicial practice is conducive to the legal protection of shareholders' rights and interests.

For SOEs, the owners are absent. In this case, the responsibility undertaker is the state-owned assets which are nominally owned by the state while the senior directors who make decisions do not have to undertake any responsibility. Milton Friedman has a very witty statement:

> When a man spends his own money to buy something for himself, he is very careful about how much he spends and how he spends it. When a man spends his own money to buy something for someone else, he is still very careful about how much he spends, but somewhat less what he spends it on. When a man spends someone else's money to buy something for himself, he is very careful about what he buys, but he doesn't care at all how much he spends. And when a man spends someone else's money on someone else, he doesn't care how much he spends or what he spends it on.

Due to their vague fiduciary duties, SOEs with owner absence have obviously become a typical example of spending someone else's money on someone else.

Second, the pyramidal holding structure extends the principal-agent relationship, even blurring the vague fiduciary duty of the manager in the absence of the owner.

The SOEs, both centrally owned and locally owned, lie in the enterprise groups of various sizes with a pyramidal holding structure. The pyramidal holding structure resulted from the organizational system designed to meet the financing needs of the enterprises on the one hand, and on the other hand, it is related to some special policies made during the SOE reform and industrial restructuring. Every level of pyramidal holding structure implies that the controlling shareholders enter a principal-agent relationship with the controlled company, and the more levels there are, the more extended and complicated the relationship becomes.

In many of the state-owned holding groups, which frequently have seven or eight levels of controlling shareholders and in which thousands of legal entities participate, the managers are responsible to the major shareholder above them but give little consideration to the state-owned assets that ultimately bear losses due to the wrong decisions they make and assurance of rights and interests of public shareholders behind the state-owned capital. In this way, in each level of state-owned assets with a pyramidal structure, the presidents as the heads of major shareholders become the actual controllers of their levels. If the principal-agent relationship is extended, insider control in the absence of owners tends to aggravate.

Third is the theory of soft budget constraints. Zombie enterprises and excessive production capacity have drawn much attention from theorists and practitioners as important issues in the supply-side structural reform we are pushing ahead with. However, Professor Xu Chenggang says, "These are old problems and these arise as expected."[1] If his idea is true, zombie enterprises and excessive production capacity actually resulted from the soft budget constraints proposed by János Kornai many years ago.

The so-called soft budget constraints refer to the financial institution's failure to adhere to the business agreement to supply capital to an enterprise which in turn borrows more money than its profit and ability to return. For equity financing, dividend distribution should not be an obligation of the company unless the board of directors make a commitment; thus the enterprises engaged in equity financing are bound by soft constraints.

Different from the soft-constraints equity financing, enterprises engaged in debt financing in the form of bank loans or issuance of corporate bonds are bound by hard constraints. The enterprise will face legal proceedings initiated by the bank and other creditors and liquidation or bankruptcy if it fails to repay its principal and interest on time. But for SOEs that are politically associated with the government in nature, the state-owned banks will not liquidate the insolvent ones; they will provide them with more loans to save them from bankruptcy in order to maintain employment, tax increases and social stability, thus softening the hard constraints. Practice like this is figuratively called state paternalism by Kornai. Dongbei Special Steel Group Co., Ltd. is a good case in point of debt-to-equity swap. In order to resolve the debt crisis of Dongbei Special Steel, the local government proposed a debt-to-equity swap plan without liquidation again in 2016, but had to give it up because the creditors were unanimously opposed to it. The crisis was finally resolved by Shen Wenrong, a private steel magnate in Jiangsu who came to hold a controlling interest in Dongbei Special Steel Group Co., Ltd. This case shows that the accidental privatization as interpreted by the media was the last-ditch move of the local government that had made repeated efforts to resolve the crisis. The last example indicates that debt-to-equity swaps manipulated by the government are regarded as the soft budget constraints in the guise of the market operations.

In the Chinese capital market, there is another kind of implicit soft budget constraints. When a poorly run listed state-owned company is warned of risks in its stocks, it will gain support from the state-owned holding enterprise groups that control it. But this company remains poorly performed long after it gets support and even loses more money with more support and ends up being another type of zombie enterprise.

Zombie enterprises and excessive production capacity are real background and direct causes for this round of SOE reform with the mixed ownership as the breach.

Behind zombie enterprises and excessive production capacity are the soft budget constraints under the banner of state paternalism. The soft budget constraints not only led to the inefficiency of SOEs in the era of the planned economy but also caused their profits to decline nowadays. It has troubled SOEs since their inception. The key to making them become business entities responsible for their own profits or losses is to change state-owned assets from managing enterprises to managing capital and share risks with other social capitals, and the mixed-ownership enterprises will be real competitive entities in the market.

Fourth, there are conflicts in multi-objective incentives in the governance model of managing both capital and enterprises. For SOEs which have finished shareholding system reform, in addition to establishing capital management approach by directly holding controlling shares, the central government and local governments have adopted the traditional top-down evaluation mechanism of personnel appointment, removal and promotion to enterprises management. This is how the management of capital and enterprises has taken shape. In addition to the holding group of SASAC with controlling shares of listed companies to carry out its duties as a major shareholder, SOEs generally adopt the top-down method to appoint the chairman and chief executive officer (CEO) by superior departments. Although the procedure requires nomination of the board of directors and voting at the shareholders' meeting, the dominant share inherent in the ownership structure of the SOEs and the political and economic influence of state-owned assets (SOA) management system make it hard to question and challenge appointments made by higher authorities. As a result, the directors, CEOs and other senior executives find that they shall undertake fiduciary duty for shareholders as stipulated in the Company Law and Articles of Incorporation on the one hand, and on the other hand, they shall be subject to supervision and assessment of higher authorities and state property management organizations.

Under such a system, senior executives of SOEs prefer to achieve promotion in ranks or politics through image projects and face jobs to attract attention from their superiors, which has become a focus of consideration for some SOE executives in their short term of office. However, these image projects will damage the interests of shareholders in the long run and become a special agency cost that outside shareholders have to bear. Therefore, some practices that seem to strengthen supervision and promote incentives have distorted the behavior of some SOE executives.

The governance model described above determines the direct engagement of state property management organizations in managing enterprises by means of appointing and assessing directors, CEOs and senior executives. This entrusts the shareholders' ownership interest to the third party that can partly and even rarely shoulder responsibility, further blurring the vague fiduciary duty between the SOE shareholders and the directors. The shareholders who have to bear consequences brought by decisions have no right to make decisions, while the third party who cannot take full responsibility has the right to make decisions.

What's more, when shareholders and the third parties run into conflicts of interest, the introduction of the third parties will put the directors in a position of multiple management. For example, the SOE hemmed in the governance model of managing both capital and enterprises, in contrast to the private enterprise, has to operate for profit, and has to perform its social obligations to stabilize prices, promote employment, increase taxes, maintain social order and perform public service like poverty relief, which puts SOEs in a multi-tasking, multi-objective business management situation. Theoretically, in the situation of multiple responsibilities, the SOE directors may damage shareholders' interest on the pretext of avoiding harming the third party's interest and even pursue their personal gains on the pretext of protecting the rights and interests of the third party and shareholders but damaging their interest in the end. This circumstance bears out what Friedman says: "The social responsibility of business is to increase its profits" (Friedman, 1970).

We realize that the SOE governance model of managing both capital and enterprises led to incentive conflicts of senior executives in a multi-objective situation and blurred fiduciary duties between shareholders and directors. It was because of this realization that the administrative department of the state-owned assets clearly charted the course for the new round of SOE reform featuring a change from managing enterprises to managing capital, and market-based selection and employment of professional managers instead of the bureaucratic top-down model.

Fifth, there is the problem of Chinese-style insider control around the presidents of SOEs. Since SOE senior executives are chosen through the top-down mechanism, directors who are appointed as presidents usually have special seniority and status. Let's take Cai Guohua, the former chairman of Hengfeng Bank, as an example. Before he started working in Hengfeng Bank, Cai Guohua was a member of the Standing Committee of Municipal Party Committee, vice mayor and secretary of the Party Committee of SASAC of Yantai City. Neither Yantai Lantian Investment as the superior holding company of Hengfeng Bank nor Yantai SASAC, which wholly controls Yantai Lantian Investment, had limited leverage on Cai Guohua. The largest shareholder of Hengfeng Bank had little control over the insider control headed by Cai Guohua; it became the power for Cai to oppose other shareholders who have the power of veto and even send them the message "I am the largest shareholder. Your opposition doesn't count." The cases of the division of public funds by senior executives, the scandalous employee stock ownership plan and the equity mystery which happened in Hengfeng Bank are all typical of insider control.

It is worth pointing out that the problem of insider control at Hengfeng Bank is different from that inherent in UK and US companies. In the latter, a high dispersion of corporate equity and the equity incentive plans for managers have gradually created entrenchment effects, which leads to the insider control problems centered on managers who are the objects of equity incentives. In contrast, the insider control problems of Hengfeng Bank were obviously not due to the above two reasons but to the top-down appointment mechanism of senior executives and the special status of chairman of SOEs, and also have special relations to the political, social, historical, cultural and economic factors under the background of China's capital market system. We call the problem of insider control, which is centered on the chairman rather than the manager, formed in this unique institutional background, Chinese-style insider control. It is an urgent problem worthy of our attention and efforts to address in the corporate governance peculiar to the Chinese capital market.

How do we describe SOEs obsessed with problems such as soft budget constraints, blurred fiduciary duties, conflicts of multi-objective incentive and Chinese-style insider control? A study of the history of enterprise organizational evolution shows that there are two dimensions. Based on the degree of specialized division of labor, the first dimension includes enterprises with low and high specialization. Due to the emergence of modern joint-stock limited companies, the improvement of efficiency brought by the social division of labor realized by capital socialization and managerial professionalization has become one of the important reasons for the substantial growth of human wealth in the past 250 years. Therefore, the joint-stock limited company is "one of the most important inventions in modern human history", in Butler's words. The efficiency improvement brought by the specialized division of labor realized by the separation of ownership and management is the essence of modern joint-stock companies.

The second division includes enterprises with less and serious agency problems according to the organizational type of enterprises. Conflicts between managers and shareholders occur when ownership is separated from the right of management in modern stock companies.

The two dimensions described above enable us to divide the enterprises into the four types illustrated in Table 0.1. At the top left is the type of enterprise with a low degree of social specialization but less serious agency problems. The family workshop is a typical example of this enterprise organizational type. In the family workshop, the owner is not only the proprietor but also the operator. The degree of specialization is low, and the production efficiency is correspondingly low. However, because the ownership and management rights of the family workshop are unified, there is no agency conflict between professional outside managers and shareholders, therefore the agency problem is not serious. At the bottom right is the enterprise type with a high degree of specialization but serious agency problems. In the United States in the 1920s and 1930s, many companies failed to establish reasonable governance structure when they completed specialized

Table 0.1 Enterprise Types Based on Specialized Division of Labor and Agency Problem Severity

	(Managing capital and enterprises) Low degree of specialized division of labor	(External financing, risk sharing, professional managers) High degree of specialized division of labor
Less serious agency problems	Family workshop (neoclassical capitalist enterprises)	Modern joint-stock limited company with good corporate governance structure
Serious agency problems	SOE (longtime absence of principal agent and owner)	Joint-stock limited companies without a good corporate governance structure

division of labor with capital socialization and managerial professionalization and improved efficiency. At that time, agency conflicts occurred frequently which was one of the causes of the global economic depression.

The top right of the chart shows the type of enterprises with a high degree of specialized division of labor and less serious agency problems. These companies are characterized by a high degree of capital socialization and managerial professionalism on the one hand. On the other hand, they solve the agency conflict between managers and shareholders by the design of a performance-based manager compensation contract, the launch of a stock option incentive plan, a small scale and centering on independent directors (even the others being independent directors except CEO as the internal director), the establishment of the board of directors based on the separation of the CEO and the chairman, as well as the construction of institutional environment such as legal system to protect investors' rights. After numerous corporate governance experiments which began in the 1920s and 1930s, many companies have grown into models with a high degree of specialized division of labor and good corporate governance.

Based on the two dimensions mentioned above, the four types of enterprises include those indicated at the bottom left, whose rights of management and ownership are not separate and whose capital and enterprises are still mixed in management with low degree of specialized division of labor and sharp agency conflict. Some SOEs, when measured against this criterion, are possessed with two characteristics as shown above: the central government and local government manage capital through the state-owned assets management chain and also exert actual influence on operation and production by adopting a top-down personnel appointment system and promotion and assessment of SOE leaders. Besides operation and production for profit, SOEs have to perform their social obligations to stabilize prices, promote employment, increase taxes, and maintain social order and perform public service like poverty relief, which puts SOEs in a business performance and management situation where they have multiple tasks and objectives to take. They have to suffer from various restraints and restrictions – management of personnel, affairs and enterprises – which disables them from real separation of ownership and rights of management, and they are organizationally similar to capitalist enterprises of new classicism. Meanwhile, they are also obsessed with problems like the owner absence, the extended principal-agent relationship, the Chinese-style insider control centered on the chairman, and the agency problems of SOEs. To a great extent, neither have they gotten rid of the intervention of the ownership to the rights of management like a family workshop nor improved the work efficiency by specialized division of labor to solve the agency problem that a family workshop does not have. All of this makes SOEs look like neoclassical capitalist enterprises with agency problems. We have seen SOEs are usually prosperous for the first few years before they sink into the vicious cycle of profit decline, successive losses, heavy debts, government-directed merger and reorganization, and rebirth.

The two objective dimensions of enterprise's organization type remind us that for the goals of the corporate governance policy, we should not only see the agency conflict caused by the separation of ownership and management rights of modern joint-stock companies but also the great efficiency improvement brought by the specialized division of labor with capital socialization and manager professionalization. Specialized division of labor (separation of ownership and management) is essential to the improvement of efficiency of modern stock companies, Meanwhile, it causes agency problems between managers and shareholders. Literature of the traditional corporate governance focuses too much on the agency problem between the manager and shareholders during the separation of ownership and the right of management while ignoring the improvement of efficiency brought by such separation. Alibaba's partner system and JD's unequal voting rights are positive explorations and beneficial attempts to realize the specialized and in-depth division of labor through the specialization of business management decisions made by the entrepreneurial team and the specialization of risk-sharing with dispersed outside shareholders. Therefore, the correct design concept of modern corporate governance should be how to achieve a balance between the improvement of efficiency brought by specialized division of labor and the reduction of agency cost to realize the win-win cooperation between shareholders and managers. This concept of modern corporate governance is applicable not only to new economic enterprises like Alibaba and JD.com but also to SOEs actively engaged in mixed-ownership reform. It is one of the goals of the new round of SOE ownership reform to realize the separation of ownership and the right of management and mutual benefit for managers and shareholders on the basis of specialized division of labor between them.

As the breakthrough of the new round of SOE reform, the mixed-ownership reform is not only an important means to realize the purpose of maintaining and increasing the value of state-owned assets under the condition of establishing the market mechanism as the basic system of resource allocation, but also a reform that includes and accepts private capital for competitive neutrality, thus helping ease the public's dissatisfaction with the monopoly and unfair competition of state-owned assets.

The Theoretical Underpinnings of the SOE Mixed-Ownership Reform and Three Levels of Reform

It can be argued that the introduction of strategic investors has been the focus of the 40-year SOE reform for the most part. We sometimes emphasized the capital socialization realized by the joint-stock system transformation, so that some well-performed SOEs were listed, for instance. We sometimes focused on the capital socialization of the employee joint-stock cooperative system that used to be popular within enterprises. Confronted with problems like the absence of owners, soft budget constraints, blurred fiduciary duties, multi-objective incentive conflicts and Chinese-style insider control, mixed ownership that emphasizes more on the introduction of strategic investors with private capital background is once again expected to be an important breakthrough in the current round of SOE reform.

In practice, the new round of SOE mixed-ownership reform focuses on the following two levels. First, at the level of real economy, it aims to achieve mixed ownership through the introduction of strategic investors with private capital background in order to improve the governance structure and transform the operation mechanism. Second, at the level of the state-owned assets management system, it aims to shift from managing personnel, affairs and enterprises to managing capital so as to realize the purpose of preserving and increasing the value of state-owned assets.

If we look for the theoretical support of the SOE mixed-ownership reform by introducing strategic investors with private capital background from the theoretical origin and literature development, we will find the modern property rights theory and decentralized control theory playing this role.

Modern Property Rights Theory

The modern property rights theory put forward by scholars represented by Professor Oliver Hart of Harvard University, winner of the 2016 Nobel Prize in Economics, has always been one of the theoretical foundations of China's SOE reform.

From the perspective that contracts in reality are rarely fully detailed, Hart points out that if investors are worried that they will be fleeced after investing under incomplete contracts, their incentive for investment will be insufficient. Then, how to encourage investors to invest? Hart thinks that investors are only willing to invest when they become owners and have residual control over the matters not specified in the incomplete contracts. This theory well explains the mystery of the modern joint-stock company, that is, why investors are willing to invest in a public company although its CEO is a stranger to them. The reason is that after they buy shares of the company, the listed company makes a credible commitment to them who, as shareholders, will enjoy collective legal protection of their rights and interests.

Hart's modern property rights theory reveals why investors are willing to become shareholders on the one hand. On the other hand, it explains who is the most motivated to supervise managers among many stakeholders such as employees, suppliers and communities of modern joint-stock companies. As Hart sees it, shareholders who collectively enjoy the owner's equity should enjoy the following two basic rights. The first of these rights, the so-called residual claim, refers to the right to claim the enterprise income after deducting the fixed contract payments such as the salary of employees, the interest of bank loans and so on; that is, the shareholders who become the owner rank behind the beneficiaries of contract such as creditors and employees, and bear limited liability within the limit of capital contribution. This is the obligation of shareholders as owners. The benefit ranks after other stakeholders means that shareholders taking risks are more concerned about the operation of the enterprise than other stakeholders. Therefore, shareholders who take risks become a group with a clear profit motive and a strong willingness to actively participate in corporate governance among many stakeholders in modern joint-stock companies. This is the motivation behind the new round of

SOE mixed-ownership reform that hopes to solve the problems of the absence of owners and blurred fiduciary duties which have long existed by introducing strategic investors with clear profit motive and private capital background.

The second right that shareholders enjoy is residual control. Residual control refers to the right to decide unspecified in the (incomplete) contracts by which shareholders vote for final decision on important issues that are unspecified in incomplete contracts at general meetings, which is a right enjoyed by all shareholders as owners. The residual control endows shareholders with the right to make the final decision at the shareholders' meetings on important issues; this means that they not only have motivation but also have the legal right to supervise managers in comparison with other stakeholders. The shareholders who collectively enjoy the owner's equity can bear the company's future business risks within the limit of their capital contribution on the one hand, and on the other hand, they make a final decision on the major issues of the company's development by voting at the general meeting of shareholders, on account of which the shareholders become the authority of corporate governance. The new round of SOE mixed-ownership reform aims to resolve the owner absence faced by SOEs by way of introducing strategic investors with private capital background. These investors are supposed to share risks with state-owned assets and to supervise managers and return the authority of corporate governance to shareholders to facilitate transformation of SOEs into the modern enterprise system on the strength of platforms of boards of shareholders and directors and legal protection. The property rights system is important in the new round of SOE mixed-ownership reform because it fundamentally solves the long-term incentive problem for shareholders by introducing and designing the incentive mechanism for managers. Therefore, the modern property rights theory is still one of the theoretical bases on which the new round of SOE mixed-ownership reform depends.

Decentralized Control Theory

With the aim of solving the problem of the owner absence prevalent in SOEs and under the guidance of modern property rights theory, the 40-year SOE reform has undergone at least three periods of arduous exploration and beneficial trials.

The first period was the early stage of capital socialization through the joint-stock cooperative system. The joint-stock enterprises in China were gradually established and developed through the transformation of traditional SOEs or collective enterprises under the planned economic system. Employee stock ownership was in a way the starting point of China's joint-stock reform of SOEs. Through the joint-stock cooperative system, employees of SOEs became shareholders with capital socialized within the enterprise at the same time.

The second period was the stage of capital socialization through listing and joint-stock reform. Listing and joint-stock reform made the socialization of capital extend to the outside and realized the capital socialization in the whole society. The joint-stock reform of SOEs directly promoted the establishment of China's capital market in the 1990s. Some SOEs with excellent assets after reorganization were given priority to go to public, and a standardized corporate governance framework was established, so that SOEs began to move forward towards a modern enterprise system. Professor Li Yining put forward his famous theory of "well-performed SOEs go to public first" (he described it figuratively as "pretty girl marries first")[2] under the given background.

For those state-owned listed companies which had already completed capital socialization through listing, long before 2015 when China's capital market entered the era of decentralized equity, the state-owned assets often held controlling shares as the controlling shareholder and developed a governance paradigm of domination of a single shareholder. Although listed companies, as representatives of excellent enterprises, had taken a crucial step in the establishment of modern enterprise system and corporate governance norms, retail investors could not effectively participate in corporate governance and form equity checks and balances. As a result, state-controlled listed companies performed worse than the listed private enterprises over the long term, and those unlisted SOEs yet to complete capital socialization and without the governance structure of power checks and balances performed even worse.

With regard to SOEs which have completed capital socialization and unlisted state-owned assets companies troubled with the lack of power checks and balances and effective supervision, it is clearly pointed out in the new round of SOE mixed-ownership reform that the introduction of strategic investors with private capital background for achieving the mixed-ownership is critical to realize capital socialization in the reform. Therefore, the SOE mixed-ownership reform underway is the third period of capital socialization of the 40-year SOE reform in China.

Unlike the previous SOE reforms that focus on capital socialization realized by the change in the shareholding system, the new round of reform gives priority to introducing strategic investors with private capital background to realize mixed ownership, for which we should look for special theoretical support besides the modern property rights theory of capital socialization.

Like Hart's modern property rights theory – the point of which is to reveal how authority is distributed in a corporation and to answer the mystery of the modern joint-stock company as to why investors are willing to buy shares issued by the joint-stock companies – the decentralized control which is used to address the problem of excessive intervention is taken as the other basic theory of the new round of SOE reform.

The core decentralized control theory lies in the prevention of excessive supervision conducted with the supremacy of a single share. The introduction of new investors is conducive to the establishment of the competitive relationship between major shareholders and an automatic error correction mechanism, which can help effectively avoid the excessive supervision and decision-making errors caused by the dominance of major shareholders and constraints on managers and avoid the problem of insider control. This theory can provide good suggestions for SOEs on how to introduce strategic investors through the mixed-ownership reform and solve the various problems we are facing at present. Therefore, it is quite necessary that we take the decentralized control theory as one of the important theories for the new round of SOE mixed-ownership reform.

The Vanke equity dispute in 2015 marked that China's capital market has entered into the era of decentralization, and the institutional environment of decentralized control among the main shareholders of state-owned listed companies has formed. In the future, the corporate governance of SOEs can rely on the competition between major shareholders to alleviate excessive supervision from major state-owned shareholders who manage both capital and enterprises under the previous ownership structure of domination of a single shareholder and the tension brought by the insider control due to owner absence.

The new round of SOE mixed-ownership reform was supposed to help restore the legal status to shareholders as the authority of corporate governance by introducing strategic investors with private capital background, so as to clarify the legal fiduciary duties between directors as trustees and all shareholders. The directors of the company must strictly fulfill the obligations of loyalty and diligence to maximize the value of all shareholders, not just some shareholders.

In the process of SOE mixed-ownership reform, we should actively promote the reform on three levels in order to make SOEs real modern enterprises by focusing on how to solve the common problems of owner absence, soft budget constraint, multi-objective conflict and Chinese-style insider control shared by SOEs.

The first level concerns shareholders. The introduction of strategic investors with clear profit motive and private capital background enables us to reestablish the authority of shareholders in corporate governance and put the absent owners in position. The analysis made above shows that in the three periods of the 40-year SOE reform, we once tried to put the absent owner in position by making the employee-turned shareholders through introducing the joint-stock cooperative system and dispersed outside shareholders through the joint-stock system reform. The reform during that stage seemed to have introduced shareholders through capital socialization, but it failed to make them take the place of the absent owners who could supervise the entrusted directors. The new round of SOE mixed-ownership reform clearly proposes the introduction of strategic investors with clear profit motive and private capital background to form the decentralized control of equity check-and-balance SOEs as a possible solution to the absence of owners at a deeper level. This is the direction that must be made clear in the new round of SOE mixed-ownership reform.

As we can see, the strategic investors with private capital background introduced into the mixed-ownership reform should first become the risk sharers who may make mistakes in their decision-making. They have to share risks with other shareholders. This can avoid the situation where previous decision-making mistakes have to be paid for by financial subsidies from taxpayers and harden previously softened budget constraints. Second, the power balance formed by strategic investors has become an important error correction mechanism for wrong decisions. Strategic investors with a clear profit motive and their appointed directors prevent major shareholders from making business decisions that may damage their own interests.

The second level concerns the state-owned asset management system. SASAC can change its role of managing personnel, affairs and enterprises to managing enterprises through the newly constructed and reorganized investment and operating platform. This reform can not only avoid the conflict between regulators and managers embodied by SASAC but also promote the establishment of the authoritative position of shareholders in corporate governance, thus helping solve the problem of the owner absence of SOEs through the changed role of SASAC.

The third level concerns the shareholding structure. The flat and pyramidal structure can match the cash flow rights reflecting capacity of responsibility with the control right reflecting influence. The pyramidal shareholding structure has by far caused many social (widening gap between the rich and the poor), political (collusion between officials and businessmen) and economic problems (tunneling,[3] capital operation and minority shareholders' speculation). The extended principal-agent relationship of pyramidal holding structure, has furthermore directly aggravated the absence of owners, which has become one of the institutional predispositions for the formation of Chinese-style insider control. In order to create an external environment for SOE mixed-ownership reform with the goals of addressing the problem of the owner absence and eliminating the demerits inherent in the pyramidal holding structure, it is time for the Chinese capital market to say no to the pyramidal shareholding structure.

Implementation Paths for SOE Mixed-Ownership Reform

Although there has been a goal set for shortening the controlling chain of SOEs, what we do for the time being is most to increase the management and control efficiency which is not inevitably related to the improvement of the external capital market and the goal of solving the problem of owner absence. We believe that it will take a long time to reach a consensus on the elimination of pyramidal holding structure in theory and practice. Therefore, at present, the SOE mixed-ownership reform mainly concentrates on the adjustment of equity structure and the rationalization of state-owned asset management system. In order to achieve the purpose of the above two levels of mixed-ownership reform, we have gradually formed three implementation paths in practice.

Path One: Introduction of Outside Investors in the Real Economy

The choice of outside investors in the real economy should be closely related to whether the SOE belongs to the basic and strategic industry. SOEs in different industries should be selected for classified reform. State-owned assets should maintain controlling shares in basic and strategic industries even though they require a large amount of external capital, while in non-basic and strategic industries, controlling stakes can be transferred to private capital. In this way, two models of SOE mixed-ownership reform have been developed for introducing external capital: (1) the Unicom model, being the first central enterprise to press ahead with the mixed-ownership reform; and (2) the Northern Trust model carried out in the practice of the SOE reform in the city of Tianjin. The former is a case of the reform of centrally controlled enterprises belonging to the basic and strategic industry, and the latter is a typical example of the local SOEs belonging to the non-basic and strategic industry.

In August 2017, China Unicom Group reduced its shares in China Unicom from 60% to 36.67% after attracting strategic investors such as China Life and BATJ (Baidu, Alibaba Corporation, Tencent and JD.COM) to hold 36.19% of its shares. In the equity structure of China Unicom, which had completed its reform, Tencent and Baidu, two strategic investors with private capital backgrounds, held 5.18% and 3.3% of its shares, respectively. But the other five major shareholders held far fewer shares than China Unicom Group, which continued to have control of the company according to paragraph 2 of Article 84 of the *Measures for the Administration of Acquisition of Listed Companies*.

Of those strategic investors attracted to invest in the mixed-ownership reform of China Unicom, China Life with its state-owned assets background became the largest shareholder by buying 10% of China Unicom's shares, exceeding those of Baidu and Tencent with private capital background. As a state-owned investment and operating company, China Structural Reform Fund held 8.96% of the shares of China Unicom in this mixed-ownership reform. In addition, China Unicom granted 850 million restricted shares to its core employees.

The China Unicom Group, holding 36% of China Unicom's shares, retained more power than a one-vote veto, which is sensitive enough to show that China Unicom is still in the hands of the state-owned assets with the participation of China Life and China Structural Reform Fund, and those Internet giants backed by private capital are more competitive than cooperative. This is because China Unicom is a large, centrally controlled enterprise, and more importantly, it belongs to the basic and strategic industries.

As we know, the strategic investors with clear profit motive and private capital background will have enough motivation to participate in SOE mixed-ownership reform only on the premise that their own rights and interests are fully protected. How could China Unicom attract strategic investors like BATJ being incentive compatible to participate in its mixed-ownership reform despite the fact that China Unicom Group was still in control of the company?

The answer was given when China Unicom declared its new board of directors on February 8, 2018. Besides the expansion of the board of directors from 7 to 13 people, of the eight non-independent directors, five came from strategic investors such as China Life, Baidu, Alibaba, Tencent and JD.com. Robin Li, Hu Xiaoming and other business stars joined the new board of directors of China Unicom. Among them, Baidu, which held about 3% of the shares, had one of the eight non-independent director candidates on the board of directors of China Unicom, accounting for 12.5% of the total number of the candidates, and became a typical example of excessive appointment of directors by non-controlling shareholders. By accepting more or over-appointed directors from the strategic investors in the board of China Unicom, the controlling shareholder China Unicom Group has taken into account the interests of strategic investors at least at the board level, offsetting the lack of effective protection to the interests of strategic investors when there was a single large shareholder, so as to make them incentive compatible to some extent. Thus, allowing strategic investors to over-appoint directors to protect their interests becomes an important experience for China Unicom to make investors with the private capital background incentive compatible and participate in the mixed-ownership reform of their own accord while maintaining a controlling stake of China Unicom Group at the equity level. From the case of China Unicom's mixed-ownership reform, we can see that only by fully protecting the interests of all parties involved in the reform and encouraging them to be compatible with one another in terms of incentive can all parties concerned truly achieve win-win cooperation and the mixed-ownership reform finally succeed.

The reform experience of China Unicom can thus be summarized as the Unicom model characterized by state-owned assets dominant in the shareholding structure while strategic investors dominant in the board of directors. The former characteristic is determined by the attribute of the basic and strategic industry, which contains China Unicom. And, China Unicom Group has a controlling interest to exercise the one-vote veto if necessary. The board of directors mainly involves daily operations, management and decisions; consequently, opinions from business elites like Robin Li need to be taken more frequently. The combination between them reflects the transformation of the corporate governance philosophy that we emphasize – it should gradually shift from the traditional concept of merely highlighting the protection of shareholders' rights and interests to the new concept of striking a balance between guaranteeing shareholders' rights and interests and encouraging entrepreneurial teams to invest in human capital as far as business model innovation is concerned.

Another example of introducing outside investors to the real economy is the mixed-ownership reform practice of Northern International Trust Co., Ltd., a local SOE in Tianjin.

On November 20, 2018, the official signing on the mixed-ownership reform of Tianjin Northern International Trust Co., Ltd. marked the completion of mixed-ownership reform of the first non-banking financial institution of state-owned shareholding system in Tianjin. Founded in October 1987, Northern Trust is one of the earliest trust companies in China.

Through the mixed-ownership reform, there were three new shareholders of private enterprises successfully introduced into Northern Trust: Rizhao Steel Holding Group Co., Ltd.; Shanghai Zhongtong Ruide Investment Group Co., Ltd.; and Yike Zhengrun Investment Group Co., Ltd. They accepted a total of 50.07% transferred equity. Among them, Rizhao Steel held 18.30% and became the largest shareholder, Shanghai Zhongtong Ruide held 17.65% and Yike Zhengrun held 14.12%. TEDA Investment Holding Co., Ltd., originally the largest shareholder with state-owned assets background, had its equity diluted to 17.94%, thus becoming the second largest shareholder. In fact, during the mooted stage, Northern Trust had made it clear that it did not seek control. In the description of relevant documents, Northern Trust clearly puts forward that "the private enterprises shall be in an absolute controlling position whether in single shareholding proportion or over-all shareholding proportion."[4] We can see that the mixed-ownership reform mode of not seeking control is largely a practical measure that some local governments have to take to get rid of the financial and operational difficulties of locally administered SOEs that are not in basic and strategic industries. For the same reason, not seeking control may also become a common practice for local governments to implement SOE mixed-ownership reform pertaining to non-basic and strategic industries.

Rizhao Steel Holding Group Co., Ltd., the new largest shareholder of Northern Trust, held 18.30% of the shares. It was only 0.36% higher than the second largest shareholder, TEDA Investment Holding Co., Ltd. which holds a 17.94% stake, and which in turn was merely 0.65 higher than the 17.65% share of the third largest shareholder, Shanghai Zhongtong Ruide. As the largest shareholder with a slim advantage, Rizhao Steel was entitled to recommend the chairman of the board. As we can see, although the chairman was appointed by Rizhao Steel, Northern Trust would play the model role in equity balance in corporate governance practice. The largest shareholder Rizhao Steel and its appointed chairman would not only be under the supervision of TEDA Investment Holding with state-owned background but also shareholders such as Shanghai Zhongtong Ruide and Yike Zhengrun Investment with private capital background.

Comparatively speaking, Northern Trust pertaining to the non-basic and strategic industry, whose mixed-ownership reform seems to be more thorough than that of China Unicom in terms of shareholding structure and the board of directors, better helps SOEs change their roles from managing personnel, affairs and enterprises to managing capital. TEDA Investment Holdings, the second largest shareholder with a state-owned background, will participate in the corporate governance of Northern Trust acting as an investor and the counterweight.

Path Two: Launching the Employee Stock Ownership Plan (ESOP) While Introducing Outside Investors to the Real Economy

In August 2016, the State-Owned Assets Supervision and Administration Commission (SASAC), the Ministry of Finance (MOF) and the China Securities Regulatory Commission (CSRC) jointly issued *Opinions on the Pilot Project of ESOP for State-Owned Holding Enterprises With Mixed Ownership* to launch the employee stock ownership plan, improve corporate governance structure, and shift the operation mechanism while encouraging SOEs to carry out mixed-ownership reform. As the last piece of the puzzle of its mixed-ownership reform, China Unicom launched the employee stock ownership plan on March 21, 2018. It granted no more than 847.88 million restricted shares to 7,855 middle managers, core managers and professional talents ranging from secretaries of the board of directors to financial chiefs, which accounted for about 2.8% of its total equity at that time.

Path Three: Transforming the Regulatory Function From Managing Enterprises to Managing Capital by the Capitalization of State-Owned Assets in the Reform of the SOA Management System

"Managing capital" refers to an access to reforming operational state-owned assets, enabling the state-owned capital to transform from SOEs with a special form of value physically to the one that can be clearly defined in financial language, has a sound liquidity, and enter the market for operation. The capitalization of state-owned assets can be achieved by the establishment or restructuring of investment and operating agencies acting as the interface between government and market, and the transformation of corporate system in former SOEs. The SASAC has become the watchdog for state-owned investment and operating agencies. Thus, after separating from the state-owned investment and operating institutions, SASAC has no direct bearing on entity enterprises invested by the investment and operating companies of state-owned capital in terms of property rights. In addition, it can no longer bypass the investment and operating institutions and never be entitled to interfere with their invested companies. As a matter of course, government functions and enterprise management can be separated.

Since 2016, the SASAC has launched a pilot project in eight companies including the State Development and Investment Corporation (SDIC); China National Cereals, Oils and Foodstuffs Import and Export Corporation (COFCO); China Shenhua Energy Company Limited; China Baowu Steel Group Corporation Limited; China Minmetals Corporation; China Merchants Group; China Communications Construction Company (CCCC); and Poly Group. This was aimed at delegating 18 items of its original powers such as asset allocation, compensation distribution, market-oriented employment and institutional reform to state-owned investment and operating companies (industry groups). Meanwhile, China Chengtong Holding Group Co., Ltd. and China Reform Holding Corporation Ltd. were designated by SASAC as state-owned capital companies.

Taking practice in Tianjin as an example, we focus on how to transform the regulatory function from managing enterprises to managing capital by the capitalization of state-owned assets in the reform of state-owned asset regulation system. According to the division of industries, state-owned capital companies including Jinlian Investment Holding Co., Ltd. (corresponding to the manufacturing industry), Jincheng Capital (corresponding to the non-manufacturing industry) and Tianjin Guoxing Capital Operation Co., Ltd. (corresponding to the high-tech industry) were set up in Tianjin successively. In July 2017, Tianjin SASAC established Jincheng State-Owned Capital Investment and Operation Co., Ltd., a wholly state-owned company with a registered capital of 12 billion yuan, responsible for the investment and operation of non-manufacturing SOEs after the capitalization of state-owned assets. On April 19, 2018, based on the recorded assessment value, Tianjin SASAC invested in Jincheng Capital with 100% stock of the Tianjin Real Estate Group Co., Ltd. which was held by itself. By establishing institutions mentioned above and allocating assets, theoretically speaking, as for Tianjin SASAC, it will prove to be the regulatory body for state-owned investment and operating companies such as Jinlian Investment, Jincheng Capital and Guoxing Capital in the future and has no direct bearing on operating entities like Tianjin Real Estate Group, so as to achieve the transformation from managing personnel, affairs and enterprises to managing capital. As for Jincheng Capital, it will participate in the relevant corporate governance as a shareholder along with strategic investors being introduced into Tianjin Real Estate Group by the mixed-ownership reform. As for Tianjin Real Estate Group, it is to achieve the capitalization of state-owned assets by transforming the corporate system. Under the balance of the rights and interests of multiple shareholders and stakeholders, the effective corporate governance and a modern corporate system will come into being by means of the board of shareholders and directors.

Implementation Modes Exemplified by the Mixed-Ownership Reform of the Steel Industry

If the debt financing decisions made in the daily operation of enterprises mainly involve risks, SOE mixed-ownership reform is more concerned with equity financing through the introduction of strategic investors, so that all shareholders are bound together to share the uncertainty. Therefore, the new round of SOE reform–themed mixed ownership has largely become the issue of who to share uncertainty with. Therefore, in this section we will reveal who the state-owned assets should choose to share the uncertainty with, as exemplified by the practice of mixed-ownership reform in the steel industry.

The first case is Dongbei Special Steel, which once partnered with banks to share uncertainty. Dongbei Special Steel and its predecessor Dalian Iron and Steel (Group) Co., Ltd. had experienced debt-to-equity swap several times in history. In 2000, China Orient, China Cinda and China Huarong, the three asset management companies jointly invested with Liaoning SASAC, Heilongjiang SASAC and Fushun Special Steel, and the above three asset management companies became the debt-to-equity shareholders of Dalian Special Steel, accounting for 35% of the total registered capital. In 2008, Liaoning SASAC repurchased the equity of the above three asset management companies according to the debt-to-equity swap contract, and its shareholding ratio of Dongbei Special Steel once rose to as high as 62.8%.

But on March 24, 2016, Yang Hua, then the chairman of Dongbei Special Steel, suddenly committed suicide. Three days after this emergency, the company announced that the 15 Dongbei Special Steel CP001 bond had virtually defaulted on its debts. Since then, news of defaulted bonds of Dongbei Special Steel kept coming, and defaulted bonds of various terms of maturity periods (medium, short and ultra-short) issued through different channels (public or non-public) amounted to a total debt of 8.57 billion yuan. When the new chairman proposed to turn 70% of the debts of Dongbei Special Steel into equity again, the creditor, realizing that the Liaoning government was under financial strains, unanimously refused this proposal at the bondholders' meeting. On September 26, 2016, they formally applied to the Dalian Intermediate People's Court for reorganization of Dongbei Special Steel. On October 10, 2016, Dongbei Special Steel formally entered the process of bankruptcy reorganization. Just as we see, Shen Wenrong's control of Dongbei Special Steel, later interpreted by the media as accidental privatization, was actually a last-ditch move taken by the local government to resolve the debt crisis. To a certain extent, Dongbei Special Steel's debt crisis is a reenacted scene of how bank loans gradually turn into bad debts account of their soft budget constraints, as noticed by Hungarian economist János Kornai decades ago. Therefore, we tend to understand debt-to-equity swaps under the government intervention as soft budget constraints in the disguise of market-oriented operations. We can see that whether the debt-to-equity swap can enable SOEs in a mixed-ownership reform to share uncertainties with banks largely depends on whether the swap is a real market-oriented behavior based on the value judgment and investors' will.

The second case is Tianjin Bohai Steel, an amalgamation of several local enterprises that stuck together against uncertainty. In 2010, four SOEs, including Tianjin Pipe Corporation (TPCO), Tianjin Iron and Steel Group Co., Ltd., Tianjin Tiantie Metallurgical Group Co., Ltd. and Tianjin Metallurgy Group Co., Ltd., were combined to create Bohai Steel. In 2014, after financial statements were consolidated, Bohai Steel made it to the Fortune Global 500 list. However, at the end of 2015, less than two years later, Bohai Steel fell into a serious debt crisis, owing 192 billion yuan to 105 banks and financial institutions after rapid expansion.

How did Bohai Steel resolve its new debt crisis? The first thing it did was to move out the enterprises it had absorbed. In April 2016, Tianjin Pipe Corporation was stripped of Bohai Steel, although it did relatively well. On the other hand, Bohai Steel went back to the idea of SOE mixed-ownership reform when it introduced Delong Steel, a strategic investor with private capital background to its core business. This shows that the so-called sticking together against uncertainties adopted by the amalgamation could only cover up temporarily the real problem of system and mechanism faced by SOEs by its large size but increased the uncertainties.

The third case is Ma'anshan Iron & Steel Company Limited (MA Steel), which chose to share uncertainty with excellent peers. On June 2, 2019, MA Steel announced that it would be restructured by China Baowu, to which Anhui SASAC would transfer its 51% equity of MA Steel free of charge. This enabled China Baowu to become the indirect controlling shareholder of MA Steel by directly holding its 51% of the equity and indirectly controlling 45.54% of the shares. By this move, the SASAC of the State Council, as the controlling shareholder of China Baowu, became the actual controller of MA Steel. Some media took this event as a landmark of the new mixed-ownership reform trend in which centrally controlled enterprises were introduced into local SOEs, for the mixed-ownership reform which was afoot in recent years with the actual controller was changed from the local SASAC to the SASAC of the State Council after mergers and acquisitions (M&A). Whether the uncertainty sharing with excellent peers launched by MA Steel will really help to realize the expected system and mechanism for SOE remains to be further seen in the specific measures to improve the basic corporate governance.

The fourth case is Chongqing Iron and Steel Group, which chose to share risks with excellent strategic investors. At the end of 2017, the actual controller of reorganized Chongqing Iron and Steel became Four Rivers Investment Company consisting of China Baowu, China-US Green Fund, China Merchants Group and WL Ross & Co. of the United States. As Zhou Zhuping, chairman of Chongqing Iron and Steel, said, Four Rivers Investment Company as the actual controller "neither sent technicians, nor invested in facilities other than maintenance, nor replaced workers and middle-level staff"; instead, it retained the original outside directors but only sent "five executives who had no experience in steel making".[5] Chongqing Iron and Steel, which had been teetering on the brink of bankruptcy for ten years, stopped the bleeding and came back to life in one year. The restructuring case of Chongqing Iron and Steel once again shows that the key problem to be solved in SOE mixed-ownership reform may not lie in resources or the market but in how to mobilize people's initiative to change the original management mechanism. After the reorganization, Chongqing Iron and Steel was under huge pressure to pay the return on investment of the original shareholders, the new shareholders after debt-to-equity swap and the Four Rivers Investment Company as the actual controller. To make profit as soon as possible apparently became the only driving force for Chongqing Iron and Steel Group to change its outdated management mechanism, which would surely help it solve the long-term problems like multi-objective conflicts that had long ailed traditional SOEs.

Generally speaking, Chongqing Iron and Steel made two adjustments to its corporate governance structure, driven by the Four Rivers Investment Company as the actual controllers. The first is an incentive mechanism for managers and employees based on the principle of marketization. After the restructuring in 2018, the annual salary of the CEO of Chongqing Iron and Steel was 5.5391 million yuan, about ten times the general manager's annual salary of 548,900 yuan before the restructuring in 2017. Many incentives such as the *Executive Compensation Incentive Plan of Chongqing Iron and Steel* and the *Employee Stock Ownership Plan from 2018 to 2020* were successfully launched in restructured Chongqing Iron and Steel, although they had ended in failure in other SOEs. Second, backing the CEO as the decision-making center of operation and management realizes the reasonable division of labor between the CEO and the board of directors, which in a way solved the main problems that had long beset SOEs, including the fuzzy boundary between controlling shareholders, board of directors and managers, and ownership and management rights bound in one.

After reorganization, the board of directors of Chongqing Iron and Steel clearly authorized its CEO the power to set up institutions, making technological transformation and other matters, and even allowed the CEO to act before reporting to the board of directors for approval. The board of directors returned to the basic functions of selecting and appointing the CEO and evaluating the CEO. On the issue of who to share the uncertainty with, Chongqing Iron and Steel has pioneered a new pattern by introducing excellent strategic investors with a clear profit motive, creating pressure to transform the operation mechanism and overcome the institutional obstacles, which worked well to create win-win cooperation among all parties as a key point and breakthrough for the rebirth of Chongqing Iron and Steel.

Now let us briefly summarize the experience of the four SOEs mentioned above in choosing uncertainty-sharing partners. They come from the same industry and were once deep in the debt crisis. Dongbei Special Steel chose to share its uncertainty with banks through debt-to-equity swap, later became an enterprise of soft budget constraint under the disguise of market-oriented operation, and finally had to be privatized. Bohai Steel shared its uncertainty by merging local enterprises and chose to stick together against uncertainty, but when a short-lived glory vanished, they had to part company and more fundamentally introduced strategic investors with private capital background. Ma'anshan Steel, which was restructured by Baowu, chose not only excellent peers but also peers from centrally controlled enterprises to share the uncertainty. The actual effect of this newly emerged practice of local SOEs sharing uncertainty by introducing centrally controlled enterprises in the same industry for mixed-ownership reform remains to be further seen. By contrast, in choosing to share the uncertainty with excellent strategic investors, the restructured Chongqing Iron and Steel took this as the key point and breakthrough of the mixed-ownership reform to create pressure to transform the traditional operation mechanism and overcome the institutional obstacles, which worked well to create win-win cooperation among all parties and lead to the rebirth of Chongqing Iron and Steel.

The essence of introducing strategic investors and achieving mixed ownership through SOE reform can be broken down into the following two directions around the over-appointment of directors by major shareholders. The excessive appointment of directors by major shareholders here refers to the situation where major shareholders appoint more directors than their equity percentage on the board of directors. A typical example is that in the board of directors of Vanke in 2017, Shenzhen Metro, the largest shareholder holding 29% of Vanke, appointed 50% of the non-independent directors – a case of over-appointing directors by the largest shareholder.

The first direction is to reduce the number of over-appointed directors appointed by the controlling shareholders. This issue involves the logical test of SOE mixed-ownership reform carried out by us with listed companies as the research object. Our research shows that in the current state-owned listed enterprises, if the actual controller cannot appoint more directors, it will not only increase the possibility of directors voting no in the future, but it will also have a more obvious supervisory effect on improving enterprise performance. The key to truly achieving the goal of mixed-ownership reform and promoting the improvement of efficiency is to reasonably ensure the seats of other shareholders in the board structure so that the private capital newly absorbed can fully participate in the governance process. Only by the means of appointing directors to access internal information and participate in the decision-making process of the board of directors can private capital effectively alleviate the original problem of excessive supervision and bring about the substantial improvement of business performance.

The second direction is to increase the number of directors over-appointed by the non-largest shareholders. A typical example is China Unicom, which has completed the mixed-ownership reform. Baidu, with 3% of the shares, appointed 12.5% of its non-independent directors. Our research attempted to check whether the over-appointment of directors by non-largest shareholders has helped to improve the efficiency of state-owned listed companies so as to carry out a logical test on SOE mixed-ownership reform from the opposite direction. The results show that the appointment of non-independent directors by non-largest shareholders has significantly reduced the amount of money and the number of related party transactions. By distinguishing the nature of non-largest shareholders, we find that the appointment of non-independent directors by non-state-owned and non-largest shareholders had a significant inhibitory effect on the related party transactions of listed companies, while the appointment of directors by state-owned non-largest shareholders had no significant impact on the related party transactions of listed companies. In the sample of local SOEs, the non-state-owned and non-largest shareholders' appointment of non-independent directors had a stronger inhibitory effect on related party transactions compared with the non-largest shareholder of centrally controlled enterprises.

The above-mentioned four cases of SOE mixed-ownership reform which chose uncertainty-sharing partners and the logical test we carried out around the over-appointment of directors by major shareholders in listed companies clearly show that in the practice of SOE mixed-ownership reform, perhaps only mixed ownership can make changes, and mixing is better than merger, just as opening-up promotes reform.

Then, what are the changes in the SOE governance structure and the operating mechanism after the completion of the mixed-ownership reform? The governance paradigm of domination of the single shareholder has inhibited the potential of benefit promotion stimulated by the improvement of governance structure and the transformation of the operating mechanism of many state-controlled listed companies after capital socialization, so that the performance of state-controlled listed companies is still worse than that of private listed companies. Nevertheless, following the logic of the above listed companies to carry out SOE mixed-ownership reform, we can still detect the impact of SOE mixed-ownership reform from the state-owned listed companies.

On December 12, 2018, at the 2018 CCTV Financial Forum Chinese Listed Companies Summit, relevant personnel of SASAC disclosed that 65.2% of SASAC's total assets and 61.7% of its net assets had invested in the listed companies, and 61.2% of its operating revenue and 87.6% of its total profits came from listed companies. To a large extent, the governance structure of listed companies was the goal and direction of SOEs actively engaged in the mixed-ownership reform.

After introducing strategic investors and completing the mixed-ownership reform, an enterprise should become a model of capital socialization like state-owned listed companies in terms of equity structure. Its shareholders should include both state-owned assets and private assets as a product of capital socialization. Private capital with a clear profit motive and its appointed directors should be an important force to restrict managers from pursuing personal benefits and damaging shareholders' interests. The post–mixed-ownership reform enterprises should set up a board of directors composed of those representing the interests of shareholders of all parties, like state-owned listed companies where major issues need to be negotiated and voted on by the general meeting of shareholders. These enterprises should even introduce social elites who are from outside, interest neutral, reputed and proficient in law, accounting and finance as independent directors for supervision and consultation, just like state-owned listed companies. Through the establishment and improvement of the above corporate governance framework, these enterprises will effectively separate the management right in the hands of professional managers from the control right in the hands of shareholders, which will lead to the improvement of efficiency based on the specialized division of labor between the professionalization of managers and the socialization of capital.

Summary

In view of their historical position and special role in the national economy and people's livelihood, SOEs have always been a constituent of China's economic system reform, and their reform has become the epitome of China's 40 years of reform and opening-up. Due to the existence of soft budget constraints, blurred fiduciary duties, multi-objective incentive conflicts and Chinese-style insider control, they are like family workshops, have not gotten rid of the intervention of the control right over the management right, and have also failed to take advantage of social specialization to improve efficiency and solve the agency problem which, however, does not exist in family workshops. All these have made SOEs look like neoclassical capitalist enterprises troubled with agency problems. Therefore, they may prosper for a few years before plunging into a vicious circle of benefit decline, successive years of losses, heavy debts, government-directed merger and reorganization, and rebirth.

The mixed-ownership reform is currently widely adopted as a new breakthrough in the new round of SOE reform. On the one hand, SOE mixed-ownership reform needs to introduce strategic investors with clear profit motive and private capital background at the shareholder level to solve the problem of the owner absence; on the other hand, through the mixed-ownership reform, the competitive relationship between major shareholders is formed, and an automatic error correction mechanism is established to effectively avoid the excessive supervision and decision-making errors which could be easily caused by the dominance of major shareholders, set up restriction on managers, and avoid the problem of insider control. Therefore, the theoretical basis of the new round of SOE mixed-ownership reform are the modern property rights theory and the decentralized control theory. SOE mixed-ownership reform can help realize decentralized control by introducing strategic investors with private capital background at the level of the real economy and implementing employee stock ownership plans. In the state-owned asset management system, it can initiate the transformation from managing enterprises to managing capital by setting up or reorganizing state-owned capital investment and operating companies. In terms of the implementation mode of introducing strategic investors with private capital background for mixed-ownership reform, they can choose two models. One is the Unicom model as the model of mixed-ownership reform of basic and strategic industries, in which state-owned assets are dominant in the ownership structure and strategic investors are dominant at the organizational level of the board of directors. The other is the Northern Trust model, which is a model of mixed-ownership reform in non-basic and strategic industries, and both the ownership structure and the board of directors are dominated by strategic investors. The key to the success of the mixed-ownership reform is to address the issues concerning incentive compatibility of private capital and other strategic investors in order to effectively protect the rights and interests of private capital.

The essence of mixed-ownership reform is to choose who to share uncertainty with. In the practice of the steel industry, excellent strategic investors with a private capital background are more appropriate uncertainty-sharing partners than banks, local peers and excellent peers for SOEs. By choosing to share risks with excellent strategic investors, SOEs under mixed-ownership reform can establish a new incentive system on the one hand, restore the original function of the board of directors on the other hand, and realize the effective separation of management right and ownership. On the realization mode of the SOE reform, we stress that, just as only opening-up can promote the reform, only mixing can make changes, and it is better than merging.

Notes

1 参见许成刚，中国经济这五年，第十期：对话许成钢，《凤凰财知道》，2017年10月25日。原话为"僵尸企业、产能过剩的根源在软预算约束". *ifeng.com.* https://finance.ifeng.com/news/special/zhonggong19th10/ (China's economy in the past five years).
2 厉以宁：靓女先嫁直须嫁. Li Yining. Pretty girl marries first. *China Collective Economy.* http://www.ce2293.com/qkglxt/showlm.asp?id=8182.
3 Tunneling is an illegal business practice in which a majority shareholder or high-level company insider directs company assets or future business to themselves for personal gain.
4 原话是：泰达控股资产管理部经理崔雪松表示，"泰达控股将让出北方信托第一大股东的位置，对此，新进大股东需要支付混改后北方信托净资产总额1%的额外款项。" Sina Comprehensive. (2018). 直击北方信托混改招商会：众多明星企业兴致满满 [Direct attack on the Northern Trust Mixed Reform Investment Promotion Conference: Many star enterprises are full of interest]. *Sina Finance.* http://finance.sina.com.cn/trust/xthydt/2018-01-16/doc-ifyqqciz7607561.shtml.
5 原话是：没有派去技术人员，也没有做除了维修以外的设施方面的投入，没有更换过工人、中层，只换了董事会和高管，外部董事保留了. Xuefeng, Y. & Y. Xuan. (2019). 公司治理是企业发展最重要的因素 [Corporate governance is the most important factor for enterprise development]. *FX361.com.* https://www.fx361.com/page/2019/0619/5221249.shtml.

1 Problems with the Insider Control in the Chinese SOEs Under Pyramidal Holding Structure

In terms of the basic form of corporate governance, SOEs, together with their controlling parent companies and grandparent companies, constitute a large-scale enterprise group, which is under a pyramidal holding structure with different size and complexity.

The extended principal-agent chain resulting from the pyramidal holding structure not only further aggravates the institutional defects of the SOE owner's absence, "spending someone else's money on someone else" but also gives rise to potential negative economic, political and social effects. It may be time for China's capital market to say no to the pyramidal structure.

Due to the absence of real owners, some major shareholders of SOEs cannot effectively perform the function of supervising managers, leading to a vacuum of corporate governance and giving facility to insider control. The insider control of Hengfeng Bank is a unique Chinese-style problem under the background of China's capital market system, and so different from the traditional sense of insider control in the United Kingdom and the United States. This is the real problem faced by China's SOEs in corporate governance practice.

As for the reason for the predicament of corporate governance that has emerged in China's capital market since 2015, the analysis shows that we need to interpret not only from the perspective of frequent invasion of barbarians[1] and chaos caused by financial crocodiles[2] hidden in various pyramidal holding structures, but also from the perspective of Chinese-style insider control. The reason for the predicament of China's corporate governance is neither simply a barbarian invasion nor a dilemma for insiders, but the encounter of barbarians with Chinese-style insiders.

1 Disadvantages of SOE System Under Pyramidal Holding Structure

In recent years, various capital forces hidden behind the complex pyramidal holding structure have been making waves in China's capital market. When we examine the ownership structure of listed companies, we find that in China's capital market, a large proportion of listed companies are either in enterprise groups backed by state-owned assets or are inextricably related to the financial empire built by the

DOI: 10.4324/9781003361404-2

capital forces. These capital forces usually try to acquire the controlling shares of company B by holding controlling shares of company A with the help of leverage, and then acquire company C through B in the same way. They have done this again and again. In addition to listed companies, they control or participate in a large number of non-listed companies through a chain of holdings. Through layers of equity control, the actual controllers at the top of the pyramid have thus constructed huge financial empires. This kind of huge pyramidal ownership structure, traditionally called XX System, is established with the help of a complex shareholding chain, such as the centrally controlled China Resources System with multiple listed companies, and the COFCO System, which holds shares in a number of listed companies. They lie in the pyramidal holding structure chain of different lengths and complexities and constitute the basic governance format of SOEs.

Arguably, the pyramidal holding structure with Chinese listed companies as its subsidiaries or sub-subsidiaries was established on the institutional system not only designed to guarantee financing for enterprises but also in relation to the special policies launched by the government during SOE reform as well as industrial restructuring.

First, China's capital market was far from mature and effective in the 1980s and 1990s. During this period, the pyramidal holding structure functioned as an important internal capital market and a supplement to the external capital market, which was far from mature and even substituted the external market. This constitutes the most direct reason for the first appearance of the pyramidal holding structure in the capital market.

Second were the actual needs of the restructuring of SOEs then. In order to promote the restructuring of SOEs with serious losses and lack of funds, high-quality assets removed from them were listed to raise funds, as the famous adage "pretty girl marries first" had it. But those listed assets, as "married girls", still had to bear the implicit responsibility of helping their poor parent companies tide over the difficulties in the future. Consequently, the listed companies and other parts of the group companies naturally developed a holding relationship between subsidiaries and the parent companies.

Third, in order to be rid of people's suspicion that SASAC would play the role as both a referee and an athlete in the process of the SOE reform, group companies for holding shares were artificially established between listed companies and SASAC. SASAC then controlled listed companies indirectly through group companies.

Fourth, in the subsequent rounds of M&A and industrial structure adjustment, some enterprises in difficulty were implanted into some relatively powerful enterprise groups by the government, so as to solve problems like poor benefit, inability to guarantee basic salary and laid-off workers.

Finally, due to the long queue for audited companies to be listed, some enterprises chose backdoor listing as a shortcut. After the assets were injected into a shell company, a new chain of control naturally took shape between the new listed company and the original company.

Concerning the above reasons, the pyramidal holding structure has gradually formed in many enterprises backed by state-owned assets, both listed and non-listed companies. Since 1999, when they began to be listed in a large number, private enterprises also adopted the state-owned equity structure. This has made the pyramidal holding structure prevalent in enterprises of both state-owned and private backgrounds in China's capital market.

The internal capital market formed by the pyramidal holding structure indeed once played a historic role in promoting enterprise groups to achieve economies of scale and rapid expansion in the early stage of reform and opening-up when the external capital market was yet to develop. However, when the external capital market was well developed and effective, the pyramidal holding structure began to show more of its disadvantages.

Theoretically, the pyramidal holding structure has a system design that easily can cause many negative effects. The root cause is that the responsibility of the actual controller of the parent company is not symmetrical with its impact on the sub-subsidiaries at the bottom of the pyramid. This may create conditions for the actual controller to use asymmetric responsibilities and rights to seek personal benefits while damaging the interest of dispersed minority shareholders.

Let us take a company as an example. Suppose the parent company holds 30% of the shares of its subsidiary while the subsidiary holds 30% shares of its own subsidiary (sub-subsidiary of parent company), which is a typical three-level pyramidal holding structure. Through the shareholding chain, the actual controller of the parent company can obtain at least 30% votes in the voting of major matters of its sub-subsidiary company. Whereas the subsidiary has a strong influence on the board of directors and relevant proposals voted at the general meeting of shareholders of the sub-subsidiary, the successful passage of the subsidiary's proposal to occupy the sub-subsidiary's funds in the form of other receivables through the voting of the latter's general meeting of shareholders tends to become highly probable. This makes the parent company with 30% cash flow right of the subsidiary obtain at least 30% of the income from the occupied funds mentioned above. However, the parent company's capital contribution to its sub-subsidiary company accounts for only 9% (30% × 30%) of the total capital of the latter, the parent company's loss caused by the free occupation of funds (even to the risk of failure to repay due in the future) is limited to 9% cash flow right invested in its sub-subsidiary. Here, we call the influence on the company's major decision-making through the board of directors and the voting of the general meeting of shareholders as the control right, and the responsibility bearing capacity reflected through the actual capital contribution as the cash flow right.

From this example, we can see that, with the help of the pyramidal holding structure, the actual controller can successfully separate control right from the cash flow right. This is in fact the realization mechanism by which the actual controller uses the pyramidal holding structure to tunnel to the sub-subsidiary company at the bottom, as described by Simon Johnson and Andrei Shleifer. The reason why it is called tunneling is that the actual controller uses its control right over the sub-subsidiary company to transfer the resources of the sub-subsidiary company to the subsidiary company by means of capital occupation, and then from the subsidiary company to the parent company, making this chain look like a long tunnel.

When it comes to China's capital market, the pyramidal holding structure has shown the following increasingly obvious negative effects.

First, the actual controller uses the complex pyramidal holding structure to tunnel to its subsidiaries and sub-subsidiaries and fail to guarantee the interests of minority shareholders, which forces the latter to vote with their feet. As for the short average duration of retail investors in China's capital market, there are two main reasons. The first one is related to the less severe supervision and punishment of insider trading so that some people still take chances. The other one is that the pyramidal holding structure deprives minority shareholders of the possibility to participate in corporate governance but they do not want to be innocent victims and therefore have to vote with their feet.

Second, for some non-core holding subsidiaries, the actual controllers usually pay more attention to capital operation and even market speculation than to corporate governance and operation management. They frequently hype about asset replacement, additional issuance of new shares, M&A and even renaming. The holding groups under their control pay more attention to the capital operation than the business management. The dispersed minority shareholders are likewise difficult to focus on the value investment itself but are busy seeking inside information through various channels. We can see that the preference of capital operation of the actual controller under the pyramidal holding structure has further exacerbated the speculative psychology of minority shareholders.

Finally, the complex pyramidal holding structure not only brings difficulties for regulatory authorities to supervise the related party transactions of the companies related by equity but also provides diversified ways for the actual controller to bribe corrupt officials. The capital tycoons ultimately form an interest alliance with some corrupt officials to make power-for-money deals, resulting in the loss of state-owned assets. The stories of Yongjin System and Tomorrow System are good lessons from the past.

A review of the history of capital markets in some countries shows that the pyramidal holding structure is not only a popular equity control model in family enterprises prevalent in Asia and Europe, but it also once appeared in the United Kingdom and the United States, where equity dispersion is the typical governance model. The equity control governance model in US enterprises typified by Rockefeller and other trusts in Lenin's eyes has evolved into a highly decentralized corporate governance model because the US government realized the negative effects of the pyramidal holding structure mentioned above and adopted a series of reform measures in the Progressive Era. It can shed some light on China's capital market in its efforts to eliminate the pyramidal holding structure and its negative effects.

To begin with, the levy of inter-company dividend tax puts the parent company, which controls subsidiaries and sub-subsidiaries in the pyramidal structure, in an unfavorable state of tax burden. This is considered to be one of the most important causes for some huge trust organizations to break up in the United States in the early 20th century. Considering the fact that the tax burden is high for enterprises in China and the expanding financial expenditure needs to tap tax sources, and the healthy development of the capital market needs to restrain the pyramidal holding structure, the foreign experience can provide feasible ways for China's future capital market – on the one hand revitalizing enterprises by reducing their tax burden, and on the other hand levying the inter-company dividend tax to make up for the lack of financial expenditure funds – so as to curb the spread and development of the pyramidal holding structure.

Then, we should formulate preferential tax policies for dividend returns of institutional investors who hold preferred shares to encourage them to hold more non-controlling preferred shares issued by listed companies so as to avoid excessive intervention of institutional investors in the operation and management of listed companies.

For some time, after declaring the significant shareholding[3] to become the largest shareholders, some insurance companies driven by profit pressure have not been intended for long-term value investment and even do not hesitate to recall all the directors who once led the enterprise all the way from difficulties. This is the result that ordinary investors, regulatory authorities, management teams and even insurance funds themselves do not want to see. And if these insurance funds held only preferred shares, the arrangement can not only systematically avoid intervention in the microeconomic agents, such as the tragedy of "bloodbathing" the board of directors but also be more helpful in maintaining and increasing the value of insurance funds.

For the SOE mixed-ownership reform underway, the above discussion gives us illumination that some SOEs may consider converting common shares into preferred shares. After the introduction of the above preferential tax policies for preferred shares, the state-owned capital dominated by preferred shares can take advantage of the tax preference and the preferential payment of dividend of preferred shares so as to achieve the purpose of preserving and increasing the value of state-owned assets on the one hand, and fundamentally help realize SOE reform from managing enterprises to managing capital on the other hand.

Third, inheritance tax should be levied to encourage financial tycoons to change from equity control to public welfare funds. Once their nature is changed, public welfare funds will focus more attention on the safety of funds and the stability of returns, rather than simply seeking the control of the company, capital operation and market speculation.

Now let us suppose if the common shares of listed companies in the capital market are mainly held by individual investors, while institutional investors such as insurance companies mainly hold preferred shares, then there is little complex pyramidal holding structure. For individual investors, since there is no possibility of tunneling by the actual controller of the original pyramidal holding structure, the holding companies will not be used as the object of market speculation. Their speculative motivation will be weakened accordingly, and they will be forced to turn to value investment, and even begin to care about the governance and management of listed companies. Institutional investors who hold preferred shares but do not have voting rights are basically short of any incentive of market speculation, capital operation and corresponding conditions; they only want to maintain and increase the value of their shares. In this way, the bloodbath which has been caused by the significant shareholding of insurance companies in the capital market will never stage again. Without the complex pyramidal holding structure as an umbrella, corrupt officials will find it hard to continue colluding with capital. Listed companies will not have to worry about the barbarian invasion and will turn their attention to the improvement of corporate governance and management. A sound capital market of a healthy trend will take shape as a result.

2   Problems With Chinese-Style Insider Control in Hengfeng Bank

On the evening of November 28, 2017, various mainstream media reported the case of Cai Guohua, the former chairman of Hengfeng Bank. In fact, as early as 2016, *Caixin Weekly* and the *21st Century Business Herald* published reports titled "Equity Control Gimmicks of Hengfeng Bank" and "Whose Hengfeng Bank?", respectively, to reveal the scandalous employee stock ownership plan and the case of suspected executives' private sharing of public funds in Hengfeng Bank, a joint-stock commercial bank headquartered in Yantai, Shandong Province. According to the information publicly disclosed then, Yantai Lantian Investment Holding Co., Ltd., wholly owned by Yantai SASAC, held 19.4% of the shares as the largest shareholder of the bank. Among Hengfeng's shareholders, there were not only institutional investors from Jiangsu, Shanghai, Beijing and Xiamen but also international strategic partners such as United Overseas Bank (UOB) of Singapore. In terms of equity structure arrangement, whether it is the degree of equity diversification, international openness and equity checks and balances, Hengfeng Bank could be regarded as a model in joint-stock commercial banks. But why did the media still ask "Whose Hengfeng Bank?"

The public reports clearly Indicate that the executives' private sharing of public funds, the employee stock ownership plan scandal and the equity mystery in Hengfeng Bank are all consequences of insider control. The Company Law commonsensically tells us that anything involving equity changes certainly needs the consent of existing shareholders, let alone issuing the additional employee stock ownership plan to dilute existing shareholders' equity. At that time, Hengfeng Bank's senior executives got 8 million yuan or 21 million yuan, respectively, while Cai Guohua alone got 38.5 million yuan. If it had been a normal compensation for executives, it must have been not only given on the basis of the compensation contract but also discussed by the board of directors and even approved by the general meeting of shareholders.

The so-called problem of insider control discussed here refers to the behavior of executives or executive directors using their actual control over the company to damage shareholders' rights and interests and challenge shareholders' corporate governance authority. Insider control first emerged in corporate governance practices in countries such as the United Kingdom and the United States. UK and US companies have highly dispersed ownership and they hope to coordinate the conflict of interest between managers and shareholders through the equity incentive, so they continue to give managers equity incentive. The two factors work jointly to push up the proportion of managers' shareholding higher and higher, like a trench dug around the actual control of managers to make it difficult for external supervision and threats to impact and shake managers. Therefore, managers protected by deep trenches can obtain private benefits by seeking control and can even pay themselves excess compensation to harm the interest of shareholders. As an important manifestation of manager agency, insider control has attracted the attention of theorists and practitioners of corporate governance in the United Kingdom and the United States.

If we carefully compare the insider control of Hengfeng Bank with that in the United Kingdom and the United States, we will find that there are obvious differences between them. First, the insider control of Hengfeng Bank was not due to the high dispersion of equity. Following Yantai Lantian Investment as the largest shareholder with a shareholding of 19.4%, United Overseas Bank of Singapore held as high as 12.4% of the shares of Hengfeng Bank which was yet to be listed, and even the third- to fifth-largest shareholders held about 10%. According to the calculation method of equity checks and balances commonly used in empirical research, Hengfeng Bank, whose equity percentage of the largest shareholder was lower than that of the second- to fifth-largest shareholders combined, precisely fell into the type of equity structure with a high degree of equity checks and balances. Therefore, such an ownership structure was far from being highly decentralized, which sowed the seeds of insider control.

Second, in Hengfeng Bank, the chairman, instead of the CEO (president), was the core of the insider control. By contrast, in UK and US corporate governance, the chairman is often only the convener of the board of directors who has no extra power in performing his duties as a director. Due to the high equity incentive, the CEO is protected by the trench effect and becomes the core of insider control in equity decentralized companies in the United Kingdom and the United States. In Hengfeng Bank, however, it is the chairman appointed by the largest shareholder to perform the responsibility of supervision of state-owned assets on behalf of SASAC is the core of the company's insider control pattern in China. The manager is more like a CEO in a foreign company in terms of positions and title but is demoted to chairman's executive assistant here. In the empirical research on Chinese listed companies, it has become a common understanding that the chairman, rather than the manager, is the key object of corporate governance.

Third, the formation of insider control is not due to the implementation of an equity incentive plan but it is due to the trench effect formed around the chairman that makes his control position unshakable. Moreover, readers familiar with the relevant provisions of China's capital market can easily find that China has strict restrictions on directors appointed by state-owned superior holding companies to obtain equity incentives. From the data disclosed at present, we can't perceive that Cai Guohua, the former chairman of the board, holds a direct stake.

The three reasons discussed above reveal to us that the insider control problem of Hengfeng Bank is different from that which has traditionally existed in the companies of the United States and the United Kingdom. We therefore cannot find the answer to the above problems from the practical experience of corporate governance in these countries. In order to distinguish two different types of insider control, we have to use the popular discourse of the current media for reference to summarize the insider control with typical Chinese institutional characteristics in Hengfeng Bank as Chinese-style insider control.

A research team led by Professor Andrei Shleifer of Harvard University made an observation of 27 countries around the world and has found that the equity of large enterprises is concentrated in the hands of major shareholders. They believe that the importance of the original agency conflict between managers and shareholders has been replaced by the new corporate governance problem of how controlling shareholders exploit minority shareholders to a certain extent. Although we agree with Professor Shleifer that the agency conflict between shareholders cannot be ignored, to our knowledge of the reality of China's corporate governance, we believe that the agency conflict between traditional managers and shareholders is still serious in China's capital market; even under the shield of the complex pyramidal holding structure, the problem of insider control caused by the agency conflict between managers and shareholders has become more complex. This is the real problem of corporate governance under the specific institutional background of China's capital market, which needs special attention from the theoretical and practical circles of corporate governance in China.

What, then, is the real reason for the Chinese-style insider control of Hengfeng Bank? There are at least two reasons.

The first is the generation mechanism of the chairman and the chairman's unique identity. In China's corporate governance practice of enterprises with state-owned assets as the largest shareholder, the key positions are often appointed by the superior organization department of the enterprise according to the cadre assessment procedure, although it still symbolically needs to go through the procedures of nomination by the board of directors and voting at the general meeting of shareholders. Due to the above-mentioned top-down ways of personnel appointment, the appointee often has a special status. Let us take Hengfeng Bank as an example. In the relevant announcement issued by Hengfeng Bank, it was mentioned that

> The board meeting was held on December 19, 2013. According to the appointment, dismissal and recommendation decision against the bank's major shareholders made by Yantai Municipal Party Committee and Municipal Government and the qualification review of the Nomination Committee of the Board of Directors Mr. Cai Guohua was elected as the director and chairman of the company.

If we look further back for Cai Guohua's identity before he served as chairman of Hengfeng Bank, we found that he used to be a member of the Standing Committee of the Yantai Municipal Party committee, vice mayor and party secretary of SASAC. This piece of information shows that the appointment of Cai Guohua as chairman of Hengfeng Bank is only a link in the overall arrangement of major party and government leading cadres in the area of Yantai. To some extent, even the leaders of Yantai City could not decide on the appointment either.

The second is the owner absence in the state-owned shareholder. In theory, shareholders with strong profit motive will prevent any behavior of the board of directors as shareholder agents from infringing upon the interest of shareholders, which is mainly reflected in that the largest shareholder usually votes against relevant resolutions that may damage the interest of shareholders at the general meeting of shareholders, and even proposes to replace incompetent board members who damage the interest of shareholders. However, whether it is Yantai Lantian Investment as the superior holding company of Hengfeng Bank, or SASAC which wholly controls, the bank could not fully check Cai Guohua simply because he had the background of once serving as a member of the Standing Committee of Yantai Municipal Party Committee, the vice mayor and the party secretary of SASAC. Yantai Lantian Investment, as the largest shareholder of Hengfeng Bank, could not exercise effective restriction on the insider control of the board of directors headed by former chairman Cai Guohua; instead, it became an available force to counter the objections that might be put forward by other shareholders, and even send a signal to other shareholders that it is useless to oppose because he is the largest shareholder. To some extent, the case of Hengfeng Bank shows that due to the absence of real owners, major shareholders failed to perform the function of supervising managers, which created corporate governance vacuum and led to insider control, and which is the reason for the emergence of Chinese-style insider control. When the above-mentioned Chinese-style insider control was formed, the employee stock ownership plan scandal, executives' private sharing of public funds and the equity mystery of Hengfeng Bank were consequential.

How should we eliminate the chronic disease of Chinese-style insider control in the practice of China's corporate governance?

In fact, as an important measure of SOE reform, transformation from managing enterprise to managing capital which has been adopted is the key to solve the problem of Chinese-style insider control in Hengfeng Bank. Through the fundamental changes mentioned above, shareholders will really become the authority of corporate governance to replace the corporate governance vacuum created by the absence of owners. In this way, similar cases to Hengfeng Bank will be reduced to a certain extent, so as to fundamentally eliminate the employee stock ownership plan scandal, senior executives' private sharing of public funds and the equity mystery.

Since 2015, the average shareholding ratio of the largest shareholder of China's listed companies has been lower than 33.3% (index of relative control), indicating that China's capital market has entered the era of decentralized equity. In the future, China's capital market must firmly establish the conviction that shareholders are the real authority of corporate governance, and make the voting of the general meeting of shareholders on important matters an important platform to reflect the wishes and demands of different shareholders and protect shareholders' rights and interests. At the same time, companies should be encouraged to hire more employees and more independent directors with neutral interest from the outside and let them put forward more professional countermeasures, opinions and suggestions on preventing damage to the interest of minority shareholders. We should even encourage takeover threats to be launched by institutional investors, including insurance funds and pensions, to make them important external forces to improve corporate governance.

3 How to Interpret the Predicament of Corporate Governance in China

After a long-term accumulation of problems, China's capital market has entered a period of concentrated outbreaks of various chaos and oddities since 2015. First, the capital market in 2015 experienced a large fluctuation of stock prices, which was vividly called a stock market crash by some media. Second, the outbreak of a series of disputes over control rights represented by Vanke's equity dispute in July 2015 and the insurance companies' significant shareholding appeared in China's capital market as a barbarian that attracted the attention of investors and the public for a time. Last, the bloody storm caused by the insurance companies' significant shareholding in China's capital market came to a climax after the board of directors of CSG Holding Co., Ltd. was bloodied. Industrialists, who were all in danger, stood up one after another to condemn the atrocities of barbarians. Among them, Dong Mingzhu pointed out that "those who destroy the real economy are sinners".[4] In this context, on December 3, 2016, the China Securities Regulatory Commission (CSRC) publicly criticized the barbarians and denounced that these insurance companies and other financial crocodiles making waves in the market were local tyrants, demons and evil monsters.

We know that disputes over control rights and even the barbarian invasions have appeared throughout the development history of capital markets in various countries. But why is the dispute over control in China's capital market so bloody and the confrontations so fierce? How should we logically and consistently interpret the chaos and oddities that have occurred in China's capital market in recent years? This section tries to put forward a unified logical analysis for interpreting the predicament of corporate governance in China.

To sum up, the key to interpreting the predicament of China's corporate governance lies in grasping the three separate and intersecting logical threads: first, the beginning of the era of dispersed ownership in China's capital market; second, the prevalence of pyramidal holding structures that have historically worked but now do more harm than good; and third, the long-standing problem of Chinese-style insider control. We can see that, on the one hand, China's capital market has entered the era of dispersed ownership with frequent incursions of barbarians and the chaos caused by financial crocodiles who are hidden behind various pyramidal holding structures; on the other hand, there is the long-standing problem of Chinese-style insider control. When barbarians encounter Chinese-style insiders, the predicament of China's corporate governance appears. The interweaving and conflict of the three logical threads has become the practical cause of the current predicament of corporate governance in China. Therefore, the three logical threads and their interweaving and conflict constitute a logic analysis framework for interpreting the predicament of China's corporate governance. Figure 1.1 depicts the

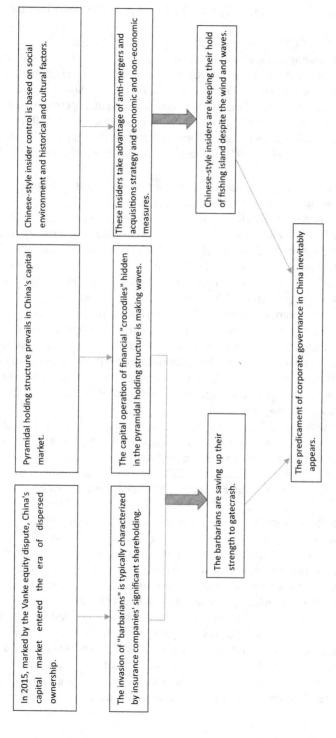

Figure 1.1 Logic analysis framework for interpreting the predicament of corporate governance in China.

three logical threads for interpreting the predicament of corporate governance in China and the framework of logic analysis formed on the basis of the three logical threads.

The entry of China's capital market into the era of dispersed ownership is the first and most important logical thread for interpreting the predicament of China's corporate governance. After the transformation of the shareholding structure of listed companies from the dominance of a single shareholder to the dispersed ownership, China's capital market has entered the era of dispersed ownership. The factors that have contributed to this shift can be summarized as follows.

First, the split-share structure reform and the completion of the full circulation of stock from 2005 to 2007 made the transfer of control rights technically possible.

Second, improving the protection of shareholders' rights and strengthening the risk sharing awareness make the original controlling shareholders tend to choose a dispersed ownership structure. Traditionally, when rights are not adequately protected by law, shareholders tend to choose a concentrated ownership structure to counter the agency behavior of managers that undermine their interests. This is an important reason why some traditional markets and emerging market countries in the civil law system have opted for a model of concentrated ownership governance, where the legal protection of investors' rights is not satisfactory. After years of development, a certain function of risk diversification has not only emerged in China's capital market, but also a variety of internal and external governance frameworks and legal systems that can protect shareholders' rights and interests have taken shape. Obviously, it is not the optimal choice for the former controlling shareholders to concentrate a large proportion of the shares in the same company.

The above two aspects constitute the internal reasons for China's capital market to enter the era of dispersed ownership.

Third, with the increasing funds that can be invested in stocks, institutional investors such as insurance companies began to enter the capital market in a big way and even became the largest shareholders of some listed companies in the secondary market for a time. Since 2010, successive acquisitions by insurance companies have accelerated the process of ownership dispersion in China's capital market.

Fourth, the ongoing SOE mixed-ownership reform, which is typically characterized by attracting private enterprises as strategic investors, will further dilute the shares of the original relatively concentrated state-owned controlling shareholders, thus forming the basic structure of dispersed ownership in China's capital market. Take China Unicom's mixed-ownership reform as an example. After attracting strategic investors including China Life and BATJ (Baidu, Alibaba, Tencent and JD.com) to hold 35.19% shares, China Unicom Group's total shares in China Unicom became 36.67%, and previously it was over 60%. Significant shareholding of insurance companies and SOE mixed-ownership reform have become external factors leading China's capital market into the era of dispersed ownership.

We can see from Figure 1.2 that the average shareholding ratio of the largest shareholders in China's listed companies has been declining over the past decade

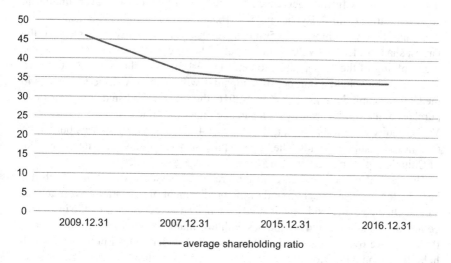

Figure 1.2 Changes in the average shareholding ratio of the largest shareholder.

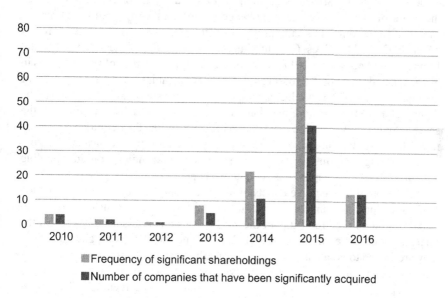

Figure 1.3 Changes in significant shareholdings.

or so. In 2007, when the split-share structure reform was completed, the average shareholding ratio of the largest shareholder of China's listed companies dropped from over 40% before the reform in 2005 to about 35%. In 2015, when the insurance funds entered the capital market on a large scale and Vanke equity dispute broke out, the average equity percentage of the largest shareholders of China's listed companies further decreased to about 33%, which was even unable to achieve relative control. By the end of 2016, among nearly 3,000 listed companies in China, there were more than 500 companies with the equity percentage of the largest shareholder below 20%, and about 50 listed companies had less than 10% shareholding of the largest shareholder. Figure 1.3 shows that since 2010, insurance funds have held a number of companies with relatively dispersed shares in the Chinese capital market. As of mid-2016, the stock of 77 listed companies was purchased in a significant way by insurance funds 119 times. In 2015, the year the Vanke equity dispute broke out, the stock of 41 listed companies was purchased 69 times by insurance funds. The Vanke equity dispute has thus become the symbol of China's capital market entering the era of dispersed ownership.

The capital market has entered the era of dispersed ownership, which has become the historical background of the predicament of corporate governance in China. On the positive side, the institutional investors represented by the insurance companies acquired listed companies with low market valuation, forming a direct threat to take over some listed companies with insider control problems, which helps these companies to improve their governance structure. On the negative side, it is possible for some institutional investors to invade companies with relatively dispersed equity as barbarians, to compete for control right or even "bloodbathe" the board of directors, posing a challenge to the investment incentive of human capital of some companies' entrepreneurial teams. According to the research report "A-share Capital Families: Current Situation and Thinking", released by Mr. Xing Liquan, as of February 7, 2017, there were 178 capital families of various types in Shenzhen and Shanghai, involving 1,045 listed companies, accounting for 34% of the total number of A-share listed companies in the same period. We note that the report refers to two or more listed companies held or actually controlled by the same actual controller as the capital system. If we follow the definition of a pyramidal holding structure as an enterprise group established by means of equity control through intermediary enterprises, there are far more pyramidal holding structures in China's capital market than we expect.

We discussed the negative effects of the pyramidal holding structure in section 1 of this chapter. To summarize: first, the actual controllers use the complex pyramidal holding structure to tunnel the subsidiaries and sub-subsidiaries, and the interests of dispersed minority shareholders cannot be effectively guaranteed, so they are forced to vote with their feet frequently. Second, for some non-core holding subsidiaries, the actual controller pays more attention to capital operations and market speculation than to corporate governance and management. Third, the complex pyramidal holding structure not only brings difficulties for regulatory authorities to supervise the related party transactions of equity related companies but also provides diversified ways for financial crocodiles to bribe corrupt officials, which eventually allows them to form an alliance of interest, resulting in the loss of state-owned assets.

The corporate governance predicament faced by China's listed companies in recent years, in addition to the frequent significant shareholdings of insurance companies, is largely related to the speculation of the financial crocodiles in the invisible pyramidal holding structures. The prevalence of the pyramidal holding structure and the resulting political, economic and social harm are the second logical thread to interpret the predicament of corporate governance in China.

The predicament of China's corporate governance, on the one hand, is related to the fact that China's capital market has entered the era of dispersed ownership, the invasion of external barbarians and the disturbance caused by capital crocodiles in the invisible pyramidal holding structure. On the other hand, it is related to the problem of Chinese-style insider control in some listed companies. When insiders encounter barbarians, the predicament of China's corporate governance emerges. The problem of Chinese-style insider control is the third logical thread in interpreting the predicament of China's corporate governance.

So what is the problem with Chinese-style insider control? So-called insider control refers to the phenomenon that the senior executives make decisions to seek personal benefits by taking advantage of the control right they actually enjoy, which exceeds their ability to assume responsibility, but the shareholders are forced to bear the consequences of decisions that harm their interests. The reason why it is called Chinese-style is that in some listed companies in China, the insider control is not caused by the highly dispersed ownership and the equity incentive plans for management – which used to be the cause of insider control in the United Kingdom and the United States – but related to the special political, social, historical, cultural factors and interest in the context of China's capital market system.

The first is the absence of owners due to the pyramidal holding structure. In addition to the disadvantages pointed out in section 1, the pyramidal holding structure is also a direct institutional inducement of the Chinese-style insider control problem. The major shareholders at the top of the pyramid (especially the state-owned controlling shareholders) either do nothing or are unable to do anything. It seems that there are major shareholders, but due to the absence of the owner and the inaction of the major shareholders, the chairman often becomes the actual controller of the company. With the extension of the control chain of the pyramidal holding structure, the owner absence and the insider control become more and more serious.

The second is the insider control based on political connections. Although formally it needs to go through the procedures of nomination by the board of directors and voting at the general meetings of shareholders, in the practice of China's corporate governance, key positions in enterprises whose controlling shareholder is state-owned are often appointed by the superior organizational department of the enterprise according to the cadre assessment system. Due to the above-mentioned top-down personnel appointment and removal approach, the appointee often has a special status.

The third is the insider control based on social ties. Let's take Shanshui Cement as an example. Zhang Caikui, an entrepreneur with a low shareholding, became the actual controller of Shanshui Cement, which is related to his meritorious deeds in the history of the company. Under Zhang Caikui's leadership, Shandong Cement (Pilot) Plant, which had been losing money for 13 consecutive years, has gradually developed into a cement enterprise listed in Hong Kong, with a number of branches throughout the country and once ranked among the top four cement companies in China. It can be said that without Zhang Caikui, Shanshui Cement would not be what it is today. In the short development course of China's modern enterprise since reform and opening-up, almost every successful enterprise has an entrepreneur like Zhang Caikui as its soul and core figure. This is a very important and unique historical factor in the formation of Chinese-style insider control in some companies in China.

Last is the insider control based on cultural traditions. In the case of Shanshui Cement, those employee shareholders who did not go to court against Zhang Caikui and his son were largely not motivated by the fact that their interests were unharmed but by the fact that they did not want to bear the reputation of betrayal. While this behavior gave those employee shareholders a reputation for loyalty and psychological satisfaction, objectively they contributed to the problem of Chinese-style insider control by not distinguishing right from wrong.

In addition to the traceable factors mentioned earlier, there may be various interests that we cannot observe. The combination of these factors makes a chairman, who does not seem to hold many shares and therefore does not have much responsibility, to be a typical Chinese-style insider controller.

Due to the various restrictions imposed by the state-owned system on the implementation of equity incentive plan and the buyout plan for managers, the historical contributions of many entrepreneurs have not been recognized in the form of equity. Faced with barbarians banging on the door, if the founding entrepreneurs with low equity percentage entrust the enterprise to a management team they have trusted and nurtured for a long time, they cannot convince other shareholders to accept their proposals; and if the founding entrepreneurs use their influence to continue to actually control the company, they will overstep the boundary from time to time while they have power, which will inevitably make them unable to take responsibility for the limited shares they hold. However, if they simply follow the logic of shareholder primacy and give up their insistence and allow new shareholders to lead the formation of a new management team, management experience and ideas established over the years will sometimes be unsustainable. When faced with the barbarian invasion in the capital market, not only do they seem powerless to resist, but their resentful resistance seems impulsive. This implicitly reinforces the antagonism of the dispute over control. In the face of public sympathy for the management teams threatened by barbarian invasions and the fierce resistance from disgruntled and even irritated management teams, the insurance funds pushed to the forefront are destined to play an unsavory role in the development stage of China's capital markets.

We see that when China's capital market enters the era of dispersed ownership and the Chinese-style insider control based on political and social connections encounters the barbarian invasions, the predicament of China's corporate governance appears. On November 15, 2016, eight senior executives of CSG Holding, including its founder Zeng Nan, resigned in succession after experiencing a dispute over control rights with Baoneng System. Some media reported this event publicly: one headline read "Yao Zhenhua Bloodbathed the CSG Boards, Causing Its

Senior Executives Collectively Resigned".[5] From the occurrence of this event, we see that the transfer of control and the threat of takeover did not bring the improvement of corporate governance and performance for the listed company as expected by the traditional corporate governance theory. On the contrary, the result is a bloodbath of the board of directors by the new shareholders, which neither the ordinary investors nor the management team and even the acquirers would like to see. If the dispute over Vanke's equity marks the beginning of the era of dispersed ownership in China's capital market, then the collective resignation of CSG's senior executives is a new climax of corporate governance events in the dispersed ownership era. In a certain sense, the transfer of control rights through bloodbathing the board of directors has become the institutional cost that China's listed companies, which, accustomed to the governance mode of dominance of a single shareholder, have to bear during the course of entering the era of dispersed ownership hurriedly.

So what kind of supervision and governance policies should we formulate to deal with the predicament of China's corporate governance when the capital market enters the era of dispersed ownership? Generally speaking, on the one hand, institutional design is needed to prevent the bloody invasion of barbarians so as to encourage entrepreneurial teams to invest more specific human capital in business model innovation; on the other hand, it is necessary to actively guide and regulate institutional investors, including insurance companies, so that the takeover threat becomes an important external force to improve the governance structure of China's listed companies. Achieving a balance between the two has become the logical starting point for the formulation of relevant corporate governance policies.

First of all, we encourage innovative enterprises to introduce the control right arrangement with unequal voting rights, so as to prevent the bloody invasion of barbarians and enable entrepreneurial teams to invest more human capital in business model innovation.

The incentive for entrepreneurs to start up will be weakened if they foresee that their hard-earned businesses may be easily invaded by barbarians in the future. Failure to set a bar high enough for barbarian invasion will undoubtedly discourage the enthusiasm of entrepreneurs. In reality, one institutional design that helps guard against barbarians from invading is the dual-class share structure. By locking control right in the entrepreneurial team innovating the business model, the unequal voting rights stocks, which seem to violate the rule of One Share–One Vote, have completed the transformation from short-term employment contract to long-term partnership contract between the entrepreneurial team and outside shareholders, to realize win-win cooperation between both sides. For example, JD.com, which went public on NASDAQ in 2014, issued two types of stock simultaneously: Class A shares have one vote per share and Class B shares 20 votes per share. Liu Qiangdong, the founder with only 20% of the capital contribution, gained absolute control of JD.com by holding 83.7% of the voting rights through Class B shares. Under the dual-class share structure, Class A stockholders hand over the business model innovation and other related decisions that they cannot grasp to the entrepreneurial team holding Class B stock, which has the advantage of information, thus realizing more specialized division of labor and efficiency improvement. When the entrepreneurial team fails to achieve the expected increase in profit, the Class B shares that are forced to be sold will automatically be converted into Class A shares, returning the company to the traditional governance model of One Share–One Vote, so as to realize a state-contingent of control rights and a smooth exit of the management team. Due to excellent characteristics in the design of control right arrangement, such as the change from short-term employment contract to long-term partnership contract and the state-contingent of control rights, unequal voting rights represented by dual-class stock structures have become the preferred way for US technology companies such as Google and Facebook to go public. Not only that, but by allowing companies to issue shares with unequal voting rights, the United States has become a target market for well-known Chinese companies such as Baidu and JD.com to go public.

In addition to dual-class shares, Alibaba's partnership system is also a model of control right arrangement worthy of reference for emerging enterprises. Currently, from the perspective of Alibaba's equity structure, Softbank (owned by Masayoshi Son of Japan), the largest shareholder, holds 25.8%. Alibaba's directors and senior managers (including Jack Ma) hold 9.0%, while Jack Ma himself holds only 6.1%. Obviously, we cannot regard Alibaba as a Japanese-owned enterprise according to the traditional way of understanding the equity structure. According to the relevant provisions of Alibaba's Articles of Association, the 38 partners represented by Jack Ma have the right to appoint the majority of Alibaba's board of directors to become the actual controllers of the company. Alibaba has thus reached the state of constant managers and changing shareholders and created the myth of labor employing capital in the Internet era.

US companies such as Google and Facebook, as well as many Chinese companies listed in the United States such as Alibaba, Baidu and JD.com, favor the control right arrangement with unequal voting rights. To some extent, this reflects the US industry and academia's renewed awareness of unequal voting rights – which were previously considered to be detrimental to the protection of investors' rights – after the wanton invasion by barbarians in the takeover wave. In the face of barbarian invasion, the introduction of dual-class shares will encourage entrepreneurial teams to invest in long-term human capital around the business model. Seemingly unequal voting rights, on the one hand, allow the entrepreneurial team who holding Class B shares to focus on business model innovation, and on the other hand, make the dispersed shareholders who holding Class A shares avoid interfering in the business model which they are not good at, only focus on risk sharing, and ultimately realize the equality between the two types of shareholders in terms of return on investment. As we have seen, the introduction of unequal voting rights is not the worst method for protecting investors' interests, nor is One Share–One Vote the best rule when it comes to the choice of control right arrangements.

On March 2, 2017, Snap Inc. of the United States attempted to issue Class A, B and C shares simultaneously, becoming one of the few companies in the world to issue shares with a triple-class structure. The Stock Exchange of Hong Kong Ltd.

issued a market consultation paper on June 16, 2017, proposing to attract technology networks or start-ups with the Weighted Voting Rights to list in Hong Kong. The reason why the Vanke equity dispute is remarkable is precisely because the management of Vanke, the object of merging, is an entrepreneurial team headed by Wang Shi. The Vanke equity dispute soon fell into a debate over whether to follow the shareholder primacy theory of the capital market or to provide sufficient incentives for entrepreneurs to invest in human capital. Therefore, there is an urgent need for China's capital market entering the era of dispersed ownership to learn from the successful experience of capital market development in various regions and accelerate institutional innovation in control right arrangements, including unequal voting rights, to achieve a good balance between encouraging human capital investment of the entrepreneurial team and playing the role of external governance of institutional investors such as insurance funds.

Second, to gradually reduce and eliminate the number of layers of the pyramidal holding structure through the formulation of tax policies and necessary regulatory measures, and change the motives and ways of speculation of the financial crocodiles who are hidden in the pyramidal holding structure, so as to promote their future conversion to public welfare and family trust funds.

For the elimination or layer reduction of the pyramidal holding structure, the direct and effective means are to enact anti-monopoly regulatory bill and tax policy to increase the overall level of tax burden of the pyramidal holding structure. Reviewing the development history of capital markets in various countries, it is easy to find that many countries have gone through the process of the prevalence of the pyramidal holding structure and concentrated ownership to dispersed ownership structure. Let's take Standard Oil of the Rockefeller family as an example. Standard Oil, founded in 1870, is a typical trust in Lenin's eyes; that is, the so-called form of capitalist monopoly organization composed of many enterprises producing similar goods or closely related products. At the beginning of the 20th century, Standard Oil produced 90% of the oil in the United States. Although Congress enacted the Sherman Antitrust Act in 1890 – the first antitrust law in US history – it was not until 1911 that the Supreme Court split Standard Oil into more than 30 independent enterprises, including ExxonMobil and Chevron, according to the Sherman Antitrust Act. During the Great Depression of the 1930s, the bankruptcy of ComEd led to the introduction of the Public Utility Holding Company Act (PUHCA) in 1935. The PUHCA limited the number of subsidiaries and cross-shareholdings of public utility holding companies to guard against the financial risks associated with pyramidal mergers. In addition to no more than two layers of control, the Act also limits the industry and region of public utility holding companies. As the US power industry enters the era of regulation, the equity of public utility holding companies is becoming more and more dispersed, resulting in a large number of "widow-and-orphan" stocks.

In addition to anti-monopoly law and regulatory policies restricting holding and cross-shareholding, increasing the tax burden of the pyramidal holding structure has also been an important measure to promote the corporate governance model of dispersed ownership in the United States. On the one hand, the US government has put the parent company, which controls subsidiaries and sub-subsidiaries, at a tax disadvantage by imposing an inter-corporate dividend tax; on the other hand, it has encouraged institutional investors to hold more non-voting preferred stocks by providing tax incentives to institutional investors who hold preferred shares, thus avoiding their excessive intervention in the management of listed companies. At the same time, by levying estate tax and gift tax, financial crocodiles are encouraged to shift from the equity control to public welfare and family trust funds. After the change of nature, public welfare funds are more concerned with the safety of capital and the stability of returns, rather than simply seeking the control of companies, capital operation and market speculation. On March 20, 2017, the American billionaire David Rockefeller died. We can gather from numerous memorial articles that the unique institutional arrangement of the Rockefeller family helped to realize the centennial wealth transmission. Through the introduction of a family trust fund, the Rockefeller family, on the one hand, kept property as a whole to benefit future generations, so as to avoid the phenomenon of a rich family unable to stay rich for no more than three generations, caused by family separation. On the other hand, the management of assets was entrusted to a professional trust, avoiding family members' direct intervention in the management, effectively solving the conflict of trust and competence that existed in the family business succession. The direct inspiration brought by the Rockefeller family's hundred years of wealth inheritance is that it seems to give up the control right, but in fact to realize the perpetuation of wealth.

Through the series of regulatory and tax policy adjustments mentioned above, the United States initially developed a corporate governance model characterized by equity dispersion in the 1920s and 1930s. The introduction of mandatory regulatory policies is often prone to policy distortions. Learning from the practice of the United States back then, we can adopt similar regulatory measures in certain industries at specific periods to reduce or even eliminate the layers of pyramidal holding structures. If we see the introduction of unequal voting rights and other control right arrangements as a passive response of listed companies to prevent the barbarian invasions, then the elimination of the pyramidal holding structure and its negative effects will be a proactive adaptation of China's capital market to the era of dispersed ownership.

Finally, to solve the problem of Chinese-style insider control by constantly improving the current corporate governance mechanism. The formation of Chinese-style insider control is not only due to historical reasons, but it is also caused by the complex reality. The solution to Chinese-style insider control is a long-term challenge for corporate governance theorists and practitioners in China. At present, the following approaches are available for reference and adoption.

First, to realize the marketization of the selection and remuneration of SOE senior executives, completely abolish the administrative ranks, truly open recruitment by the board of directors to the whole society and offer market-oriented compensation package, so as to promote the transformation of SOEs from managing enterprises to managing capital. China has issued two important documents on SOE reform: the "Guidance on Further Improving the Corporate Governance

Structure of SOEs" and the "Plan for SASAC to Accelerate the Function Trans-formation by Focusing on Capital Management". The core spirit of the documents is to return the authority of selection and recruitment, performance assessment and reward management of executives to the board of directors. The appraisal, appoint-ment and removal of managerial cadres, namely professional managers, is shifted from SASAC and the Organization Department of the CPC Central Committee to board of the companies, thus accelerating the transformation of SOEs from manag-ing enterprises to managing capital.

Second, the awakening of shareholders' awareness of their rights. When insiders and barbarians fight with each other, it is often the dispersed outside shareholders whose interests are harmed. Shareholders need to realize that their shares are not only marketable securities that can be realized, but also votes. On March 31, 2013, Wang Zhenhua and Liang Shusen, individual shareholders with a total sharehold-ing of 3.15%, submitted "A Proposal on the Removal of All Directors of the Com-pany" to Dong Fang Hotel. At the 2013 annual general meeting of shareholders held on April 15 of that year, although the proposal to remove all directors submit-ted by the above two shareholders was rejected, the proposal on the related party transaction of Dong Fang Hotel's investment in Da Jiao Shan Hotel was also rejected at this general meeting after the controlling shareholders avoided voting. This event was called the "uprising of small shareholders" by some media because it changed the previous corporate governance practice that dominated by control-ling shareholders, and minority shareholders were forced to vote with their feet, and not only opposed the controlling shareholders, but also put forward their own new proposals.

As a matter of fact, the Dong Fang Hotel's event is just one of the small share-holder uprisings that have occurred within China's listed companies in recent years. With the improvement of the legal environment of China's capital market and the enhancement of small and medium shareholders' awareness of rights, small shareholder uprisings have increased explosively in recent years. From 2010 to 2015, listed companies in China have had at least 207 small shareholder upris-ings. We understand that these events are not only one of the typical events mark-ing the entry of China's capital market into the era of dispersed ownership but also will have a profound and lasting impact on the governance practices of China's listed companies. This also reminds the theoretical researchers and practitioners of corporate governance to put on an important research agenda that making share-holders truly become the authority of corporate governance and the voting at share-holders' general meeting as a basic platform that reflects shareholders' will and protecting their rights and interests.

Third, the board of directors (mainly independent directors) plays an impor-tant mediating role in the disputes over control rights between insiders and bar-barians. Under the dispersed ownership structure in the United Kingdom and the United States, if the insider control occurs, the receiver will often redeem the actual control through a plan such as the golden parachute, thereby minimizing the losses of both parties in the dispute. With a strategy of compromise and the wisdom of giving up, the golden parachute has become one of the market-oriented solutions to disputes over control rights. In theory, a board of directors dominated by independent directors with more symmetrical information will play an important mediating role in the control rights disputes between insiders and barbarians. Under the mediation of the board of directors dominated by independent directors, the golden parachute is eventually introduced to incumbent entrepreneurs through voting at the general meeting of shareholders, so that they voluntarily give up their anti-merging resistance. On the basis of listening to the opinions of incumbent entrepreneurs and the new shareholders, the nomination committee of the board of directors led by independent directors appoints a new management team in accordance with the principle of achieving the sustainable and stable development of the company. This is actually the reason for the board organization mode popular in many listed companies in the United Kingdom and the United States, in which all board members except the CEO are independent directors. However, due to the lack of independence and good market reputation, independent directors still have a long way to go to play the role of mediator in equity disputes.

Fourth, let the standard insurance capital become a positive force for the healthy development of China's capital market. The positive implication of the wave of M&A characterized by the significant shareholding of insurance companies is to warn insiders who still rely on the iron rice bowl:[6] although the former state-owned major shareholders may not let you go easily, the new shareholders may force you to leave. We need to strike a good balance between alerting inactive managers with the threat of external takeover and protecting the human capital investment of entrepreneurial teams characterized by business model innovation, and finally make the takeover threats initiated by institutional investors, including insurance and pension funds, as an external governance mechanism and an important force for perfecting corporate governance.

Now let us imagine a bright future for China's capital market under the above corporate governance and regulatory policies. The common shares of listed companies are mainly held directly by individual investors, while institutional investors such as insurance funds mainly hold preferred shares, and there is little complex pyramidal holding structure. For individual investors, since there is no possible tunneling by the actual controllers of the former pyramidal holding structure, and the companies in which they hold shares will not be subject to market speculation, their speculative motives will be weakened accordingly, and they will turn to value investment and even start to care about the governance and management of listed companies. For institutional investors who hold preferred shares and thus have no voting rights, they lack both incentives and conditions for market speculation and capital operation for the purpose of preserving and increasing value. Therefore, the frequent equity disputes we have observed in China's capital market in recent years have disappeared. Without the complex pyramidal holding structure as the cover and carrier, the collusion between capital and power of some corrupt officials in the past is unsustainable, and listed companies can thus launch institutional innovations in control right arrangements such as the dual-class share structure. They need not worry about the barbarian invasion and can just focus on the improvement of corporate governance and the enhancement of business management. A healthy and benign capital market has begun to take shape.

4   The Status Quo of SOE Governance

Reviewing the course of China's economic system reform in the past 40 years, it is evident that the reform of state-owned enterprises has always been the central link and core content of China's economic system reform because of their unique position and extensive influence in China's national economy. In 2015, China's SOEs launched a new round of mixed-ownership reform. The success or failure of the new round of SOE reform is crucial to the final realization of China's market-oriented economic transformation. Before putting forward concrete reform measures, it is necessary to understand the status quo of SOE governance and clarify the historical logic of the new round of SOE reform characterized by mixed ownership. We hope that SOEs can form reasonable and effective equity and corporate governance structures through the true mixture of ownership and take more solid steps in the process of transformation to modern enterprises.

Although several rounds of SOE reform have been carried out since the reform and opening-up, the following characteristics still exist in the corporate governance of SOEs.

First, some SOEs make high profits by virtue of their monopoly position in the market and compete unfairly with private enterprises, which leads to the public's discontent and anger over monopoly operation and unfair competition.

The profits of SOEs mainly come from monopolies. Let's take the profits of central enterprises in 2010 as an example. In 2010, central enterprises made a total profit of 134.5 billion yuan, accounting for 67.5% of the total profits of SOEs. In 2009, ten companies, including PetroChina, China Mobile, China Telecom, China Unicom and Sinopec, accounted for more than 70% of the profits of central enterprises. Among them, PetroChina and China Mobile earned 128.56 billion yuan and 148.47 billion yuan, respectively, accounting for more than one-third of the total profits of central enterprises. Compared with private enterprises, the nominal performance of state-owned and state-owned holding enterprises was not satisfactory. From 2001 to 2009, the average return on equity (ROE) of state-owned and state-owned holding industrial enterprises was 8.16%, while that of non-state-owned industrial enterprises was 12.9%. In 2009, the ROE of SOEs was 8.18%, and that of non-state-owned industrial enterprises was 15.59%. It can be seen that compared with private enterprises, the nominal performance of SOEs is not good enough.

We can get a glimpse of the current situation of the development of Chinese enterprises through the list of top 500 enterprises in 2014 before the launch of the new round of mixed-ownership reform. Among the 43 loss-making enterprises in the Top 500 List of China Enterprise Confederation and China Enterprise Directors Association, only one was private enterprise, and SOEs became the hardest hit. Unprofitable enterprises were concentrated mainly on coal, iron and steel, nonferrous metals and chemicals, building materials, water transportation and other fields. As many as 14% of the 300 SOEs are in the red, and these 42 enterprises had a total loss of 72.66 billion yuan, of which ten central enterprises lost 38.57 billion yuan in total. In contrast, only one out of 200 private companies lost money, and the loss was only 50 million yuan.

The profits of SOEs are mainly derived from low financing costs, land and resource rents, government subsidies and tax breaks. The nominal performance of SOEs is not their real performance but the image project of unequal competition with private enterprises by enjoying various preferential policies. First of all, in terms of financing costs, the average real interest rate of state-owned and state-owned holding industrial enterprises is 1.6%, while the weighted average interest rate of other enterprises (regarded as market interest rate) is about 4.68%. If the interest payable by SOEs is recalculated according to the level of market interest rate, the interest payment differential from 2001 to 2009 is about 2,753.9 billion yuan, accounting for 47% of the total nominal profits of state-owned and state-owned holding industrial enterprises. Second, from the perspective of land and resource rent, the industrial land rent is calculated according to the 3% proportion of the price of industrial land. Therefore, state-owned and state-owned holding industrial enterprises should pay 3,931.2 billion yuan of rent from 2001 to 2009, which accounts for 67.2% of the total nominal profits of state-owned and state-owned holding industrial enterprises. If we consider commercial service land, SOEs should pay 1,210.4 billion yuan in rent alone in 2008. The average resource tax on oil is only 26 yuan per ton. Coupled with the resource compensation fee calculated at 1% of the sales revenue, the resource rent levied on oil is less than 2% of the price, which is far lower than the 12.5% levied on joint ventures in China. According to the above proportion, it is estimated that from 2001 to 2009, the oil resource rent owed by state-owned and state-owned holding industrial enterprises was about 243.7 billion yuan. Together with natural resources such as natural gas and coal, state-owned and state-owned holding industrial enterprises paid 497.7 billion yuan less in resource rent from 2001 to 2009. And then, as for the government subsidies to SOEs, from 1994 to 2006, national financial subsidies for losses of SOEs reached 365.3 billion yuan. Among them, state-owned and state-owned holding industrial enterprises received about 194.3 billion yuan in financial subsidies from 2007 to 2009. Finally, the tax burden of SOEs is much lower than that of private enterprises. From 2007 to 2009, the average income tax burden in 992 SOEs was 10%, while that of private enterprises reached 24%, making the tax burden of private enterprise much heavier than that of SOEs. Therefore, if a total of about 7,491.4 billion yuan of unpaid and payable costs and subsidies are deducted from the total nominal profits to restore the real cost of enterprises from the book financial data, the average ROE of state-owned and state-owned holding industrial enterprises would be −6.29% from 2001 to 2009. And from the new round of SOE mixed-ownership reform, private capital is expected to have a finger in the pie.

Natural political connections and regulatory monopolies lead SOEs to occupy the dominant position in resource allocation. The role of SOEs as the "eldest son of the Republic" and the double identity of the SOE executive as both enterprise manager and government official makes the executive naturally connected to the government. This gives SOEs an advantageous position in resource allocation and even affects the government's policy direction, making many policies preferential and favorable to SOEs. Some state-owned listed companies employ retired government officials as independent directors, which not only enables those companies to get more implicit benefits such as greater policy tilt and support, less administrative control and regulatory penalties due to violations, but also obtain the actual benefits in terms of tax incentives and government subsidies.

SOEs have little incentive to innovate and reform because of the strong policy and resource advantages, and on the other hand, unfair competition squeezes the development space of private enterprises, hindering the healthy and balanced development of the national economy.

Second, in addition to managing capital through state-owned asset management, the government also exerts substantial influence on enterprise operations through the top-down personnel appointment and dismissal system and the promotion assessment of senior executives, which makes SOEs become neoclassical capitalist enterprises with agency conflicts.

The modern corporation is one of the greatest inventions of mankind. Nearly 99% of the wealth creation in human history has been achieved in the past 250 years, and the organization of the modern corporations is largely responsible for this. The essential difference between the modern company and the family workshop–style neoclassical capitalist enterprise is capital socialization and management professionalization based on the specialized division of labor. Through the separation of ownership and management rights, modern corporations can avoid non-professional investors intervening in the management decisions of professional managers, so as to improve the operation efficiency. In addition, due to the absence of owners and the long chain of principal-agent, state-owned listed companies have gradually formed the internal control pattern with the chairman as the core, and there are serious principal-agent problems and high agency costs. As a result, state-owned listed companies neither get rid of the intervention of control right over management right that often existed in the family workshops, nor do they make use of the social specialization to improve efficiency, and also they do not have a good solution to the agency problem that does not exist in the family manual workshop. The agency problem caused by the separation of ownership and control rights in modern companies should be solved by the improvement of corporate governance structure, rather than returning to the neoclassical capitalist enterprises like family workshops, in which control rights intervene in business management. In the above sense, China's SOEs need a modern corporate revolution in the future, and the first goal is to make a real separation between ownership and management of enterprises.

The corporate governance of SOEs faces conflicting multi-tasking goals. Due to their special status in China's national economy and social development, SOEs not only have the characteristics of ordinary enterprises, but they also bear the social responsibilities which are hard to imagine for ordinary enterprises, including stabilizing prices, promoting employment, and even maintaining social stability.

When SOEs are regarded as tools of national policies, in order to realize the political and economic intentions of the country, SOEs need to obey the overall situation of national economic construction and social development and serve the macro political and economic policies. For example, SOEs are used as a means of counter-cyclical adjustment to expand investment during recessions, to lower the prices of their products to curb inflation, and to hire more workers to avoid unemployment. In foreign economic policy, SOEs are also used as an important weapon against international competition. The multi-tasking of SOEs obviously hindered the effective operation of the market mechanism, making SOEs a mixture of administration and market. This makes SOEs unable to realize the capital socialization and manager professionalization based on the idea of specialized division of labor, and unable to improve the efficiency of enterprises through a true separation of ownership and management to avoid the intervention of non-professional investors in the decision-making process of professional managers. In fact, the most important social responsibility of enterprises is to create profits.

As one of the forms of public ownership, SOEs have a special position in China's national economy. Most of the SOEs invested and controlled by central or local governments at all levels are distributed in key industries and critical areas related to the national economy and people's livelihood, so the control rights of SOEs are uniquely arranged. In order to maintain the control of the government or its agents over state-owned listed companies, China's capital market once launched the split-share structure, that is to say, part of the state-owned shares could not be listed and circulated, and the same shares had different rights and different prices. In recent years, with the completion of the reform of the split-share structure and the call for the reduction of state-owned shares, the controlling shareholder's stake has decreased year by year. However, in order to control the listed companies, the SASAC system or state-owned legal persons as the largest shareholder still holds a controlling stake, and the situation of one share being dominant has not fundamentally changed. Along with the unique arrangement of control rights of SOEs, a unique system of personnel appointment and removal of senior executives has gradually developed in China's SOEs. The appointment of SOE executives formally depends on ownership, but in essence it is achieved through top-down personnel appointment from higher authorities.

Under the top-down personnel appointment and removal system of SOEs, on the one hand, the senior executives are the managers of enterprises and also the maker and the implementer of business development plans; on the other hand, they belong to certain political ranks and have the same opportunities and channels for political promotion as government officials. This makes SOE executives who are both economic men and political men more like government officials than professional managers (see research by scholars such as Yang Ruilong). This political promotion channel exists not only within SOEs, between parent companies and subsidiaries, and between subsidiaries of enterprise groups under the same controlling shareholder, but also between SOEs and government departments. According to the research by Wang Zeng et al., promotions accounted for 30% of the 1,125 observations of executive changes in China's listed companies between 2005 and 2011.

Similar to government officials, SOE executives are forced to place a high value on internal promotion channels due to the lack of external employment opportunities for professional managers provided by a vibrant market. This is reflected in the fact that SOE executives are more concerned about performance appraisals in the form of job checks by government authorities because these appraisals directly affect whether they receive political promotions. Also, because political promotion brings not only higher pay, social status and prestige, but also more power, SOE executives, like government officials, have strong motives to strive to increase their chances of political promotion.

In order to win the attention of the media, the public and the higher authorities so as to win the tournament for political promotion, SOE executives are willing to launch image projects which help to improve their personal images in the short term but are detrimental to the sustainable and stable development of the enterprise in the long term. Therefore, there is an incentive distortion in the political promotion of SOE executives in China. For SOEs, public welfare donations seem to be an indispensable responsibility and essential economic behavior in their daily management due to the special nature of enterprises. A study based on A-share state-owned listed companies shows that the public welfare donations given by SOEs increase significantly as executives' tenure is extended (job changes increase the likelihood of political promotion). However, the significant increase in public welfare donation is, on the one hand, associated with the self-interest motive of SOE executives for preserving the position of chairman and gaining opportunities for their future political promotions; on the other hand, some donations fail to improve or even hinder the future performance of enterprises to perform the expected function of strategic marketing. As a result, the implicit incentive for promotion has been distorted in the actual operation of the political promotion system of SOE executives. Under the background of the above system, public welfare donation, which was supposed to reflect corporate social responsibility, has to some extent become an image project carried out by SOE executives for political promotions. The image projects of SOEs, including public welfare donations, media reports and overseas M&A, have thus become special agency costs that dispersed outside shareholders need to face under the insider control of SOEs.

There is no unified and open market for professional managers in China, so the operation mechanism of the managers market, such as career concerns and manager reputation, cannot work as well as expected. A total of 896 out of 1,271 sample observations came from internal promotion, accounting for 70.5% of all managers replaced during the sample period, and 232 observed managers came from the job rotation within their corporate group, accounting for 18.25%. If managers generated by internal promotions and job rotations are regarded as insiders in a broad sense, nearly 90% of managers replaced in China's listed companies from 2005 to 2011 are not from outside but from inside of the enterprise. Only 143 observed managers were recruited from outside, accounting for 11.25%. This shows that the professional manager market in China is still at an early stage of development, and there is no unified and open professional manager market.

The top-down personnel appointment system in SOEs actually poses a challenge to the board of directors as the authority of corporate governance and undermines the effectiveness of professional managers market that operates based on the career concerns and manager reputation to identify manager's competence. Good performance does not guarantee the long-term tenure of the current manager, which leads them to focus on short-term performance and neglect long-term accumulation. Compared with the mature external managers' market in Western countries, the top-down appointment system in China reduces the professionalization of managers of listed companies and makes the operation mechanism of the managers' market, including career concern and manager reputation, fail to play the expected role. Nowadays, the competition between enterprises is getting fiercer, marketization is gradually deepening, and many SOEs need to complete the reform of modern corporate governance. It is important to choose the right method of manager selection and appointment to improve the efficiency of corporate governance.

A clear evidence of government intervention in the micro-management of SOEs is the new policy of executive pay limits launched in recent years. Equity incentives, which are considered very important in directors' compensation package, are rarely adopted. Some senior executives are not motivated enough due to the salary restrictions, and the brain drain in SOEs is serious. In November 2014, the Central Committee of the Communist Party of China and the State Council issued the *Opinions on Deepening the Reform of the Compensation System for the Executives of Centrally Administered Enterprises* (Doc. 12 [2014] released by the General Office of the CPC Central Committee), which divided the salary of the executives appointed by the central enterprises into three parts: basic annual salary, performance-based annual salary and tenure incentive income. The salary of each part is determined according to a certain multiple of the average salary of the employees in central enterprises in the previous year. For example, the basic salary cannot exceed twice the average salary of the employees in central enterprises in the previous year; the annual performance-based salary cannot exceed six times the average salary of the employees in central enterprises in the previous year; and the tenure incentive income shall not exceed 30% of the total annual salary of the executive during his term of office (about 2.4 times the average salary of the employees in the central enterprises in the previous year). Through the salary limitation policy, the salary of the executives appointed by the central enterprises will be kept within 10.4 times the average annual wage of the employees in the central enterprises. Throughout the new round of salary limitation policy, its remarkable features can be summarized as two aspects: the average salary of central enterprises' employees in the previous year as a reference system, and the top-down implementation of salary limitation is promoted by documents issued by the General Office of the CPC Central Committee. Although the above-mentioned salary limitation policy is mainly aimed at the appointed executives of central enterprises, due to the fuzzy boundary between the so-called appointed executives and professional managers and the related spillover effects, the above-mentioned practices will undoubtedly have an important impact on the managerial compensation design of SOEs in China.

When assessing whether executive compensation is reasonable, the benchmark should be how much value the executive creates for the enterprise, not anything else. The reason is that shareholders have incomplete information about the level of the manager's efforts, which is the logical and factual starting point for designing management compensation contracts. The strength of the incentive is judged by the pay performance sensitivity of managers. Sometimes paying a manager a high salary seems to increase the cost of the firm, but it is entirely worth it if the increased pay for managers (which provides sufficient incentives to the manager) allows the firm to achieve a greater value. A large number of empirical studies show that, in addition to the enterprise performance, managers' risk attitude, uncertainty of external business environment, enterprise scale and the competition in the industry significantly affect the level and structure of managerial compensation. If one company's performance (size, competitiveness in the industry, etc.) is different from that of another company, there is a reason for that company's managerial compensation to be different from that of the other company. In addition to the payment for human capital, managers' compensation includes incentives and it is also the embodiment of entrepreneurship, so fairness cannot be reflected simply by comparing with the average salary of ordinary employees. This reminds the theorists and practitioners to rethink the rationality of limiting executive pay by taking the average salary of central enterprises' employees in the previous year as the reference system.

We know that when information is incomplete, the party with information advantage should take the lead in the design and implementation of the relevant contract. For example, as the core of corporate governance, the board of directors has more information advantages in evaluating corporate performance, so in corporate governance practice, the design and implementation of executive compensation are usually completed by the board of directors (Compensation Committee). This fully reflects the principle of matching the authorization structure with the information structure of modern organizations. At present, the new round of executive pay curbs are being led by the government departments that do not have the information advantage, which is obviously contrary to the principle mentioned above.

Research shows that the phenomenon of excessive executive compensation does exist in some listed companies in China. However, the correct way to solve the excessive compensation is not through the one-size-fits-all salary limit imposed by the government departments, but through the self-examination conducted by the board of directors (Compensation Committee) of listed companies under the supervision of the regulatory authorities. In the process of self-examination, the board of directors should use the pay performance sensitivity of managers as an evaluation benchmark. If corporate performance is declining while salary of managers is increasing, it is clearly an unreasonable compensation design that should be corrected. In fact, excessive executive compensation is precisely the evidence of the existence of unreasonable corporate governance structure, which needs to be corrected by improving the corporate governance structure, rather than simply limiting salary.

Third, due to the source of the position, the managers' influence in the personnel turnover and the nepotism culture in the board of directors, independent directors cannot play the role of supervising managers as expected.

Independent directors refer to board members who have no family or business ties to the company other than being directors of the company. As an important measure to improve the governance structure of listed companies in China, and drawing on the mature experience of Western countries, China's capital market fully implemented the independent director system for listed companies since 2003. At least in form, the independent director system has become one of the most basic and important institutional arrangements for the governance of listed companies in China. Influenced by institutional design and board culture, independent directors have not played the expected role of supervising managers well.

Although SOE chairmen or managers are the objects of supervision, they interview and recommend independent directors when they take office, which makes the supervisory role of independent directors inherently inadequate. Since the chairman (manager) plays a very important role in nominating directors to the new board of directors, the remuneration, reputation and social contacts facilitated by becoming a director encourage every director who hopes to be renominated in the election of the new board of directors to please the manager. On the one hand, managers' performance appraisal and salary formulation are implemented by directors; on the other hand, managers in turn participate in setting the annual salary and allowances of the director. More importantly, once a director gives the impression that they like to antagonize managers, it is difficult for them to get invited to join the board of directors of other companies. Due to these considerations, directors are often ambiguous and easy to compromise in supervising the chairman or manager. As we can see, the root causes and defects of the institutional design make it difficult for independent directors to play the independent supervision role effectively, because they need to be interviewed and recommended by the chairmen of the board (managers) when they take office, and their compensation needs to be formulated with the participation of the chairmen (managers).

Since a mature market for independent directors has not yet been formed, independent directors generally come from friends of the chairmen (managers) or friends of their friends. The strong culture of cronyism restricts independent directors from playing an effective supervisory role. From the institutional root, the nepotistic culture may be inseparable from the power of the chairman or manager on the one hand, and it may be the result of the interaction between the culture and social connection related to the acquaintance society on the other. Given cultural and social norms of respecting the authority of managers, directors are often reluctant to damage the good co-worker relationships with managers by, for example, blocking compensation plans.

Some listed companies introduce independent directors not for supervising managers but for seeking political connections. Studies have shown that the establishment of political connections by the heads of private enterprises as representatives of the National People's Congress or members of the Chinese People's Political Consultative Conference has a positive impact on the improvement of corporate performance. Politically connected status helps private companies obtain more loans from commercial banks and government tax subsidies. Many private companies are willing to hire independent directors with official backgrounds, not to supervise the chairmen or managers but to establish political connections. In essence, it is a transaction in which the company pays salary to independent directors and the independent directors with official background seek political and economic benefits for the company. Since the purpose of hiring independent directors is to build political connections, it is clear that we cannot expect them to supervise chairmen or managers.

In order to prevent abusing power for personal gain and carrying out unfair competition through political connections, on October 19, 2013, the Organization Department of the CPC Central Committee issued the *Opinions on Further Regulating Party and Government Leading Cadres to Hold Part-Time or Any Positions in Enterprises*. After the publication of the opinion, a wave of independent directors left A-share listed companies immediately. By early June 2014, a total of 268 people had voluntarily requested to resign from their positions as independent directors, involving about 300 listed companies in both Shanghai and Shenzhen stock markets. On average, 33 independent directors submitted their resignation every month, and at least one independent director resigned per day (according to *Economic Information Daily*). It is a unique phenomenon in the governance practice of listed companies in China that so many officials serve as independent directors.

It is difficult for independent directors to actively participate in important business decisions of listed companies and make feasible policy suggestions. According to a report released by the Shanghai Stock Exchange in 2013, 38 independent directors of 26 companies raised objections to relevant matters that year, accounting for 1.23% of the total number of independent directors. According to the *2007 Analysis of the Performance of Independent Directors of Listed Companies on the Shanghai Stock Market*, only 1.5% of independent directors raised objections in 2007. We can see that dissent raised by independent directors did not change much during the five-year period (2007–2013) and even shows a downward trend. The vast majority of independent directors have never raised objections to board resolutions or against the will of controlling shareholders and management under their control. According to the 2013 report of Shanghai Stock Exchange in 2013, more than one-third of independent directors said that they could not obtain the same information as inside directors to support their independent judgment and opinion. About one in seven independent directors said the companies they worked for had deceived them or prevented them from exercising their authority. In the absence of necessary information, independent directors can neither blindly agree nor arbitrarily veto, but only abstain from voting. This makes it difficult for independent directors to actively participate in important business decisions of listed companies and make policy recommendations. Even those independent directors who express opposing opinions are still finding it difficult to materially affect the resolutions of listed companies because their negative votes are often not adopted or not fully adopted. There are many examples. The independent director of Nanning

Chemical Industry once proposed to dismiss the chairman who failed to perform his duties for a long time, but the proposal was rejected by the general meeting of shareholders and aborted. The independent director of China Television Media proposed to add a formal lawyer's opinion to the lease contract, which was also rejected. Similar situations occurred in several listed companies such as King Long Motor Group, Minfeng Special Paper, Lyrun New Material and Higrand Technology.

For independent directors, the incentives of the fixed allowance system are insufficient. Different from listed companies in mature market of economic countries that mainly rely on equity incentive plans to provide incentives to independent directors, by the end of 2011, about 94% of China's listed companies still paid fixed wage subsidies to their independent directors. However, the equity incentive plan, which is very important in the design of compensation contract, is explicitly not allowed to be adopted in the compensation plan of independent directors in China. Article 8 of *Equity Incentive Measures for the Administration of Listed Companies (for Trial Implementation)* promulgated by the China Securities Regulatory Commission in 2005 clearly stipulates that the objects of equity incentive plan can include directors, supervisors, senior managers, core technical (business) personnel of listed companies, and other employees whom the company thinks should be motivated, but should not include independent directors. In contrast, more than 50% of the world's top 500 companies offer equity incentives to independent directors, and independent directors in 5% of companies earn all of their income from stock. It is a clear fact that the differentiated compensation design based on individual performance and risk sharing will obviously provide stronger incentives to independent directors and will be superior to a fixed compensation.

We note that the previous corporate governance theory and practice paid more attention to the compensation of managers. The independent directors design incentive compensation schemes for managers, but their own compensation has long been either ignored, or it has simply been assumed that the independent directors have been well incentivized; thus they have the motivation to perform the duties of supervising managers and strategic consulting. However, as some scholars have pointed out, while the board of directors plays a potential role in solving the agency problems caused by conflicts of interest between managers and investors, it also faces its own agency problem (independent directors are agents of shareholders) and corresponding incentive problems. Therefore, how to motivate independent directors to think like shareholders is as important as designing the manager compensation – the traditional concern of corporate governance theory and practice.

The turnover of independent directors is chaotic, accompanied by serious reverse elimination. In theory and in practice, the turnover of independent directors from outside the company does not need to and should not be synchronized with the unconventional turnover of the chairman. However, in some companies, unrelated to the company's restructuring, poor corporate performance, punishment by regulatory authorities and reserved opinions issued by independent directors, the independent director who has not expired is unexpectedly resigned soon after the unconventional replacement of chairman. Therefore, the phenomenon of "a new chief brings in new aid" and the board culture of cronyism exist in the change of independent directors of listed companies in China. For an enterprise with a board culture of nepotism, the chairman of the board will become the emperor who makes daily management decisions and decides on the promotion of board members, while the board members, including independent directors, will be accordingly alienated into tame courtiers. This kind of culture will undoubtedly change the original intention of the independent director system to provide external and independent supervision by employing independent directors and weaken the effectiveness of independent director's supervision, which is one of the practical reasons why independent directors cannot play the expected role in corporate governance.

In addition to the phenomenon of a new chief brings in new aid – when the former chairman steps down, the independent director also resigns – there is other chaos in the turnover of independent directors, which is the manifestations of the board culture of nepotism in China's listed companies. For example, Mr. Jie, an independent director of a real estate company, was reappointed as an independent director after he had served two terms for six years and left for three years; Mr. Kang, an independent director of a cement company, was recommended as a supervisor after his two terms as an independent director expired, and he became the independent director again when the board changed. These examples not only show that there are irregular practices and cronyism in the process of selecting and hiring independent directors in the case companies, but also reveal to a certain extent that in China's corporate governance practice, many listed companies only regard the independent directors as a measure to meet the regulatory requirements rather than the independent supervisor.

Another important issue related to the turnover of independent directors is the reverse elimination. If an independent director puts forward a reserved opinion, it will be difficult to be hired by other companies, thus creating what is known as reverse elimination. In the culture of reverse elimination and cronyism, independent directors expect that if they say no, they will not only be more likely to quit, but they will also find it difficult to get hired by other companies. The high cost of saying no forces independent directors to be silent, flattering, and even pandering or colluding.

It has been more than ten years since the listed companies in China fully implemented the independent director system. Although independent directors have played an important role in improving the credibility of information disclosure and increasing the cost of related party transactions of listed companies, the role of independent directors in supervising the chairman and managers is far from expectations due to the above reasons. In the future, we need to make positive improvements from both institutional design and cultural roots and strive to form a board culture of harmony without uniformity, so that the independent director system of listed companies in China can develop healthily and eventually become a basic institutional arrangement that plays an important role in corporate governance.

5   Historical Logic of SOE Mixed-Ownership Reform

On the basis of reviewing the types and problems of corporate governance of China's SOEs and summarizing the status quo, this section attempts to find out the historical logic followed by the new round of SOE reform characterized by mixed ownership.

First of all, mixed-ownership reform helps to calm public discontent and anger over the monopoly operation of state-owned assets and unfair competition. The high profits of some SOEs are closely related to their monopoly position in the market and unfair competition with private companies. However, private capital is expected to "share a piece of cake" from the new round of mixed-ownership reform.

Second, mixed-ownership reform is an important means to realize the purpose of maintaining and increasing the value of state-owned assets under the condition that the fundamental system of resource allocation based on the market is established in China. As we can see from the list of 2014 China Top 500 Enterprises recently released by the China Enterprise Confederation and the China Enterprise Directors Association, the pressure of maintaining and increasing the value of state-owned assets is very high.

And then, mixed-ownership reform is a continuation of the traditional logic of capital socialization in SOE restructuring. In the past round of mixed-ownership reform, SOEs have successively implemented restructuring forms such as the joint-stock system and the listing of some holding companies of enterprise groups. The joint-stock system was realized through employee stock ownership, while the listing was achieved through the public offering of shares. If we interpret the implementation of the joint-stock system as the socialization of capital within the enterprise, the listing of SOEs can be understood as the socialization of capital in a wider range. At present, a large number of state-owned assets are placed in the management chain of state-owned assets led by SASAC at all levels through the formation of large enterprise groups. Some enterprises at the bottom of the pyramidal holding structure are listed companies that have completed capital socialization, but at the middle and top there are still a large number of SOEs that have not completed capital socialization. These companies and other unlisted SOEs or groups will be the focus of the new round of mixed-ownership reforms.

Next, the mixed-ownership reform aims to improve the operational efficiency of state-owned capital by introducing other types of shares. This will mainly be achieved in two ways. First, to introduce strategic investors to expand the business scope while obtaining financing. Second, mixed-ownership reform will help enterprises form a reasonable governance structure. The introduction of private capital with a strong profit motive will effectively promote the reform and improvement of the corporate governance structure to protect their own rights and interests.

Finally, mixed-ownership reform will reflect the innovation of the concept of state-owned asset management – from managing enterprises to managing capital. The current basic business model of SOEs not only manages capital through the state-owned assets management but also exerts substantial influence on the business operation through the top-down personnel appointment and removal system and the promotion assessment of SOE executives. As a result, the ownership and management rights cannot be truly separated, and the SOE's organizational form is similar to that of the neoclassical capitalist enterprise of the family workshop style. However, traditional neoclassical capitalist enterprises don't have agency conflicts due to the unity of ownership and management rights, while SOEs have agency conflicts due to the absence of owners and extended principal-agent system. As for solving the agency problem caused by the separation of ownership and management rights in modern enterprises, we should rely on the perfection of corporate governance structure instead of returning to the family workshop–style neoclassical capitalist enterprise. As we can see, SOEs that manage not only capital but also enterprises have not taken advantage of social specialization to improve efficiency, and at the same time have not solved the agency problem well. In this sense, China's SOEs need a modern corporate revolution in the future.

So how can we truly realize the mixed-ownership? Generally speaking, a new reform measure will be a fundamental success only when it becomes a self-enforcing institutional arrangement (the so-called Nash equilibrium). A self-enforcing institutional arrangement needs to meet two basic conditions. The first is that by becoming (financial or strategic) investors of SOEs, private enterprises and social capital besides state-owned capital will bring themselves higher return on investment than other investments (opportunity cost). This is the so-called individual rational participation constraint. Since private capital can take advantage of the opportunity of mixed-ownership reform to participate in and share the high monopoly profits previously available only to SOEs, this condition does not seem difficult to satisfy.

The second is that state-owned capital and private capital should be incentive compatible. In other words, regardless of state-owned capital or private capital, the ownership mix should be truly profitable. The most fundamental interest of state-owned capital is to maintain and increase the value of state-owned assets in order to improve the welfare of the society as a whole. One of the fundamental purposes of carrying out a new round of mixed-ownership reform is to maintain and increase the value of state-owned capital, so it is evidently profitable for state-owned capital. However, the biggest concern of private capital participating in the mixed-ownership reform lies in the possible appropriation and hollowing out of private capital by the state-owned capital as the controlling shareholder. A large body of research literature shows that the controlling shareholders will tunnel and misappropriate the assets of the holding companies they control by means of related party transactions, fund embezzlement (receivables, payables, other receivables, other payables) and the loan guarantee, thus damaging the interests of dispersed outside shareholders. Therefore, in order to make private capital profitable from the mixing of capital, it is necessary to establish institutional arrangements that balance and protect the interests of different types of shares. For private capital, if the state-owned capital as the controlling shareholder make a credible commitment not to use the controlling position to encroach upon the interests of the private capital, the private capital will be profitable in mixed ownership and thus achieve incentive compatibility. Of course, the precondition for the incentive compatibility constraint to be satisfied is that the commitments made by the state-owned capital must be credible. Therefore, the key to the success of mixed-ownership reform is how to make the relevant commitments made by state-owned capital believable.

The bailout practice of the US government during the 2008 global financial crisis and the thinking on the innovation of corporate governance structure in emerging markets brought by Alibaba's listing in the United States have inspired us to carry out the institutional design of mixed-ownership reform. Let's first look at the US government's bailout practice. From the direct nationalization of companies in crisis by using financial funds, to holding non-voting preferred shares, and to simply providing guarantee for bank loans, the common consideration in the three phases of the US government's bailout policy is how to avoid the government's intervention in the business operation and decision-making of enterprises at the micro level, because the government is not adept at the operation and management of enterprises because it lacks firsthand information. This is considered by some analysts to be one of the reasons for the institutional design of the strong economic recovery in the United States in recent years. Alibaba successfully went public in the United States by introducing a partnership system similar to unequal voting rights. So why did Alibaba's shareholders choose to give up part of their control in favor of giving more control to the partners represented by Jack Ma? One important reason is that due to the rapid development of emerging industries, investors simply cannot understand many business models. It is obviously the optimal arrangement for outside investors to hand over more control to Jack Ma and his team who have information advantages and can effectively grasp the business model, and retreating to the backstage to be ordinary investors themselves. This is a rational choice made by dispersed outside investors based on the rapid development of emerging industries and the information asymmetry of the business model.

The above-mentioned practices brought inspiration to the mixed-ownership reform that state-owned capital may consider making a solemn commitment to private capital of excluding tunneling and direct intervention in the business operation by holding preferred shares (with certain conditions and up to a certain percentage), so as to better achieve the purpose of preserving and increasing the value of state-owned assets.

After completing the mixed-ownership reform in accordance with the above mode, state-owned capital operating institutions guide the market's evaluation by increasing or decreasing their holdings of preferred shares according to the performance and corporate governance of listed companies. This is typical market behavior rather than an administrative approach to exert external pressure on listed companies to improve performance and corporate governance. Thus, state-owned capital plays the role of an active shareholder and non-voting institutional investor. The board of directors is elected by other outside shareholders with voting rights and becomes the true authority of corporate governance. Senior executives are hired by the board of directors from the professional manager market. The independent director system, on the other hand, needs to be improved actively in terms of both institutional design and cultural origin, thus ensuring independence of the personnel procedures of independent directors including employment, performance and replacement. In this way, the independent director system will become a basic institutional arrangement that will play an important role in corporate governance. In addition to the internal governance mechanism, the companies that completed mixed-ownership reform also need to form the external institutional environment of corporate governance with the help of market supervision such as strict information disclosure, the introduction of legal measures (inversion of evidential burden and class action) and media supervision and tax enforcement to protect investors' rights.

It is to be expected that various potential problems will arise during the process of mixed-ownership reform. Two problems are very prominent. First, who should be the object of capital socialization under the conditions of limited resource allocation capabilities and approach in the capital market? How to realize capital socialization in a fair way? Blindly implementing mixed-ownership reform without adequate preparation will inevitably lead to asset loss and rent-seeking behavior under covert operations. To solve this problem, public bidding and vigorous anti-corruption can be effective countermeasures with the help of external supervision, such as the media. Among them, taking advantage of the resource allocation capabilities of the existing capital market to list as a whole is one of the feasible options. Second, how to solve the agency problem of state-owned capital? Undoubtedly, the most fundamental interest of state-owned capital is to maintain and increase the value of state-owned assets as mentioned, so as to enhance the welfare of the whole society, but the interest of agents of state-owned capital may be rent-seeking. Therefore, the agents of state-owned capital may become one of the main obstacles to promoting mixed-ownership reform. The solution to this problem depends on the continuous establishment and improvement of a democratic, scientific, fair and just decision-making mechanism and environment.

Notes

1 The term "barbarians" comes from the book *Barbarians at the Gate* by Bryan Burrough. After its publication, the word barbarian became a buzzword, often used to describe hostile buyers.
2 Financial "crocodiles" are very powerful and aggressive persons in the financial field, namely international speculators.
3 Significant shareholding: when an insurance company purchase shares of a listed company in the secondary market and the shares purchased exceed 5% or an integral multiple of 5% of the total shares, it is necessary to disclose its identity. The fund of an insurance company is relatively strong, so it will bring certain benefits to investors.
4 Zhang Yan. (2016). 董明珠谈资本敲门格力电器：如果他们破坏中国制造会成为罪人 [Dong Mingzhu Talks about Capital Knocking on Gree Electric: If they destroy Made in China, they will become criminals]. *Surging News*. https://www.thepaper.cn/newsDetail_forward_1573240.

5 重磅突发 | 南玻A高管集体辞职，姚振华"血洗"董事会？ [Big bang | The senior executives of CSG A resigned collectively, and Yao Zhenhua "bloodwashed" the board of directors?]. *Sina Finance*. https://cj.sina.com.cn/article/detail/1030341137/103246.
6 "Iron rice bowl" is a Chinese term used to refer to a secure occupation with steady income. This term is similar (but not identical) to the concept of a "job for life".

2   Theoretical Basis of SOE Mixed-Ownership Reform

The confusion faced by the practice of SOE mixed-ownership reform and the debate on the guiding theories indicate that the theoretical and practical circles need to find a new theoretical basis for the new round of SOE mixed-ownership reform. In short, SOE reform faces two major problems. One is the problem of excessive supervision under the dominance of a single shareholder. The other is that the designers of the incentive mechanism for managers lack long-term incentives due to the absence of the owner. To use a popular expression, the dilemma faced by SOEs is "absent for what should be managed and intervening in what should not be managed". Therefore, the new theoretical basis of SOE mixed-ownership reform is inseparable from the cure for SOEs' disease.

A fundamental solution to the problems faced by SOEs, such as absent for what should be managed but intervening in what should not be managed, is to form a pattern of checks and balances and decentralized control among shareholders by mixing ownership in the shareholding structure (the so-called mixed-ownership reform), establishing a competitive relationship between major shareholders, and introducing an automatic error correction mechanism. As a result, after the mixed-ownership reform, SOEs can not only effectively avoid excessive supervision and decision-making mistakes easily caused by the dominance of single shareholders, but also form constraints on managers and avoid the problems of insider control. Thus, the theory of decentralized control has become one of the theoretical foundations of the new round of SOE mixed-ownership reform. Together with modern property rights theory and long-term partnership theory, it forms the theoretical basis for the practice of mixed-ownership reform, which is actively promoted by China's SOEs today.

1   Re-discussion of the Theory of SOE Reform After Two Decades

Hart's theory of modern property rights has long been regarded as one of the theoretical foundations of SOE reform in China. For example, in a seminar on SOE reform held in 2018 with the participation of Professor Hart, starting from his modern property rights theory, some scholars pointed out that the core importance of the property rights theory lies in the core content of a large number of incentives,

DOI: 10.4324/9781003361404-3

which can be solved only after the property right is settled. Before solving the problem of property rights, it is impossible to imitate the operation of market and private ownership, which is the core content of property rights theory.

Unlike the views of these scholars, who emphasized the importance of property rights, some scholars emphasized the importance of incentive mechanism design in issues including the formulation of government industrial policies. They argue that the government's failure to design a good industrial policy is simply due to the poor use of incentive mechanism design. It is not that the industrial policy itself is bad but that the industrial policy is poorly designed. They stressed that the idea of incentive mechanism design should be widely applied to industrial governance and even national governance, and that the essence of governance is mechanism design. These scholars' views seem to be aimed at the government's formulation of industrial policies, but there is no doubt that their logic also applies to SOEs.

During the 40-year SOE reform in China, there has always been a theoretical debate about whether property rights are important or incentive mechanism design is important. In the mid-1990s, scholars such as Lin Yifu debated whether SOE reform should start from the reform of property rights or from improving the environment for market competition. After two decades, scholars have begun a new debate on the importance of property rights or incentive mechanism design in SOE reform.

For the convenience of expression, we call scholars who emphasize the importance of property rights as the property rights school and those who emphasize the importance of incentive mechanism design as the incentive school. We see that in the incentive school, the new scholars have a slightly different focus than their predecessors on the important issue of incentive mechanism design. Old scholars emphasize market competition as an exogenous incentive provided by a relatively natural institutional environment. But from the idea of modern incentive mechanism based on the principal-agent – the analytical tool of game theory – the new scholars stress how to design endogenous incentives to solve the agent's adverse selection and moral hazard caused by asymmetric private information. Similar to the differences within the incentive school, the new property rights school emphasize more on the fact that SOE reform is possible only after the problem of property rights are solved, while the old scholars emphasize that it is easier to advance SOE reform by clarifying the property rights of market players than by improving the market competitive mechanism.

Our concerns are (1) whether SOE reform can address the incentive mechanism for managers only after solving the problem of property rights; (2) whether SOE reform can formulate proper industrial policies, even if the government is a typical agent, as long as it draws lessons from the design of incentive mechanisms; and (3) whether in the SOE reform, even a typical agent like the government can formulate a proper industrial policy as long as it draws lessons from the idea of incentive mechanism design.

In our opinion, both the new property rights school and the new incentive school have some misunderstandings, at least in the context of SOE reform.

We first discuss the misunderstanding of the new property rights school: only after solving the property rights problem can the incentive mechanism for managers be solved. From the perspective that contracts in reality are rarely fully detailed, Hart points out that the incentive to invest in advance is insufficient because investors are worried that they will be ripped off after investing under incomplete contracts. So how to encourage investors to invest? According to Hart, investors are willing to invest only when they become owners and have residual control over matters not specified in incomplete contracts (specificity). This theory is a good explanation of the mystery of the modern joint-stock company, in which an investor is willing to invest in a public company and become a shareholder even though he is not familiar with the CEO of the company. The reason is that after investors buy the company's shares and become the shareholders of the company, the public company makes a credible promise to investors that they will collectively enjoy a legally protected ownership interest.

We note that Hart's modern property rights theory does involve the discussion of incentive problems and emphasizes the importance of property rights arrangements for providing incentives. However, it should be pointed out that the incentive Hart focuses on here refers to the incentive problem that investors are worried about being ripped off after (specific) investment (due to incomplete contract) and "insufficient incentive for ex ante specific investment". In other words, Hart is concerned about the investment incentive of how to encourage investors to buy the company's stock and become company shareholders through a property rights arrangement that reflects residual control rights. Obviously, this is not based on the asymmetric information framework between the principal and the agent. The principal (such as shareholders) proposes incentive contract design to the agent (such as managers) to solve the problems of adverse selection and moral hazard and reconcile the interests between them. The former emphasizes the prior arrangement of property rights in the residual rights of incomplete contracts from the viewpoint that the incomplete contract will lead to subsequent extortion, but it does not pay much attention to information issues. The latter emphasizes the incentive arrangement that the principal compensates the agent with information rent to encourage the agent to be honest from the perspective of the information asymmetry between the principal and the agent. Therefore, the incentives in Hart's modern property rights theory are not the same as the incentives in the principal-agent theory. The reason why the new property rights school made the judgment that it is possible to address the incentive mechanism for managers only after solving property rights is that they confused the property rights arrangement used to incentivize shareholders' investment with the incentive mechanism design carried out for managers. In fact, they misunderstood Hart's theory of modern property rights.

Equally important, Hart's view that property rights arrangement is important has been challenged in recent years by the practice of weighted voting rights, including the practice of Chinese enterprises such as Alibaba and JD.com. Professor Hart himself also realized this point. Let's take JD.com and Alibaba as examples. In JD.com, which issued AB dual-class shares, shareholders holding Class A shares have only one vote per share compared to 20 votes per share for the shareholders holding Class B shares. In Alibaba's partnership system, SoftBank, which previously held 31.8% of the shares, and Yahoo, which held 15.3%, gave up their right to appoint directors to the board, and SoftBank appointed only one non-voting observer. To the surprise of the new property rights school, Class A shareholders of JD.com and major shareholders in Alibaba's partnership system, such as Soft-Bank and Yahoo, have partially or even completely given up their control, but they are still willing to become shareholders of JD.com and Alibaba. This obviously cannot be explained by Hart's modern property rights theory.

If the new property rights school not only misreads Hart's theory but also has a misunderstanding of its own theory after encountering challenges from JD.com and Alibaba, the view of the new incentive school – which advocates even a typical agent like the government can formulate proper industrial policies as long as it can learn from the idea of incentive mechanism design – is also subject to theoretical error.

From the perspective of current development status, the theory of incentive mechanism is far from solving the design of one-to-many and many-to-many incentive contracts. At present, the design of SOE's incentive contracts is often faced with the problem of one-to-many and many-to-many due to the extended principal-agent relationship and the multiple identities of SOE executives as political men and economic men. In the theory of incentive contract design, the problem of incentive design between only two, or at most three (homogeneous) individuals, has been solved. The design of compensation contract with (homogeneous) shareholders as the principal and (homogeneous) managers as the agent is an incentive problem between two individuals. As for the incentive design between three individuals, see the discussion related to preventing collusion between two agents in a tripartite game carried out by Jean Tirole et al.

Due to the lack of practical operability, even some relatively mature ideas of incentive mechanism design still remain at the level of theoretical research and still have a considerable distance from real practice to a large extent. A typical example is that equity incentive, once considered by Jensen and Meckling (1976) as an important way to coordinate the agency conflict between managers and shareholders based on the idea of incentive mechanism design. However, because there is no effective way to measure a manager's true performance, events such as the Enron accounting scandal have occurred, where senior executives manipulated stock prices or even committed accounting fraud. Jensen later had to revise his previous comments and called equity incentives "the heroin of executive incentive" (高管heroin, Jensen, 2005).

Moreover, it is obviously not easy to design incentive mechanisms around individuals and organizations with different preferences and constraints, both in theory and in practice. In real economic life, suppliers and buyers, composed of different organizations and individuals, not only have different preferences, but also face different constraints. Even some suppliers themselves are also buyers. The economist Kenneth Arrow once reminded us that, due to the differences in individual preferences, it is impossible to get a total demand function of a whole society through simple ranking and aggregation of preferences so as to work out a satisfactory price for everyone in society (achieve consumer surplus).

In fact, if we compare the planned economy to an experiment of one-to-many and many-to-many incentive mechanism design, the empirical evidence shows that the market-oriented economic transformation in many countries, including China, has to some extent declared this experiment a failure. We can see that the view of the importance of incentive mechanism design in SOE reform advocated by the new incentive school is also challenged by the above theory and practices.

From the above theoretical and practical challenges encountered by the new incentive school, a more fundamental problem naturally arises. Who has the motivation to introduce and design effective incentive mechanisms for SOE managers?

In fact, this question has two implications. First, designers can benefit from designing an effective incentive contract for managers. Second, the designer also can bear the consequences of a wrong design. A modern joint stock company that has established a perfect corporate governance structure with shareholders as the managerial authority can satisfy both of these two aspects to a certain extent. For example, the design of the compensation contract seems to pay a high salary to managers, but fully motivated managers will bring more return on investment to shareholders, so shareholders have the motivation to design an effective compensation package for managers. Shareholders who invested in listed companies with their own money bear limited liability up to the amount of their capital contribution, but after all, they have to bear the economic consequences for the wrong decisions they made by voting at the general meeting of shareholders.

In terms of the current SOE mixed-ownership reform in China, compared with the previous SOEs actions (like a man "spends someone else's money on someone else, and he doesn't care how much he spends or what he spends it on"), the mixed-ownership reform carried out by introducing private investors with clear profit motives has solved the long-term incentive of who has the motivation to introduce and design the effective incentive mechanisms for SOE managers. On the one hand, in order to ensure the safe recovery of investment and reasonable return, private capital with clear profit motives has the incentive to participate in the construction of the corporate governance system, introduce and design effective incentive mechanism for SOE managers to realize win-win cooperation; on the other hand, the private capital participating in investment should bear the corresponding responsibility for the mistakes of the decisions they made, instead of passing on the loss to the government or even taxpayers. Therefore, SOE mixed-ownership reform has become one of the ways for shareholders to introduce and design incentive mechanisms for managers to solve the problems of long-term incentive.

It should be noted that, as per the previous analysis, the importance of incentive mechanism design for SOE reform is obviously not the initial concern of Professor Hart's modern property rights theory. However, from the fact that the idea advocated by the new incentive school that incentive mechanism design is important in SOE reform has encountered theoretical and practical challenges, we derive the question of who has the motivation to introduce and design an effective incentive mechanism for SOE managers. For this question, the logical inference of modern property rights theory (not the theory itself) can provide a possible theoretical explanation for why shareholders with clear profit motives are motivated to introduce and design the long-term incentive mechanism. From this perspective, we believe that Hart's modern property rights theory still plays a very important guiding role in SOE reform.

To a certain extent, the above analysis shows that the theoretical basis of the current actively promoted SOE mixed-ownership reform is simply neither the modern property rights theory advocated by the new property rights school, nor the theory of incentive contract design advocated by the new incentive school, but the inherent and natural combination of the two.

2   Theoretical Analyses of Defects in SOEs

The theoretical and practical circles have gradually reached a consensus on the necessity of SOE reform by understanding the various defects exposed in SOE management. In the process of the development of SOEs in China, existing problems have gradually been more or less exposed. Section 4 of Chapter 1 points out the necessity of SOE reform by analyzing the status quo of SOE governance. So from a theoretical perspective, how can we investigate and recognize these defects of SOEs?

The first is the soft budget constraint.

In recent years, problems such as zombie enterprises and excessive production capacity have continued to attract the attention of China's theoretical and practical circles, becoming important issues of the supply-side structural reform actively implemented in China. Xu Chenggang pointed out that these are old problems and they arise as expected. The cause of zombie enterprises and excessive production capacity is actually the soft budget constraint proposed by Kornai many years ago.

The term "soft budget constraint" refers to the case that the institutions that provide funds to enterprise fail to adhere to prior business agreement and make the enterprise borrow funds far beyond the actual profitability and repayment ability (Kornai, 1986). We know that for equity financing, the distribution of dividends should not be an obligation of the firm unless the board of directors makes a commitment, and thus firms that engage in equity financing face soft constraints. Unlike the soft constraint of equity financing, debt financing, which is realized through bank loans and corporate bonds, exposes enterprises to a hard constraint. If the enterprise fails to repay the principal and interest to the creditors such as the bank on time, it will face legal action initiated by the creditors and even liquidation and bankruptcy. However, for SOEs naturally politically connected to the government, in order to maintain employment rate, tax growth and social stability, state-owned banks will not push insolvent enterprises into bankruptcy liquidation but will instead further increase the loans to save them, thus softening the original hard budget constraint. These practices were described as "state paternalism" by Kornai. Take Dongbei Special Steel Group as an example. The company has implemented debt-to-equity swaps. In order to resolve the debt crisis of Dongbei Special

Steel, the local government proposed a debt-to-equity swap plan which did not involve liquidation in 2016, but it was forced to abandon the plan due to unanimous opposition from creditors. The debt crisis was eventually resolved by Shen Wenrong, a private steel magnate from the province of Jiangsu, who controls Dongbei Special Steel. We see that this event, interpreted by the media as accidental privatization, is actually the local government's helpless action to resolve the debt crisis of Dongbei Special Steel. In the above sense, the debt-to-equity swap under government intervention is considered a soft budget constraint under the guise of market operation.

Some SOEs have become zombie enterprises and face a decline in profit due to excessive production capacity, which is the direct cause of the current round of SOE reform which takes mixed-ownership as a breakthrough. Behind the zombie enterprises and excessive production capacity is the soft budget constraint under state paternalism. To a large extent, the soft budget constraint is not only the cause of the inefficiency of SOEs in the era of planned economy but also the reason for the declining efficiency of SOEs today. Since their birth, SOEs have not been able to solve the problem. The key to making an SOE become a self-financing operating entity is to realize the transformation of state-owned capital from managing enterprises to managing capital, and to share risks with social capital, so that SOEs can truly become major players in the market economy after the mixed-ownership reform.

Second, under the pyramidal holding structure, SOEs face the problem of owner absence and vague fiduciary duties.

According to the modern property rights theory (Grossman and Hart, 1986; Hart and Moore, 1990), shareholders collectively exercise owners' rights and interests to make the final decision on major issues (not covered by incomplete contracts) by voting at the general meeting of shareholders on the one hand. On the other hand, the shareholders bear limited liability to the extent of their respective capital contributions and assume corresponding responsibility for (wrong) decisions they made. Shareholders thus become the authority of corporate governance, and directors need to bear the legal responsibility of fiduciary duties (duty of loyalty and diligence) to shareholders. Under the above governance structure, the legal fiduciary duty of directors to shareholders is relatively clear. And a clear definition of fiduciary duties facilitates the protection of investors' rights and interests by law in judicial practice.

It is easy to know that a large number of SOEs in China belong to enterprise groups with pyramidal holding structures. The formation of the pyramidal holding structure comes from the design of organizational institution to meet the financing needs of enterprises on the one hand, and is related to some special policies launched by China's government in the process of SOE restructuring and industrial restructuring adjustment on the other. In the enterprise groups, the listed companies at the bottom of the pyramidal holding structure seem to have major shareholders, but due to the owner absence of state-owned controlling shareholder and the extended principal-agent relationship, the chairman of the board often becomes the actual controller of the listed company. With the extension of the control right of the pyramidal holding structure, the phenomenon of owner absence and insider control becomes more serious. Friedman has a famous quote on this:

> When a man spends his own money to buy something for himself, he is very careful about how much he spends and how he spends it. When a man spends his own money to buy something for someone else, he is still very careful about how much he spends, but somewhat less what he spends it on. When a man spends someone else's money to buy something for himself, he is very careful about what he buys, but he doesn't care at all how much he spends. And when a man spends someone else's money on someone else, he doesn't care how much he spends or what he spends it on.

Because of their vague fiduciary duties, SOEs have apparently become a typical example of spending someone else's money on someone else. The new round of mixed-ownership reform needs to make clear the vague fiduciary duty by introducing strategic investors with symmetrical power and responsibility.

Third are the conflicts of the multi-objective incentive under the governance model of managing both capital and enterprise.

In addition to directly holding the controlling shares of SOEs and establishing a new approach of managing capital, China's central and local governments still follow the traditional approach of managing enterprises from the era of state-owned enterprises – top-down personnel appointment and removal and the assessment and promotion system for SOE leadership – forming a pattern of managing both capital and enterprises. On the one hand, the shareholding group wholly owned by SASAC, which holds the controlling shares of listed companies, performs the duties of major shareholders. On the other hand, the higher authorities appoint the chairman and CEO, while the SASAC inspects the SOE leadership assessment and promotion system for appointing other vice presidents. Although the procedures need to be nominated by the board of directors and voted at the general shareholders' meeting, it is difficult to pose a substantive impact and challenge on the appointments of higher authorities due to the dominant structure of a single shareholder and the political and economic influence of the state-owned assets management system. Under the above-mentioned leadership assessment and promotion system, SOE senior executives become government officials of the same level or higher through a tournament of political promotion, realizing their ideal career from businessmen to officials. Attracting the attention of higher authorities through image projects and face jobs to achieve political promotion has become the core goal of SOE executives in their short tenure. However, these image projects will harm shareholders' interests in the long run and become special agency cost that outside shareholders have to bear in the context of China's SOE system. As a result, some measures that seem to strengthen the supervision and incentives of SOE executives have led to incentive distortions in their behavior. At the same time, the administrative department of state-owned assets is directly involved in managing the enterprise by appointing, removing and assessing the chairman, CEO and key executives, which is somewhat akin to placing the shareholders' ownership interests in the hands of a third party who can only partially or even not be held accountable. Shareholders who can bear the responsibility for decisions they made are not allowed to make decisions, while the third parties who are unable to take full responsibilities have the right to make decisions, thus making the fiduciary duty between the shareholders and SOE directors even more vague.

Under the governance mode of managing both capital and enterprises, the chairman, CEO and other major executives not only be responsible for the shareholders in fiduciary duties in accordance with the Company Law and the Articles of Association, but also subject to the supervision and assessment from the higher authorities and the state property management organizations in accordance with the management procedures of government officials. In addition to making profits from production and operation, SOEs need to fulfill their social responsibilities, such as stabilizing prices, boosting employment, increasing tax revenue and maintaining social order. SOEs even need to participate in public welfare activities such as poverty alleviation, which puts them in a state of multi-tasking and multi-objective management. The research of Holmstrom and Milgrom (1991) shows that when agents face multi-objectives at the same time, the incentive and emphasis on one of the objectives will induce the agent to spend too much effort on the objective and ignore the others, which leads to the distortion of resource allocation. Facing the multi-responsibilities, theoretically, SOE directors can compromise the legitimate interests of shareholders under the pretext of avoiding harming the interests of third parties, or even pursue private benefits in the name of protecting the interests of the third parties and shareholders, thus actually harming the interests of both third parties and shareholders. Friedman stressed that "the social responsibility of business is to increase its profits" (Friedman, 1970).

We realized that the previous SOE governance model of managing both capital and enterprises can easily lead to incentive conflicts of SOE executives under multi-objectives and more ambiguous fiduciary duties between shareholders and directors. Therefore, in the new round of SOE reform, state property management organizations have clearly proposed changing the direction of SOE reform from managing enterprises to managing capital, and to replace the top-down personnel system of government officials with a market-oriented professional manager recruitment system.

Finally, there is the problem of Chinese-style insider control in SOEs with the chairman as the core in state-owned enterprises.

Because SOEs are facing the problems of soft budget constraints, vague fiduciary duties, conflicts of multi-objective incentives and Chinese-style insider control, SOEs tend to fall into a vicious cycle of profit decline, successive years of losses, heavy debts, government-directed merger and reorganization, and rebirth after experiencing the first three years of prosperity.

3   Theoretical Basis of Mixed-Ownership Reform of SOEs: From Property Rights Theory to Decentralized Control Theory

Starting from the perspective that the contract in reality is always not complete, Professor Hart of Harvard University, winner of the 2016 Nobel Prize in Economics, argues that investors are willing to invest only if they become owners and have residual control over what is left unsaid in incomplete contracts. This theory has long been regarded as the theoretical basis of China's SOE reform. However, Hart's theory that property rights arrangement is important has been challenged in recent years by the practice of weighted voting rights of some enterprises, including Alibaba and JD.com in China. Professor Hart himself also noticed that his theory was challenged by the growing practice of weighted voting rights around the world.

After decades of difficult march, SOE mixed-ownership reform has gradually entered the deep-water area. SOEs have implemented forms of restructuring, such as the employee shareholding cooperative system and listing of some holding companies of enterprise groups. The employee shareholding cooperative system is realized through employee stock ownership, while the listing is realized through the issuance of public shares. If we consider the implementation of the employee shareholding cooperative system as the socialization of capital within the enterprise, the partial listing of SOEs can be regarded as the socialization of capital on a larger scale. Sometimes we emphasize the socialization of capital through shareholding reform (e.g., the listing of some well-performed SOEs, which was vividly described as "the pretty girl marries first"), and sometimes we focus on the socialization of capital within enterprise through the employee shareholding (e.g., the once-popular employee shareholding cooperative system). Why should mixed-ownership reform be achieved by introducing strategic investors in the practice of SOE reform? What is the role of strategic investors in improving the corporate governance structure and establishing a modern enterprise system? These issues have always troubled policy makers who are on the front line of SOE mixed-ownership reform.

The previous analysis in this section said that Hart's view that the property rights arrangement is important has been challenged in recent years by the practice of weighted voting rights, including Chinese enterprises Alibaba and JD.com. The confusions faced by the practice of SOE mixed-ownership reform and debates over the guiding theories indicate that the theoretical and practical circles need to find new theoretical foundations for the new round of SOE reform.

The analysis in Section 2 of Chapter 2 shows that the actual problems faced by SOE reform are excessive supervision under the dominance of a single large shareholder and the lack of long-term incentives for the designers of a manager incentive mechanism caused by the owner's absence. A popular expression for the dilemma faced by SOEs is "absent for what should be managed and intervening in what should not be managed". Obviously, the new theoretical basis of SOE mixed-ownership reform cannot be separated from the remedy for this "disease" of SOEs.

It is easy to understand that the problem of long-term incentives for shareholders who design incentive mechanisms for managers would partly involve Hart's modern property rights theory. In fact, many scholars still regard modern property rights theory as the theoretical basis for the new round of SOE mixed-ownership reform. Here we emphasize that the theoretical basis of SOE mixed-ownership reform is only partially related to modern property rights theory. The reason is that the introduction of private investors with a clear profit motive will help to establish a long-term incentive (for shareholders who design incentive mechanisms for managers), making the incentive mechanism for managers more flexible and diverse. This is in line with the spiritual essence of Hart's modern property rights theory.

However, a more fundamental solution to the problem faced by SOEs – absent for what should be managed and intervening in what should not be managed – is to form decentralized control through the mixed-ownership reform in the ownership structure. Therefore, the theory of decentralized control has become one of the main theoretical basis of the new round of SOE mixed-ownership reform. The so-called decentralized control theory was developed by Bennedsen, Bolton, Gomes, Müller, Novaes, Thadden, Wärneryd and Wolfenzon from different perspectives to explain why enterprises need to introduce strategic investors.

Bolton and Thadden (1998) pointed out that when there are fewer shareholders in the controlling position, the controlling major shareholders have incentives to prevent managers from making any business decision that reduces verifiable cash flows, even though the actual losses far outweigh the manager's private interests, resulting in efficiency costs. With the goal of avoiding excessive supervision, Bolton and Thadden encouraged the introduction of new major shareholders to realize decentralized control. A political theory of the firm developed by Müller and Wärneryd (2001) argues that, although the introduction of new outside investors will lead to new conflicts and rent-seeking behavior and become the common enemy to former controlling shareholders and managers, the new game carried out by the three parties around the distribution of residual power will reduce the deadweight loss caused by the conflict of residual allocation. The study of Bennedsen and Wolfenzon (2000) shows that in the presence of multiple shareholders, any deviation from the direction of fund use requires the unanimous consent of all members of the collusive group. The more shareholders there are, the more difficult it is to reach consensus, and the funds are more likely to be invested in the right place. The presence of a collusive group is likely to cause less distortion in the use of funds than a company controlled by a single shareholder. Gomes and Novaes (2001) noted that despite the controlling shareholders having a strong desire to avoid disagreement, the final decision resulting from subsequent bargaining often prevents managers from making business decisions that are in the interests of controlling shareholders but detrimental to the interests of minority shareholders. The above effect is called the compromise effect. Therefore, decentralized control becomes an important mechanism to achieve a balance between the excessive supervision by major shareholders resulted from the dominance of a single shareholder and the managerial insider control caused by the absence of owners. We summarize the main ideas involved in the above literature as decentralized control theory, the core of which is to prevent excessive supervision under the dominance of a single shareholder.

The starting point of Hart's modern property rights theory is to reveal how authority is distributed in enterprises and answer the mystery of the modern joint-stock company of why investors are willing to buy shares issued by a joint-stock company. However, the modern property rights theory is considered by some Chinese scholars as the theoretical foundation for the SOE restructuring. Similarly, the theory of decentralized control, which was initially used to explain the introduction of strategic investors and to solve the problem of excessive intervention (Bolton and Von Thadden, 1998; Bennedsen and Wolfenzon, 2000; Müller and Wärneryd, 2001; Gomes and Novaes, 2001), has become one of the all-important theoretical underpinnings of SOE mixed-ownership reform in China.

Here we summarize how to simultaneously solve the problems of excessive supervision caused by a single shareholder's dominance (intervening in what should not be managed) and the inadequate or distorted incentives due to agency conflicts (absent for what should be managed) through the formation of decentralized control structure in the new round of mixed-ownership reform. First of all, by introducing new strategic investors to build a decentralized control structure, the mixed-ownership reform establishes a competitive relationship between major shareholders and constitutes an automatic error correction mechanism, which can not only effectively avoid excessive supervision and poor decision-making caused by the dominance of major shareholders but also pose a restriction on managers and avoid insider control. After introducing new strategic investors in the mixed-ownership reform, it has become a basic fact that all shareholders enjoy the owner's equity equally. In a modern joint-stock company, the more shares you own, the greater the risk of business failure you bear. Therefore, the decentralized control structure formed by mixed-ownership reform clarifies that shareholders are the authority of corporate governance and that directors bear a legal fiduciary duty to shareholders in the way of mutual recognition of status.

Second, mixed-ownership reform builds a decentralized control structure by introducing private investors with a clear profit motive, which makes win-win cooperation between shareholders a consensus while avoiding excessive supervision, thus effectively solving the long-term incentives for shareholders who introduce and design incentive mechanisms for managers. We know that compared with SOEs, private investors with a clear profit motive are more motivated to introduce flexible and diverse incentive mechanisms. Private enterprises are well aware that it is worth paying high salaries to managers, because fully motivated managers can make more money for them. Through mixed-ownership reform, private investors with natural and clear profit motive are introduced to complete new property rights arrangement and corporate governance structure, and a consensus of win-win cooperation is easily formed among major investors, so as to solve the long-term incentives for shareholders who introduce and design incentive mechanisms for managers.

The Vanke equity dispute in 2015 marked the beginning of the era of dispersed ownership in China's capital market, and the institutional environment of decentralized control between major shareholders has been formed in SOEs. The future corporate governance of SOEs depends on competition between major shareholders. On the one hand, it can mitigate the excessive supervision of managing both capital and enterprises by state-owned major shareholders in a dominant position and restrain the problem of Chinese-style insider control resulted from the absence of owners. On the other hand, shareholders establish long-term incentive mechanisms through the consensus of win-win cooperation.

In addition to the decentralized control theory and modern property rights theory, the theory of long-term partnership being developed based on the innovation of control rights arrangement of Alibaba and JD.com is actually one of the important theories for present SOE mixed-ownership reform in China.

According to long-term partnership theory, by retreating backstage to be ordinary investors, on the one hand the shareholders of Alibaba and JD.com entrusted the business model innovation they are not familiar with to the professional entrepreneurial teams, and focused on risk sharing themselves, thus realizing a specialized and in-depth division of labor and improving management efficiency. On the other hand, the above arrangements help complete the transformation from the previous short-term employment contract to the long-term partnership contract, and achieve long-term win-win cooperation between constant managers and constant shareholders. Thanks to the above two improvements, the shareholders of JD.com and Alibaba have not only avoided being ripped off by managers but also have made a good profit from long-term win-win cooperation in the case of partial or even full authorization of control rights to managers.

At the same time, the innovation of the property rights arrangement of JD.com and Alibaba shows us that although the shareholders of these companies have given up their actual control, it does not seem to affect the design of vibrant incentive mechanisms for management of Alibaba under the partnership system and JD.com under the dual-class share structure. In the face of the pressure of value maintaining and increasing, how do the state-owned holding shareholders who are not familiar with business model innovation shift from managing enterprises to managing capital, or even retreat to be ordinary investors (as the shareholders of JD.com and Alibaba), so as to achieve an in-depth and specialized division of labor with manager professionalization and risk-sharing socialization and improve the efficiency of management? How to transform the short-term employment contract for retail investors in the capital market under the previous single shareholder dominance to a long-term partnership contract between the investment and operating entities representing state-owned assets and other strategic investors so as to achieve win-win cooperation? How to make professional managers and excellent staff think like shareholders and establish a risk sharing mechanism by implementing employee stock ownership plans in the mixed-ownership reform? And so on. The long-term partnership theory based on the innovative practice of the control rights arrangement of Alibaba and JD.com brings new enlightenment to the practice of SOEs.

This is a refutation of the view of some scholars that only by solving the property rights arrangement can the incentive mechanism of managers be solved. To some extent, these scholars have formed this understanding because they confused the incentives for shareholders (property rights arrangement) with the incentives for managers. Incentives for shareholders emphasize a property rights arrangement for the residual rights of the incomplete contract in advance from the perspective that the incomplete contract will lead to subsequent extortion and does not involve the problem of information. Incentives for managers emphasize an incentive system arrangement that the principal takes the information rent as compensation and encourages the agent to be honest to solve the problem of moral hazard and adverse selection from the perspective of the information asymmetry between the principal and the agent. SOEs have long been criticized because of the absence of owners in property rights arrangements. However, SOEs were once expected to prosper for years, just like other enterprises.

Therefore, Hart's modern property rights, together with the decentralized control theory and the long-term partnership theory, constitute the theoretical basis of SOE mixed-ownership reform that is actively carried out in China today.

4   Examples of SOE Mixed-Ownership Reform: State-Owned Listed Companies

The fact that state-owned listed enterprises are able to "generate 87.6% of profits using 61.7% of net assets"[1] proves the rationality and importance of introducing strategic investors and capital socialization to reform and enhance the value preservation and appreciation ability of state-owned capital in the current SOE reform. For SOEs undergoing mixed-ownership reform, an expected outcome is to establish and perfect the corporate governance structure by introducing strategic investors and socializing capital so as to effectively separate management rights from control rights, thereby realizing the efficiency improvement brought by specialized division of labor.

Since the new round of SOE mixed-ownership reform was launched in 2014, many researchers and practitioners who are concerned about SOE reform are eager to know what the overall situation of SOEs will be after the reform is completed. From the rare cases such as China Unicom (which is known as the first central enterprise to press ahead with the mixed-ownership reform) and Tianjin Northern Trust (which is the representative of mixed-ownership reform of local SOEs), it is difficult for even imaginative readers to peek into the whole scene of SOEs after successful mixed-ownership reform.

On December 12, 2018, at the 2018 CCTV Financial Forum Chinese Listed Companies Summit, relevant personnel of SASAC revealed that SASAC had invested 65.2% of total assets and 61.7% of net assets to the listed companies, and 61.2% of operating revenue and 87.6% of total profits came from listed companies.

Listed companies undoubtedly represent excellent companies. In addition to the operation means and the management philosophy, the governance structure of listed companies is, to a large extent, the goal and direction pursued by SOEs that are actively engaged in the mixed-ownership reform.

First of all, strategic investors are introduced into SOEs. After the completion of mixed-ownership reform, as a result of capital socialization, SOEs should be the same as state-owned listed companies in terms of ownership structures, with not only state-owned capital but also private capital as shareholders. Then, after the completion of mixed-ownership reform, SOEs should form a board of directors composed of directors representing the interests of all shareholders, just like state-owned listed companies, and major issues should be approved by the shareholders' general meeting through consultation and voting. Private investors with a clear profit motive and their representative directors become an important factor in preventing managers from pursuing personal profit and harming shareholders' interests. Finally, just like state-owned listed companies, enterprises that have completed mixed-ownership reform will even introduce social elites from outside who are interest-neutral, reputation-oriented and have expertise in law, accounting and finance to supervise and consult as independent directors. Through the establishment and improvement of the above corporate governance structure, enterprises that have completed mixed-ownership reform can effectively separate the management right in the hands of professional managers from the control right in the hands of shareholders, which will lead to efficiency improvement and specialized division of labor based on the professionalization of managers and the socialization of capital.

This is in fact the important reason for the ability of state-owned listed companies to generate 87.6% of profits with the 61.7% of net assets, as noted by the relevant staff of SASAC. The above facts also prove the rationality and importance of the current SOE reform to enhance the ability of state-owned capital to preserve and increase its value by introducing strategic investors and capital socialization. It is in this sense that Professor Cao Fengqi of Peking University called the current mixed-ownership reform "the relaunch of joint-stock reform of state-owned enterprises".

Therefore, for SOEs undergoing mixed-ownership reform,[2] an expected outcome is to establish and improve the corporate governance structure by introducing strategic investors and capital socialization so as to effectively separate management from the control, thus realizing efficiency improvement brought by specialized division of labor.

Similarly, a basic fact that cannot be ignored is that listed companies, even state-owned listed companies that perform well among central enterprises, are on the whole inferior to non-state-owned listed companies in terms of performance. Let's take the situation of SOEs in 2014, the year when the new round of mixed-ownership reform was launched. According to the list of China Top 500 Enterprises released by the China Enterprise Confederation and the China Enterprise Directors Association, among the 43 companies that suffered losses, only one was a private company, and SOEs became the hardest hit. Although the above situation has been greatly improved in recent years with the support of policies related to making SOEs stronger and bigger, it is still an indisputable fact that state-owned capital is inferior to private capital in terms of input-output efficiency. So how can state-owned listed companies, which seem to have completed capital socialization and mixed-ownership reform, find new ways to further improve their efficiency?

We have noted that some of the practices currently adopted in the SOE mixed-ownership reform are worth learning and referring to for state-owned listed companies. In order to realize the transformation from managing personnel, affairs and enterprises to managing capital, Tianjin SASAC established state-owned capital investment and operating companies such as Jinlian, Jincheng and Guoxing as the new regulation objects, so Tianjin SASAC no longer has direct property rights relationship with the operating entities. Jincheng and other state-owned capital investment and operating companies participate in the corporate governance as shareholders together with the strategic investors introduced into the operating entities through mixed-ownership reform, thus curbing the previous situation of managing personnel, affairs and enterprises to a certain extent.

In the future, state-owned listed companies may learn from the practice of SOE mixed-ownership reform in Tianjin and gradually change the controlling shareholders of listed companies from operating entities to state-owned capital investment and operating companies, so as to achieve the transformation from managing personnel, affairs and enterprises to managing capital. Through the above-mentioned reforms, management rights of state-owned listed companies will be separated from control rights more effectively, and the efficiency of SOEs with modern enterprise system will be further improved, so that the state-owned capital invested will be truly preserved and increased in value.

At the 2018 Central Economic Work Conference, which closed on December 21, 2018, it was proposed to accelerate the reform of state-owned assets and state-owned enterprises; uphold the principles of separation of government administration from enterprise management and from state assets management and fair competition; make state-owned capital stronger, better and bigger: speed up the implementation from managing enterprises to managing capital; restructure and establish a number of state-owned capital investment and operating companies; and actively promote mixed-ownership reform. We know that the reform of the state-owned asset management system from managing personnel, affairs and enterprises to managing capital through the establishment of investment and operating companies will become the focus of SOE reform during the period from 2019 to 2022 under the three-year action plan. It also constitutes the most iconic difference between the current SOE mixed-ownership reform and the previous SOE joint-stock reform.

It is also noteworthy that the 2019 Central Economic Work Meeting clearly put forward the principles of separation of government administration from enterprise management, separation of government administration from state assets management and fair competition, which was rarely mentioned at the Central Economic Work Meetings in previous years. To a certain extent, this shows that relevant decision-making bodies have found the key to the successful transformation of the reform of the state-owned asset management system from managing personnel, affairs and enterprises to managing capital successfully, and improving the ability to maintain and increase the value of state-owned capital.

Notes

1 2018年12月12日，在2018央视财经论坛暨中国上市公司峰会上，国资委副主任翁杰明先生透露，"有65.2%的总资产和61.7%的净资产已经进入上市公司，有61.2%的营业收入和87.6%的利润总额来自于上市公司"，Yang Ye. (2019). 国资委完善上市公司国有股权管理 [The State owned Assets Supervision and Administration Commission improved the management of state-owned shares of listed companies]. *Economic Information Daily.* http://www.jjckb.cn/2019-02/14/c_137819439.htm?from=timeline.
2 曹凤岐. (2018). 四十年股份制改革再出发. 中国金融, *894*(24): 24–26.

3 The Models of SOE Mixed-Ownership Reform

Only by fully guaranteeing the interests of all parties involved in the mixed-ownership reform and adopting the incentive compatibility mechanism will the win-win cooperation be truly achieved and the mixed-ownership reform succeed in the end. As the first central enterprise to press ahead with the mixed-ownership reform, China Unicom has partially achieved the goal of incentive compatibility among all parties involved through state-owned capital domination in the ownership structure, while strategic investors are dominant in the board of directors. Today, the Unicom model of mixed-ownership reform has become a good lesson for SOEs.

The recent phenomenon of transferring the control rights of private capital to state-owned capital is just a mixed-ownership reform completed by private enterprises in order to ease the financial strain. This is a rational choice made by private companies based on the difficult situation they face.

In mixed-ownership reform, both state-owned and private enterprises need to follow the principle of introducing strategic investors to form power checks and balances to avoid excessive supervision. It is not only the starting point, but also the model choice for mixed-ownership reform to establish a governance structure with mutual incentive compatibility, so that all parties involved can pool their wisdom and work together for win-win results.

1 The Gains and Losses of China Unicom's Mixed-Ownership Reform

In 2017, China Unicom announced the mixed-ownership reform plan, which featured the participation of BATJ (the four Internet giants) and SOEs such as China Life Insurance, and received a lot of market attention. The mixed-ownership reform of China Unicom is undoubtedly the state-owned enterprise reform in the introduction of private capital background strategic investors to take an important step. So what are the expected gains and unsatisfactory losses of the mixed-ownership reform plan announced by China Unicom?

Let's first look at the expected gains of China Unicom's mixed-ownership reform plan.

First, by attracting private enterprises to participate, the model of SOE mixed-ownership reform represented by China Unicom further dilutes the equity of the

DOI: 10.4324/9781003361404-4

controlling shareholders and accelerates the advent of the era of dispersed owner-ship in China's capital market. After the reform of split-share structure and the significant shareholdings of insurance companies, the outbreak of Vanke equity dispute in 2015 marked the beginning of China's capital market from an era of single-shareholder domination to an era of equity dispersion. According to the recently announced mixed-ownership reform plan, China Unicom Group holds about a 36.67% stake in China Unicom after attracting strategic investors, includ-ing China Life and BATJ, to hold 35.19% of shares. By contrast, since 2015, the average shareholding ratio of the largest shareholder of listed companies in China has broken through 33.3%, the critical point of the capacity of relevant control, for the first time. However, the equity structure arrangement of China Unicom's mixed-ownership reform is to some extent related to the government's dominance and control over strategic industries such as telecommunications.

Nonetheless, China Unicom's mixed-ownership reform plan surprised the mar-ket and many observers by giving private capital such a large percentage of shares. After the completion of this round of mixed-ownership reform, the basic structure of dispersed ownership in China's capital market will initially take shape and tend to remain stable. The era of single shareholder dominance in corporate governance, where the controlling shareholder has the overall control from the organization and operation of the board of directors to the daily decision-making of the manage-ment, is coming to an end. In the era of dispersed ownership, in the face of the threat of external takeover or even the invasion of barbarians, corporate gover-nance relies more on the negotiation and compromise of all parties in interest. How to adapt to the above transformation in the future has become an important chal-lenge for many restructured SOEs, including China Unicom.

Second, the mixed-ownership reform model represented by China Unicom well reflects the economic concept of decentralized control, which helps to improve the inefficient corporate governance under the single-shareholder dominant mode. Some scholars encourage the introduction of new major shareholders to achieve decentralized control from the perspective of excessive supervision by major shareholders and the frustration of managers' enthusiasm. The sharing of control rights among several major shareholders may result in a compromise effect, which is conducive to indirectly protecting the interests of a wide range of dispersed outside shareholders in the process of major shareholders bargaining for their own interests. Some scholars have further applied the rent-seeking theory to develop a political theory of the firm, emphasizing that the newly entered major shareholders become the common enemy of the original controlling shareholders and managers, thereby reducing the deadweight loss caused by the conflict of residual distribution within the enterprise. Actually, this is why we remain cautiously optimistic about China Unicom's mixed-ownership reform plan, even though we think there are many shortcomings in the plan.

So what will be the unsatisfactory loss of China Unicom's mixed-ownership reform plan?

First of all, in terms of the equity structure, the strategic investors with a private capital background who participate in mixed-ownership reform cannot form effective checks and balances on major shareholders. In China Unicom's mixed-ownership reform plan, Tencent and Baidu with the largest share of investment among the strategic investors backed by private capital only accounting for 5.18% and 3.3%, respectively, far below China Unicom Group's 36.67%. What is particularly interesting is that among the potential strategic investors announced, in addition to China Life with state-owned capital background and whose shareholding ratio is higher than that of Tencent and the others, the relationship between several Internet giants with private capital background is actually more competitive than cooperative. This makes it relatively difficult for strategic investors with private capital backgrounds to take concerted actions to form checks and balances on major shareholders. Therefore, we think that China Unicom's mixed-ownership reform plan seemingly leans on the Internet giants' moneybag, but in essence, it reflects the ingenuity of the plan designer.

Second, strategic investors with private capital backgrounds are also in a weak position in the formation and organization of China Unicom's new board of directors. According to some current media reports on the composition scheme of directors, the seats of China Unicom Group will be reduced from four to two. Tencent and Baidu also appoint board members, but three directors are appointed from government and one from state-owned enterprise, so directors with private capital background are in an absolute minority among non-independent directors. The excessive appointment of directors, which is asymmetric with the shareholding ratio, objectively makes the major shareholders bear the responsibility and enjoy the power asymmetrically, forming a negative externality in the economic sense. From relevant reports on China Unicom's mixed-ownership reform plan, we have noticed that China Unicom Group has also agreed to transfer approximately 1.9 billion shares to the China Structural Reform Fund.

In addition, the votes of potential allies of major shareholders at the shareholders' meeting are also a force to be reckoned with. In China Unicom's mixed-ownership reform plan, China Life with state-owned capital background holds 10% of the shares, surpassing Tencent, Baidu and other private companies, becoming the largest strategic investor introduced in the reform. China Life will be more cautious in future investment measures after the significant shareholding of Baoneng's insurance funds caused the Vanke equity dispute and the regulatory authorities standardized and rectified insurance funds. In addition to China Life with a state-owned capital background as the largest strategic investor, China Unicom also plans to grant about 850 million restricted shares to its core employees. We suspect that whether it is state-owned capital such as China Life, employee stock ownership, or even China Structural Reform Fund – which remains to be seen – could be a force in the shareholders' meeting to support the motions proposed by major shareholders in favor of themselves but at the expense of other minority shareholders.

As mentioned above, on the one hand, the newly issued mixed-ownership reform plan of China Unicom cannot make strategic investors with private capital backgrounds form checks and balances over major shareholders in terms of ownership structure. On the other hand, the strategic investors with private capital background are in a weak position in the organization of the board of directors and the operation of the general meeting of shareholders. Therefore, it can be imagined that these strategic investors will face challenges in protecting their own rights and interests. Nonetheless, China Unicom has taken an important step in introducing private capital in the mixed-ownership reform, opening the door for private capital to participate in the telecommunication industry, which was previously monopolized by state-owned capital. We are cautiously optimistic to foresee that China Unicom's exploration of a new corporate governance model as China's capital market enters the era of dispersed ownership will provide more valuable experience for other SOEs to learn from in their mixed-ownership reforms.

2 The Unicom Model of Mixed-Ownership Reform

After the formation of a new board of directors on February 8, 2018, the mixed-ownership reform of China Unicom, which began in August 2017, came to an end with the release of the employee equity incentive plan on February 11, 2018. Hence the employee equity incentive plan is known as the last piece of the puzzle of the mixed-ownership reform. As a large central enterprise in the monopoly sector, China Unicom's mixed-ownership reform has always been a highly concern of the media and the public, becoming a wind vane of SOE mixed-ownership reform. Although it is too early to judge whether China Unicom's mixed-ownership reform is successful, we can learn some lessons from the initial stage of the reform and can even summarize the Unicom model for other SOEs that are carrying out mixed-ownership reform for reference.

From the shareholding structure of China Unicom after the introduction of strategic investors such as China Life and BATJ for mixed-ownership reform in August 2017, strategic investors hold 35.19% shares and China Unicom Group holds 36.67% shares in total. Tencent and Baidu, which have the highest proportion of investment among strategic investors with a private background, contributed only 5.18% and 3.3% respectively, a far cry from China Unicom Group, which holds a combined 36.67% stake. China Life with a state-owned background holds a bigger stake than the likes of Tencent, while the relationship of these Internet giants with private capital backgrounds is more competitive than cooperative. According to paragraph 2 of Article 84 of the *Measures for the Administration of the Acquisition of Listed Companies*, China Unicom Group continues to have control of China Unicom. Therefore, from the perspective of the shareholding structure of China Unicom after the mixed-ownership reform, the strategic investors with private capital backgrounds are unable to form effective checks and balances on the major shareholders. China Unicom's shareholding structure, dominated by state-owned assets, once raised concerns among observers about how strategic investors would protect their rights and interests.

However, observers' concerns were partly assuaged after the appointment of a new board of directors of China Unicom on February 8, 2018. From the perspective of the composition of the new board of directors, China Unicom has undergone two notable changes. One is that the size of the new board has expanded from

7 to 13 people, with 5 independent directors accounting for 38%. This is slightly higher than the regulator's requirement that no fewer than one-third of the board be independent directors. Another change is that, in the list of eight candidates for non-independent directors, except for three China Unicom executives, the remaining five are from strategic investors such as China Life, Baidu, Alibaba, Tencent and JD.com. Among them, Robin Li, Hu Xiaoming and other business stars have joined China Unicom's new board.

We note that, with a stake of around 3%, Baidu appoints one seat among nine non-independent directors (accounting for 12.5%) on China Unicom's board, which is uncommon in China's relatively concentrated A-share market. Academics refer to the phenomenon of corporate governance – in which major shareholders nominate more directors through the board composition process and result in a separation between the actual influence of the directors in major decisions and the responsibility-bearing capacity reflected by its shareholding ratio – as over-appointment of directors. Theoretically, similar to the separation of the ultimate owner's ownership and cash flow right of the listed company under the pyramidal holding structure, over-appointment of directors also means the asymmetry of responsibility and power, forming a negative externality in the sense of economics. As a form of separating cash flow rights from control rights, the over-appointment of directors, like a pyramid holding structure and a family member serving as the chairman of a family business, is regarded as an important way for the largest shareholder to achieve corporate control.

However, it is worth noting that Baidu, which has over-appointed directors on China Unicom's new board, is not the controlling shareholder, but the strategic investor introduced in the process of mixed-ownership reform. Directors representing minority shareholders with information disadvantages can have more voting rights in the discussion of directors' proposals, which is obviously conducive to the protection of minority shareholders' interests. Therefore, if the over-appointment of directors, which seems to be associated with negative externalities, is carried out by strategic investors who are non-controlling shareholders, it is not a mechanism strengthening the control and even further tunneling shareholders' interests but a counterweight to controlling shareholders.

This is actually the reason why we remain optimistic after China Unicom announced a mixed-ownership reform plan with a structure dominated by state-owned assets. The introduction of strategic investors will make it possible to create a decentralized control structure among major shareholders of China Unicom. The result of balancing control rights among major shareholders may create a compromise effect in favor of the interests of a wide range of dispersed outside shareholders in the bargaining process of protecting their respective interests.

Let's take the board meeting of Wanda Commercial on January 29, 2018, as an example. Wanda, Tencent and Baidu once worked together to create the so-called Tencent-Baidu-Wanda Project. However, due to the lack of dominance at both the shareholder level and the board level, the opinions of Tencent and Baidu were not fully respected, so they eventually chose to quit. According to the newly signed strategic investment agreement, Suning, JD.com, Tencent and Sunac will have seats on the board of directors of Wanda Commercial. This institutional arrangement, to some extent, increases the possibility of strategic investors such as Tencent having an advantage on the board. By introducing more directors from strategic investors into the board organization, the interests of strategic investors can be taken into account, which makes up for the lack of effective protection of strategic investors' interests when the shareholding structure is dominated by single shareholders, and enables strategic investors to have incentive compatibility to a certain extent. Thus, over-appointed directors from strategic investors become an important counterweight to controlling shareholders and a credible commitment to preserving the interests of strategic investors.

In fact, China Unicom and the private enterprise Wanda follow the same business rules, that is, only when the interests of all parties involved in the mixed-ownership reform are fully guaranteed and incentive compatible with each other can they truly achieve win-win cooperation and the reform can ultimately be successful. If we summarize the mixed-ownership reform experience of state-owned China Unicom as a model, it can be summarized as follows: state-owned capital dominates in the equity structure and strategic investors dominate in the board organization. The former is determined by the strategic attribute of the monopoly sector in which China Unicom belongs to, and China Unicom Group can even exercise one-vote veto by using controlling shares when necessary. The board of directors, which is mainly concerned with daily operations and management decisions, needs to listen more to the opinions of business elites such as Robin Li. The combination of the two also well reflects the transformation of corporate governance concept emphasized by the theorists and academics in recent years: corporate governance should gradually shift from the traditional concept of emphasizing the protection of shareholders' rights and interests to a new concept of balancing the protection of shareholders' rights and interests with encouraging entrepreneurial teams to invest in human capital around business model innovation.

The model in which state-owned capital dominates in the equity structure and strategic investors dominate in the board organization may be an important lesson extracted from the initial stage of China Unicom's mixed-ownership reform. In the future, more new attempts and explorations are needed in the practice of mixed-ownership reform in terms of how to safeguard the interests of all parties involved in the reform and achieve win-win cooperation.

3   The Cycle of SOE Reform

At present, SOE reform is actually carried out at two levels in parallel. The first is to realize the transformation of supervisory function from managing enterprises to managing capital in the reform of state-owned capital management system through the capitalization of state-owned assets. The second is to achieve mixed-ownership, improve corporate governance and establish a modern enterprise system by introducing strategic investors into SOEs as operating entities. We will focus on this discussion in Chapter 5.

As for SOEs as operating entities, the main initiative of mixed-ownership reform is to attract strategic investors to participate in the reform by partially or fully transferring the controlling stake to let them dominate in the board organization or even in the proportion of shares. We take China Unicom as an example, which is in the first batch of pilot projects to push forward mixed-ownership of central SOE. With 3% of the shares, Baidu won one seat of the eight non-independent directors (accounting for 12.5%) on China Unicom's board after the mixed-ownership reform, thus creating the so-called Unicom model in which state-owned capital dominates in the equity structure and strategic investors dominate in the board organization. As we can see, the institutional arrangement of China Unicom's mixed-ownership reform, in which state-owned assets dominate the shareholding structure, ensures China Unicom Group, the actual controller, has a one-vote veto on important matters. At the same time, the predominance of strategic investors in the board organization not only encourages strategic investors to participate in the mixed-ownership reform by providing them a corporate governance mechanism to protect their rights and interests but also improves China Unicom's operation and management with the help of the rich experience of strategic investors.

Since central enterprises often belong to strategic industries, mixed-ownership reform will affect the overall situation, so relevant policies must be introduced with care and caution. In contrast, SOE mixed-ownership reform at the provincial level is much lighter in terms of both historical and practical burdens. Let's take the recent launch of mixed-ownership reform of Tianjin Building Materials Group (hereinafter TBMG) and Northern Trust as an example. On May 4, 2018, Beijing Building Materials Group (hereinafter BBMG) successfully signed a contract with TBMG at Tianjin Property Rights Exchange to acquire 55% of the latter's equity and became the new controlling shareholder. If this is the first step for enterprises in Beijing and Tianjin to jointly implement the Beijing-Tianjin-Hebei Integration Initiative, then Northern Trust, which began to issue capital and share increase projects on the Tianjin Property Rights Exchange in early April 2018, has gone further. After the completion of Northern Trust's mixed-ownership reform, the shareholding of state-owned enterprises was reduced to 34%, while new social capital held 57.56% and other original shareholders held 8.44%. According to media reports, private companies have an absolute holding in Northern Trust, regardless of the proportion of the single shareholding or the overall shareholding. At the time, both the legal representative and the chairman of Northern Trust were vacant. After the mixed-ownership reform, the new largest shareholder will have the right to elect the chairman and general manager. This means that after the completion of the mixed-ownership reform, it will not be surprising for SOE chairmen and general managers to write job applications in places like Tianjin.

The characteristics of the new round of mixed-ownership reform of local SOEs in competitive industries can be summarized as follows. First of all, state-owned capital investment and operating companies hold at least one-third of the shares and keep the right of one-vote veto on important matters of the board of directors. The second is that there are no restrictions on the geographical and state-owned background of the largest shareholder. Private enterprises can obtain controlling shares, whether they hold the shares alone or as a whole. The third is that the chairmen and general managers are nominated by the new major shareholders.

The above new trends in SOE reform show that both the state-owned asset management system and the mixed-ownership reform of SOE operating entities have reached the stage of substantive promotion. Compared with previous SOE reforms, we note that this round of reform has shown a new atmosphere.

To begin with, from "haste makes waste" to "land oneself in serious trouble". In 2015, Baoneng attempted to take control of Vanke through a significant shareholding in the secondary markets, but was beaten back by Vanke management team, as well as the local governments and even the regulatory authorities. Baoneng got a bad reputation as a barbarian, demon or evil monster and chose to withdraw from Vanke in disgrace a few years later. In the new round of mixed-ownership reform, private enterprises can not only become the controlling shareholders of some SOEs with unsatisfactory operating conditions and poor asset viability, but also the positions of chairman and general manager are vacant.

Then, from "pretty girl marries first" to "mother is exalted due to her son's rank". In the implementation of SOE mixed-ownership reform, asset evaluation, debt treatment and personnel placement will be the key factors for strategic investors to choose whether to participate in the reform. In the early process of SOE restructuring characterized by joint-stock reform, some of the high-quality assets were separated from the parent company and other parts in order to be listed first. Professor Li Yining has vividly referred to this as "pretty girl marries first". Over the years, some listed companies under state-owned enterprise groups have become scarce resources in China's capital market, which has adopted the approval-based initial public offering system. In the new round of mixed-ownership reform, the state-owned enterprise groups rely on their listed subsidiaries in the asset evaluation process, laying the foundation for the smooth progress of the subsequent reform. This may be something that the designers of the joint-stock reform plan did not anticipate.

Furthermore, from "non-melting popsicle" to "hot potato". In addition to personnel placement (positions usually remained the same for three years), the biggest challenge for strategic investors involved in SOE reform is how to deal with the high debt of many SOEs. In order to refute some economists' suggestions on speeding up the reform process of state-owned enterprises, some scholars claim that SOEs are non-melting popsicles. After several rounds of debt-to-equity swaps over a period of 20 years, Dongbei Special Steel defaulted on its debt in 2016. The new chairman once proposed to swap 70% of the company's debt for equity, but it was unanimously rejected by creditors. Shen Wenrong's holding of Northeast Special Steel, which was interpreted by the media as accidental privatization, was actually a desperate move made by the local government to resolve the debt crisis of Northeast Special Steel. Today, with the peak of corporate debt defaults, rumors of capital chain rupture in SOEs arouse the vigilance of financial trusts, as if a systemic financial risk will come right away. The SOEs in the process of mixed-ownership reform are undoubtedly the victims of the rumor of bond default risk, causing some strategic investors who are ready to enter may be deterred from this. What was once a non-melting popsicle has now become a hot potato that is hard to handle.

Finally, from the loss of state-owned assets to the inflow of private capital. In the past, state-owned assets suffered a lot of losses. Now, through the participation of strategic investors in mixed-ownership reform and the inflow of private capital, state-owned capital is actually becoming stronger, better and bigger. In this regard, I particularly agree with Chen Qingtai's speech at the SOE Reform Forum. He stated that "it is meaningless to continue to strictly define the state-owned and private background for mixed-ownership enterprises. The government should weaken or even cancel the policy of differential treatment according to the components of enterprise ownership so as to promote equal rights, equal opportunities and equal rules for all types of enterprises."[1]

4   From China Unicom to Northern Trust: Invariance and Change in SOE Mixed-Ownership Reform

On November 20, 2018, Tianjin Northern International Trust Co., Ltd. (hereinafter Northern Trust) officially signed the project of mixed-ownership reform, marking the first state-holding joint-stock non-bank financial institution to complete its mixed-ownership reform. Founded in 1987, Northern Trust is one of the oldest trust companies in China. Through the mixed-ownership reform, Northern Trust successfully introduced three new shareholders of private enterprises, namely Rizhao Steel Holding Group Co., Ltd.; Shanghai Zhongtong Ruide Investment Group Co., Ltd.; and Yike Zhengrun Investment Group Co., Ltd., and transferred 50.07% equity in total.

In August 2017, China Unicom became the first batch of central enterprise to see mixed-ownership reform through the introduction of strategic investors such as China Life Insurance and BATJ. In the deepening process of SOE mixed-ownership reform – from the pilot trial of central SOE represented by China Unicom to comprehensive implementation of local SOE represented by Northern Trust – we see new opportunities to observe and evaluate the invariance and change of the design concept of corporate governance system.

We have noticed that both China Unicom and Northern Trust have followed the following principles in the mixed-ownership reform process intentionally or unintentionally.

First of all, by introducing strategic investors with private capital background, the decentralized control structure with equity checks and balances is formed, so as to achieve a breakthrough in the reform of corporate governance institutional framework. For example, after the completion of China Unicom's mixed-ownership reform, the shares held by the controlling shareholder China Unicom Group decreased from 60% to 36.67%, and Tencent and Baidu, which accounted for 5.18% and 3.3% of the shares, respectively, became new major shareholders. Before mixed-ownership reform, Northern Trust was composed of 27 shareholders, including large SOEs, listed companies and private enterprises. Among them,

20 SOEs owned by the city government had a total shareholding of 82.1%. After the mixed-ownership reform, the new shareholders of the three private enterprises received a total of 50.07% equity. Among them, Rizhao Steel became the largest shareholder with 18.30%, while Shanghai Zhongtong Ruide held 17.65% and Yike Zhengrun held 14.12%. The stake held by TEDA Investment Holding, the state-owned former largest shareholder, was diluted to 17.94%, making it the second largest shareholder.

The theoretical basis of SOE mixed-ownership reform is to introduce a competitive decentralized control theory to avoid excessive regulation under the dominance of a single shareholder by introducing a competitive error correction mechanism. Introducing strategic investors to form a competitive relationship between major shareholders thus establishes an automatic error correction mechanism. It can not only effectively avoid the excessive regulation and decision-making errors easily caused by the dominance of a single shareholder but also form a check on managers to avoid the problem of insider control. Only through decentralized control can state-owned assets transform the role from managing personnel, affairs and enterprises to managing capital. A simple example is that even though they have a certain degree of competition and grudges, BATJ, the four Internet giants, will firmly stand together against the major shareholders that may harm the interests of outside shareholders. In the face of query of BATJ alliance, China Unicom Group is more likely to propose motions as a shareholder from the perspective of maximizing the interests of shareholders so as to avoid damaging the interests of outside shareholders.

Second, for the basic and strategic industries involved, the equity design of mixed-ownership reform still maintains the relative holding of state-owned assets through the right of one-vote veto. For example, after China Unicom completed its mixed-ownership reform, the shareholding ratio of China Unicom Group dropped from 60% to 36.67%, but it was still higher than the 33.3% required for one-vote veto right on major issues. This is obviously determined by the characteristics of the basic and strategic industry in which China Unicom belongs. We believe that in the future mixed-ownership reform, from central enterprises to local SOEs, there will be frequent equity design schemes in which major shareholders with state-owned background in basic and strategic industries hold 34%. In order to maintain the influence of state-owned assets at shareholders' meetings, some SOEs will even introduce strategic investors with a state-owned background as strategic allies. In the mixed-ownership reform of China Unicom, China Life and China Structural Reform Fund with a state-owned background undoubtedly play such a role.

Finally, the introduction of strategic investors in SOE mixed-ownership reform does not care much about whether the strategic investors are from an investment background or industrial background, and the purpose of improving corporate governance through the mixed-ownership reform is higher than the purpose of generating synergies. Theoretically, the introduction of strategic investors from related industries is more likely to generate economic synergies. However, when we look at China Unicom and Northern Trust, which have completed mixed-ownership reform, the above implications are not obvious. To a certain extent, this round of mixed-ownership reform attaches more importance to improving corporate governance than to the synergy effect. Let's take the Northern Trust's mixed-ownership reform, which has just been completed in stages. Due to the scarcity of trust company licenses, Northern Trust's mixed-ownership reform has attracted a lot of attention from strategic investors and outsiders. The three new private capital shareholders that have joined the company are both investment and industrial investors. In the above sense, SOE mixed-ownership reform has brought new opportunities for some industrial private enterprises to achieve the combination of industry and finance and leapfrog development by means of financial holdings.

If we further compare and analyze the corporate governance system of China Unicom and Northern Trust, we can see some obvious differences between them.

First, given the fact that it is impossible to attract strategic investors by directly transferring control rights due to industrial attribute, China Unicom was forced to choose the model of state-owned capital dominating in the equity structure while strategic investors dominate in the board organization to make strategic investors somewhat incentive compatible and willing to participate in the mixed-ownership reform. In contrast, Northern Trust, a local SOE that is not part of the basic and strategic industries, achieves this directly by ceding control.

Among the eight non-independent directors of the new board established by China Unicom on February 8, 2018, three directors were appointed by China Unicom Group, and the other five are from strategic investors such as China Life, Baidu, Alibaba, Tencent and JD.com.

Northern Trust made it clear from the beginning of the mixed-ownership reform that it did not seek control rights. In the explanation of relevant mixed-ownership reform, Northern Trust explained that private enterprises would have an absolute control position whether they have a single shareholding or an overall shareholding. In terms of the realization form, a total of 50.07% equity of Northern Trust was acquired by three private enterprises, which means that private capital has obtained the controlling position of Northern Trust in a practical sense. To a large extent, the mode of mixed-ownership reform without seeking control is what local governments have to take in order to get rid of the financial and operational difficulties of local SOEs that do not belong to the basic and strategic industries. For the same reason, not seeking control may become a common practice adopted by local governments for SOE reform in non-basic and strategic industries in the future.

Second, in the board organization of China Unicom, the controlling shareholder China Unicom Group holds up to 36.67% and nominates three of the eight non-independent directors. In Northern Trust, Rizhao Steel, which has become the largest shareholder by a narrow margin, is given the power to recommend the chairman. Rizhao Steel, Northern Trust's new largest shareholder, holds only 18.30%, 0.36% higher than the second largest shareholder TEDA Investment Holding (holds 17.94%), and 0.65% ahead of the third largest shareholder, Shanghai Zhongtong Ruide Investment (holds 17.65%). While Rizhao Steel appoints its chairman, Northern Trust will be a model of equity checks and balances in the practice of corporate governance. The largest shareholder, Rizhao Steel, and its appointed chairman will be supervised not only by state-owned TEDA Investment Holding, but also by private investors such as Shanghai Zhongtong Ruide and Yike Zhengrun.

In comparison with China Unicom, we can see that Northern Trust, which belongs to non-basic and strategic industries, better transformed the role of SOEs from managing personnel, affairs and enterprises to managing capital, and its shareholding structure and board organization seemed to be more thoroughly reformed. The state-owned second largest shareholder TEDA Investment Holding participates as an investor and counterbalance force in the corporate governance of Northern Trust. Shareholders from different interests and backgrounds can only achieve win-win cooperation if they work together to overcome difficulties.

It should be said that the phased completion of the mixed-ownership reform of Northern Trust plays a very important role of a wind vane to boosting the confidence of slightly sluggish SOEs and opening up a new situation of mixed-ownership reform. Northern Trust's mixed-ownership reform has also proved with facts our previous prediction that with the deepening of reform, chairmen and general managers of some SOEs began to write job applications. This is not a joke but a coming reality.

5 Possible Implementation Modes of SOE Mixed-Ownership Reform

Like any reform measures, mixed-ownership reform can become self-reinforcing only when it becomes an optimal strategic combination (the Nash equilibrium in economics) agreed upon by both or more parties. A self-reinforcing institutional arrangement needs to meet two basic conditions. One is the participation constraint. Specifically in the case of mixed-ownership reform, a financial or strategic investor of SOEs will earn a higher return on investment than other investors (opportunity cost). As it is expected to take advantage of the opportunity to enter the monopolistic strategic industry that was difficult to dabble in in the past, and thus share high monopoly profits, private capital has a strong willingness to participate in mixed-ownership reform. The ease of meeting participation constraints can be seen in the participation of BATJ, the four Internet giants, in China Unicom's mixed-ownership reform in August 2017. The second is the incentive compatibility constraint. Specifically, in the case of mixed-ownership reform, reform should be profitable and win-win for both state and private capital. The most basic interest of state capital is to promote the preservation and appreciation of state assets in order to improve the social welfare of all people. As we know, the main purposes of mixed-ownership reform are to improve the operating efficiency of state-owned capital, to get rid of financial and operational difficulties, and to promote the preservation and appreciation of state-owned capital. Therefore, it seems self-evident that mixed-ownership reform is profitable for state-owned assets. However, the biggest concern of private capital participating in mixed-ownership reform is the possible appropriation and tunneling of private capital by state-owned capital as the controlling shareholder. Corporate governance literature suggests that with the help of pyramidal holding structure, the ultimate owner will separate cash flow rights from control rights, thus tunneling the interests of listed companies located at the bottom of the pyramidal structure through capital occupation, related party transactions and other ways (Johnson, La Porta, Lopez-de-Silanes and Shleifer, 2000; Claessens, Djankov and Lang, 2000). For private capital, if the state-owned capital as the controlling shareholder can make a credible commitment not using its holding position to embezzle and tunnel the interests of private capital, private capital will benefit from the mixture of ownership and thus become incentive compatible. Of course, the prerequisite for the incentive compatibility constraint to be satisfied is that the commitment made by state-owned capital must be credible. Therefore, the key to the success of mixed-ownership reform is how to make the commitments made by state-owned enterprises credible.

Then, starting from the above evaluation benchmark, what are the possible implementation modes of SOE mixed-ownership reform?

Mode One: Holdings of Private Capital

Yunnan SASAC and New Huadu Industrial Group each hold 50% equity in Yunnan Baiyao Group. This typical case has created the Baiyao Mode – the mode of mixed-ownership reform controlled by private capital. Compared with Yunnan Baiyao, a more typical example of the private holding is the Hangzhou-Shaoxing-Taizhou high-speed railway project (see Chapter 4, section 2 of this book for a detailed discussion of this issue). On December 23, 2016, the construction of the Hangzhou-Shaoxing-Taizhou high-speed railway started in Taizhou, Zhejiang Province. As a private investment consortium holds 51% of the stake, it has become China's first railway with absolute private ownership. The shareholding structure of the Hangzhou-Shaoxing-Taizhou high-speed railway once aroused the concern of many people. Will the Hangzhou-Shaoxing-Taizhou high-speed railway project, which is in a regional monopoly position, grab monopoly profits by setting a high price, so that local residents are forced to bear the high monopoly price? Is it reasonable to hand over railway infrastructure with strong long-term positive externalities to private enterprises with strong short-term profit motives?

An obvious fact is that even if private investors have a controlling stake in the high-speed railway project, they cannot do whatever they want. We make this judgment for three reasons. First, according to Hart's theory of incomplete contracts, shareholders' rights come from the right of redress in legal principle to deal with matters not specified in the incomplete contract. For the part clearly provided in the contract, it does not need and should not be realized by shareholders in the form of residual control. It would be an abuse of shareholder power if a shareholder made irresponsible comments on the part that was already specified in the contract. Providing high-quality and low-cost railway transportation services is a solemn commitment and a contractual obligation of the project to local residents and the government. Since the price adjustment is not so much related to the incomplete contract, it is not within the scope of shareholders to exercise residual control through voting. Second, due to the regional monopoly characteristics of the Hangzhou-Shaoxing-Taizhou high-speed railway, the project, which is highly external, needs to be supervised by regulatory authorities, and even become an important regulatory object of relevant anti-monopoly authorities. If the Hangzhou-Shaoxing-Taizhou high-speed railway project sets a high price, the regulatory authorities can conduct an anti-monopoly investigation and impose penalties accordingly. Third, according to the theory of contestable market (Baumol, 1982), even if the Hangzhou-Shaoxing-Taizhou high-speed railway project has some kind of regional monopolies, there are still developed roads, sea and air transportation in the Hangzhou-Shaoxing-Taizhou area. These alternative modes of transportation are important reference factors for the pricing of this project. In theory, the excess monopoly profits obtained by Hangzhou-Shaoxing-Taizhou high-speed railway project will attract new high-speed railway projects, so as to break its monopoly on the high-speed railway service in the region.

As we can see from the cases of Yunnan Baiyao Group and Hangzhou-Shaoxing-Taizhou high-speed railway project, private capital has high enthusiasm to participate in SOE mixed-ownership reform because it has a relative or even absolute controlling stake, which can not only satisfy the participation constraints but also the incentive compatibility constraints that are usually difficult to meet, so it has high enthusiasm to participate in the mixed-ownership reform of state-owned enterprises.

Mode Two: Conversion of State-Owned Assets Into Preferred Shares

On the one hand, preferred shares are very similar to bonds in terms of setting face value, fixed rate of return, non-voting rights and tax benefits. On the other hand, preferred shares are particularly similar to equity in terms of dividend timing, corporate income tax and taxation of preferred shares held by individuals. Therefore, as an important financial instrument, preferred stock is called disguised bonds. Its remarkable feature is that it can effectively avoid excessive intervention by shareholders in enterprise management and ensure the separation of management and control. At the same time, the priority status of dividend payments helps to preserve and increase the value of state capital. Therefore, SOEs can considered making serious commitments to the private capital to exclude the behavior of tunneling, direct intervention and operation of enterprise by holding non-voting preferred stock, such as when the US government rescued the market in the financial crisis, or SoftBank and Yahoo, the major shareholders of Alibaba, so as to meet the incentive compatibility constraints and promote the substantive implementation of SOE mixed-ownership reform.

After the mixed-ownership reform is completed in accordance with the above mode, state-owned capital operation institutions will increase or decrease their holdings of preferred shares based on the past performance and corporate governance of listed companies to guide the market's evaluation of them. This is to put external pressure on listed companies to improve performance and corporate governance through market actions rather than administrative methods. Thus, the state property management organizations have completed the role transformation from managing both capital and enterprises to managing capital. Newly introduced institutional investors with similar shareholdings will implement decentralized control, and the resulting compromise effect will be conducive to protecting the interests of dispersed outside shareholders and state-owned assets. According to the legal basis provided by Hart's theory of incomplete contracts, the general meeting of shareholders, which reflects that shareholders are the authority of corporate governance, is the highest authority of the company to vote on major issues including the change of directors and M&A.

We have noted that for some time now, state property management organizations have begun to mention the policy proposals to promote mixed-ownership reform by issuing and converting preferred shares. Although there is no specific case of converting state-owned assets into preferred shares so far, we have reason to believe that the approach mentioned above may bring a major breakthrough in mixed-ownership reform and become the key to deepening the reform in the future.

Mode Three: Introduction of Outside Investors to the Subsidiary

Most of the SOEs that have been or are currently undergoing mixed-ownership reform carried out equity restructuring to the subsidiaries by attracting institutional investors (see Chapter 4, section 5 of this book for detailed discussion). Air China Cargo, a subsidiary of China National Aviation Corporation, and COFCO Capital, a specialized company in the financial sector under COFCO, have adopted a similar mode of mixed-ownership reform. The realistic rationality of this mode is as follows. First, the equity reconstruction of subsidiaries provides a physical platform for the entry of social capital to mix state capital and social capital. Second, the equity restructuring of subsidiaries is helpful to transform the role of state-owned assets management system from managing both capital and enterprises to managing capital. Third, state-owned capital can introduce social capital into its subsidiaries to adjust the industrial layout in an orderly manner, so that the limited capital can be concentrated in the main business.

We have noticed that some SOEs that have adopted the above mode for mixed-ownership reform still have some misunderstandings in terms of how to protect the rights and interests of social capital participating in the subsidiaries. For one thing, before the mixed-ownership reform plan is put forward, some enterprises do not carefully distinguish whether the reform is facing the problem of improving operational and management efficiency or financing constraints according to the principle of setting up subsidiaries and branches. For example, in some projects, social capital was mechanically introduced and subsidiaries and corresponding corporate governance structures such as boards of directors and supervisors were established. The basic systems of corporate governance such as the board of directors and the board of supervisors, which needs continuous investment to maintain, not only do not improve the efficiency of operation and management, which is the most important for the project, but they also unnecessarily increase the operating costs. Second, ignore the basic corporate governance system of subsidiaries and still manage them as branch companies. For example, directly intervene in the appointment and removal of the board of directors and the key management team of the subsidiary company, rather than negotiate with shareholders and vote at the shareholders' meeting after recommending directors according to the proportion of capital contribution. On the one hand, the part-time nature of appointed directors leads to a discrepancy between rights and obligations. On the other hand, the lack of salary incentives leads to the difficult appointment of directors. The executive orders of the parent group directly replace the decision-making effect of the shareholders' meeting of the subsidiary and its authorized board of directors, which weakens the corporate governance authority of subsidiary company, and the rights and interests of social capital cannot be effectively guaranteed. Third, some social capital enters for a short period of time due to reputation or pressure and waits for the right time to withdraw, making the seeming achieved mixed-ownership reform unsustainable and weak.

Mode Four: Launch of the Employee Stock Ownership Plan

An employee stock ownership plan (ESOP) is an incentive plan launched by enterprises to bind the return of employees to the long-term development of enterprises, so that employees will pay more attention to the long-term performance of enterprises and avoid pursuing short-term interests at the expense of the long-term interests of enterprises. ESOP is also considered one of the important ways to achieve mixed-ownership reform because it involves equity restructuring. The State-Owned Assets Regulation and Administration Commission (SASAC), the Ministry of Finance (MOF) and China Securities Regulatory Commission (CSRC) jointly issued *Opinions on the Pilot Project of ESOP for State-Owned Holding Enterprises With Mixed Ownership* (hereinafter *Pilot Opinions*) in August 2016, which has become an important policy for launching ESOPs in mixed-ownership reform. However, SOEs that have implemented ESOP in the mixed-ownership reform have the following problems to varying degrees. First, there is a lack of necessary arrangements for the corporate governance system to make shareholding employees truly become the masters of the company. In the current corporate governance system, management is often appointed by superiors and, according to the *Pilot Opinions*, is not allowed to hold shares. However, employees who are allowed to hold shares cannot effectively protect their rights and interests. This is equivalent to handing over your fate to someone who may not really care about your interests. Second, employees who are fully motivated by an ESOP will certainly attract social capital to participate in SOE mixed-ownership reform. However, an ESOP will increase the number of shareholders that social capital has to face, not to mention that these are not ordinary investors but very important stakeholders. Therefore, the question is whether an ESOP should be launched by the board of directors after the implementation of mixed-ownership reform and according to employee incentives, or whether an ESOP should be launched before the introduction of social capital. As far as the current situation of employee incentive is concerned, after scientific evaluation, the board of directors believes that the base salary plus performance-related salary is not enough to provide sufficient incentives to employees. Third, an ESOP should focus on SOEs' stock funds. The attractions and potential problems of SOEs are mainly focused on stock funds. However, the *Pilot Opinions* focus on the incremental introduction of employee shareholding in the form of capital increase, share expansion and capital contribution. At the same time, stock ownership is not free for employees. Employees should invest mainly in currency and pay on time according to their appointment. The pilot enterprises shall not provide advances, guarantees, loans and other financial assistance to employees holding shares. As we have seen, employees are not allowed to hold shares that they are interested in (such as those with high monopoly benefits in the stock of SOEs). What employees are allowed to hold is often newly issued, but they may not be interested. This makes employee ownership become the wishful thinking of the designers of the SOE mixed-ownership reform plan. Fourth, the ESOP should have a reasonable exit mechanism. In the history of China's SOE reform, the employee shareholding cooperative system ended in vain because it could not reasonably solve the problem of employee stock ownership withdrawal. According to the *Pilot Opinions*, if an employee leaves the company for reasons such as resignation, transfer, retirement, death or dismissal, his shares should be transferred internally within 12 months. In case of transfer to the shareholding platform, qualified employees or non-public capital shareholders, the transfer price shall be determined by both parties through negotiation and shall not be higher than the audited net assets per share of the previous year. Employees can transfer their shares to a specific limited market with less room for negotiation. We have seen that employee stock ownership has become less attractive for employees who have to change jobs for some reason. Employees who are truly capable are reluctant to accept ESOP for fear of being bound, while those who accept ESOP are often less competent.

On February 11, 2018, China Unicom announced the equity incentive plan to be launched. According to the plan, China Unicom granted up to 847.88 million restricted shares to 7,855 middle-level managers, core management and professional talents of the company, including the board secretary and the financial officer, accounting for approximately 2.8% of the total share capital of the company at that time. After introducing strategic investors, as a listed company, China Unicom launched the ESOP by issuing restricted shares, which alleviating or even partially circumvented the concerns mentioned above to a certain extent. However, the arrangement of the corporate governance system and the exit mechanism for incentive targets are still inevitable problems for most unlisted SOEs when implementing mixed-ownership reform. Therefore, for most SOEs, the ESOP plays only a very limited role in mixed-ownership reform. Even for China Unicom, which has relatively mature conditions in implementing ESOP, it only took some members of the management team, such as secretary of the board and the head of finance, as the incentive targets, but not the CEO and other key members of the management team. The final effect of the equity incentive plan remains to be further observed.

Three-in-One Mode: Subsidiary + Strategic Investor + ESOP

In the actual implementation process of mixed-ownership reform, many SOEs will consider introducing strategic investors and launching ESOP in the subsidiary at the same time, thus forming the so-called three-in-one mode of mixed-ownership reform mode. China Unicom, which launched the mixed-ownership reform plan in August 2017, adopted the three-in-one mode. In the mixed-ownership reform arrangement of China Unicom, China Unicom Group introduced strategic investors to the listed company China Unicom and adopted ESOP.

The other five top shareholders of China Unicom all have much smaller stakes than China Unicom Group. By introducing more directors from strategic investors to the board organization, China Unicom has taken into account the interests of strategic investors and compensated for the lack of effective protection of strategic investors' interests when the shareholding structure is dominated by a single shareholder. At the same time, it made strategic investors, to some extent, incentive compatible. The over-appointed directors of strategic investors thus serve as an important counterbalance to controlling shareholders and a credible commitment to protect the interests of strategic investors.

Therefore, only by fully protecting the interests of all parties involved in the reform and being incentive compatible with each other can they truly achieve win-win cooperation and ultimately achieve success in mixed-ownership reform.

Note

1 国务院发展研究中心原党组书记陈清泰在5月12日举行的第四届思想中国论坛的发言："对混合所有制企业再继续严格界定国有和民营已经失去了意义，政府应该弱化直至取消按企业所有制成分区别对待的政策，促进实现各类企业权利平等、机会平等和规则平等。". Li Xiaodan. (2018). 陈清泰：重新定义国企、从管企业转向管资本 真改革要做这两件事 [Chen Qingtai: Redefining State owned Enterprises and Changing from Managing Enterprises to Managing Capital]. *eastmoney.com*. https://finance.eastmoney.com/a2/20180513871049747.html.

4 Routes to Realizing SOE Mixed-Ownership Reform

In the process of mixed-ownership reform, SOEs face many problems. For example, the succession problems left over by the history of SOE reform, the amendment of relevant Articles of Association is opposed by minority shareholders, and a large number of practical and theoretical workers worried about private capital will control SOEs after the reform and do whatever they want. These seem to be just details of the realization route, but they are related to the success or failure of SOE mixed-ownership reform.

In the process of choosing the route of mixed-ownership reform, on the one hand, the government should not simply adopt national special management to seek the control asymmetric with responsibility, but needs to make all parties involved in the reform incentive compatible. On the other hand, the government should not overstep its authority or transfer the responsibilities that originally belonged to its regulation to SOEs through property rights control.

For SOEs in financial distress, debt-to-equity swap under the government intervention constitutes a soft budget constraint in the guise of market-oriented operation, which only delays the outbreak of debt crisis but cannot fundamentally eliminate or truly resolve the problem.

As for the mixed-ownership reform of subsidiaries, only when a corporate governance system that effectively protects the rights and interests of all shareholders is established and developed, and when credible commitment and sincerity are conveyed to social capital through flexible and diverse selection and arrangement of shareholding structure, can social capital have an incentive to participate in the reform. This is the only way to achieve a real change in the concept and practice of China's SOEs from managing enterprises to managing capital.

1 Special Succession-Related Problems Caused by SOE Reform

With the aging of the older generation of entrepreneurs, the inability of the next generation to succeed in their fathers' businesses is a typical problem faced by private family businesses. Unlike the succession problems faced by private family enterprises, many listed companies in China that were reformed from SOEs in the early years are facing succession problems. This is also the problem faced by

DOI: 10.4324/9781003361404-5

companies with high media exposure, such as Ge Wenyao's Shanghai Jahwa, Zeng Nan's CSG Holding, Wang Shi's Vanke and Dong Mingzhu's Gree Electric Appliances. These famous entrepreneurs have a lot in common. First, they have made half a lifetime of efforts to lead SOEs that were small and suffered serious losses to grow step by step into the leading enterprises in their industries. Second, according to the shareholding structure, they do not have many shares, so they are not the real owners of the company. Third, these experienced and outstanding entrepreneurs have a decisive impact on their companies and even entire industries.

However, while these entrepreneurs ponder how to pass on their business to the next generation of entrepreneurs, China's capital market has rushed into an era of dispersed ownership. The conflict between the new significant shareholders who took ownership in the secondary market and these entrepreneurs has become the most characteristic corporate governance story of our times and institutional context. On the one hand, the new significant shareholders (e.g., Ping An Leasing, the owner of Shanghai Jahwa, and Baoneng Group, the owner of Vanke) kept pressuring the listed companies for short-term profit due to the high cost of M&A and even have the motivation to transfer control rights. On the other hand, entrepreneurial entrepreneurs continued to pursue established M&A development strategies even after the new significant shareholders took over. For example, Ge Wenyao of Shanghai Jahwa acquired Seagull Watch and Dong Mingzhu of Gree acquired Zhuhai Yinlong New Energy. As a continuation of such conflicts, events such as Ge Wenyao's sudden "retirement" are inevitable. Conflicts between new significant shareholders and these entrepreneurs will continue to affect the future practice of corporate governance in China.

The reason for these conflicts has more or less to do with the crossover between these new significant shareholders and entrepreneurs. First, new significant shareholders intervene in the traditional operation and management of the business. The separation of ownership and control is precisely the key to realizing the socialization of capital and the professionalization of managers, and to improving efficiency through the specialized division of labor. Therefore, it is the soul of modern joint-stock limited companies. In the event of Baoneng's bloodbath to the board of directors of CSG Holding, even Baoneng System itself did not want to see the collective resignation of the senior management team represented by Zeng Nan. The bloodbath of the board of directors becomes the institutional cost that China's listed companies have to pay for the absence of the corresponding adjustment of corporate governance system and psychological preparation when they rush into the era of dispersed ownership. Second, these powerful entrepreneurs put aside the production and operation of traditional businesses and engage in capital operations such as M&A.

The past performance of these entrepreneurs proves that they are experts in business operations, but there is no evidence that they are also experts in capital operations. Whether due to the crossover of new significant shareholders or to the crossover of entrepreneurs – or even both at the same time – today we see a wonderful corporate governance story with a plot of twists and turns playing in China's capital market.

Behind this lies the succession problem faced by listed companies reformed from SOEs in the early years. Entrepreneurs with low shareholdings ratios will not be able to convince other shareholders to accept their proposals if they entrust the companies to a management team they trust and have long cultivated. If these entrepreneurs use their influence to continue to control the company or even cross over from time to time, they will grow old one day, which will inevitably lead to the inability of their shares to bear the responsibility. The reason the succession problem is unique is precisely because these entrepreneurs lack the control that is so important to modern joint-stock companies. If entrepreneurs simply follow the theory of shareholder primacy and give up their insistence and allow new significant shareholders to lead the formation of a new management team, the company's long-developed management experience and philosophy may become unsustainable. In the case of the executive turnover at Shanghai Jahwa, the newly established management team led by the new significant shareholders has caused so many controversies in just a few years, which to some extent indicates that this is not necessarily an ideal model of succession. Therefore, just as thinking about how to encourage entrepreneurial teams to invest in human capital characterized by business model innovation in the face of the barbarian invasion, as China's capital market enters the era of dispersed ownership, the theorists and practitioners of corporate governance also need to think about how to address the special succession problems faced by listed companies that were reformed from SOEs in the early years.

At present, the more urgent problem is how to stop the one-way or even two-way crossover of entrepreneurs and new significant shareholders. Collective voting at shareholders' meetings led by new significant shareholders can be an effective practice in deterring entrepreneurs from crossover. Admittedly, Gree's dividend returns to shareholders have been commendable, but shareholders still blocked Gree's move to acquire Zhuhai Yinlong New Energy at the general meeting. Under the leadership of new significant shareholder Ping An Leasing, the shareholders' meeting once blocked the acquisition of Seagull Watch by Shanghai Jahwa proposed by Ge Wenyao. Preventing the crossover of new significant shareholders is clearly more problematic than preventing the crossover of entrepreneurs.

Dispersed shareholders are too accustomed to the control of major shareholders under the single shareholder dominance mode and are unwilling to stand up and cast their sacred vote, which makes it seem that there is no effective mechanism to prevent the crossover of new significant shareholders. This is the reason why the Baoneng System can bloodbathe the board of directors of CSG Holding.

In the long run, an ideal mechanism to prevent new significant shareholders from crossover would be the proposal of independent directors to hold special shareholders' meetings. The reason it is independent directors rather than board of directors is precisely because inside directors are susceptible to the influence of entrepreneurs or new significant shareholders and are not in a position to make objective and fair judgments on proposals from the perspective of the interests of dispersed outside shareholders. By simple comparison, we can find that in mature market economies where the ownership of listed companies is highly dispersed, the ideal organizational model of the board is that all the directors except the CEO are independent directors. These independent directors, who come from outside and are relatively independent and concerned with reputation and career development, become an important third party to protect the interests of dispersed shareholders and mediate conflict of interests between entrepreneurs and new significant shareholders. If necessary, independent directors should initiate a special general meeting of shareholders to make a final decision on the disputed matters by voting. After all, all shareholders can and will be responsible for decisions made within the limits of their capital contributions. For example, the proposal of 840 million yuan salary increase for 70,000 employees put forward by Gree's management should also be submitted to the general meeting of shareholders for discussion and approval before implementation by the independent directors with neutral interests, since it involves the major investment and the redistribution of shareholders' dividends. There is no doubt that this mechanism is not yet mature in China's capital market. Its effective operation needs to meet two necessary conditions. The first is the maturity of shareholders. This is mainly reflected in the awakening of shareholders' awareness of their rights: the shares in their hands are not only marketable securities but also votes. As one of the main constituents of future shareholders, institutional investors can also become an important force to check and balance entrepreneurs and new significant shareholders. For example, in the case of Shanghai Jahwa, institutional investors made efforts to counterbalance the new significant shareholder Ping An Leasing, restructure the board of directors and recommend preferred directors. The second is the maturity of the independent director market and corresponding system. From the selection mechanism to the compensation system and the institutional arrangements for the performance of rights and obligations, independent directors will need to gradually get rid of the image of eye candy or tool of signature and become a third-party force independent of the parties under the constraints of reputation incentive and legal risk. As China's capital market enters the era of dispersed ownership, and the shareholding proportion of the largest shareholder continues to shrink, independent directors with increasing stakes should gradually replace part of the corporate governance role originally played by major shareholders at the concentrated ownership era.

As shareholders and independent directors mature, the board dominated by independent directors will gradually become the new authority for corporate governance in China's capital market. For example, under the coordination of the board of directors, and finally through the vote at the general meeting of shareholders, implement equity incentive plans such as the golden parachute for entrepreneurs to let them land smoothly. On the basis of listening to the opinions of entrepreneurs and new significant shareholders, the nominating committee of the board of directors led by independent directors shall select and appoint the new management team in accordance with the principle of realizing the sustainable and stable development of the company.

In addition to the aforementioned adjustment of corporate governance system, the solution to the special succession problems faced by entrepreneurs with SOE genes also depends on a shift in concept. Entrepreneurs should be aware of the limits of their career longevity and take the initiative to exit at the right time. The shift from holding industrial capital to public welfare funds is a gradual shift from taking the risk of specific investment to diversified investments that rely on risk sharing. A typical example of this is the role change of Bill Gates, the former president of Microsoft. New significant shareholders need to break the traditional mindset of shareholder primacy and "the boss hires employees" and establish a win-win long-term partnership with entrepreneurs to share the dividends of enterprise development. New significant shareholders should respect entrepreneurs and their authority in business management, while entrepreneurs should be grateful to new significant shareholders for sharing the risk.

2   Can Private Capital–Turned–Controlling Shareholder Act Willfully?

On December 23, 2016, the Hangzhou-Shaoxing-Taizhou high-speed railway project started construction in Taizhou, Zhejiang Province. As the private investment consortium holds 51% of the stake, it has become China's first railway in which private capital has absolute control, which has attracted a lot of media attention. Some people worry that the Hangzhou-Shaoxing-Taizhou high-speed railway project, which has a monopoly position in the region, may gain monopoly profits by forcing local residents to bear high prices. Some people further questioned whether it was reasonable to trust railway infrastructure with strong long-term positive externalities to private capital with strong short-term profit motives. In fact, behind these doubts, there is an important misunderstanding: can private capital act willfully when it becomes a controlling shareholder?

For the following four reasons, even if private capital becomes the controlling shareholder of the high-speed railway project, it does not mean that it can do whatever it wants.

First, from a legal point of view, shareholders' rights come from the right of redress to ex post disposition for matters not specified in the incomplete contract. According to Professor Hart, the 2016 Nobel laureate in economics, since the contract signed between shareholders and managers is incomplete, shareholders are reluctant to invest in the modern joint-stock company in anticipation of being ripped off by managers, unless they have the final say on matters not stipulated in the incomplete contract. In order to encourage shareholders to invest, modern joint-stock companies need to make a commitment that shareholders, as owners, have the final right to make major decisions. This is reflected in the fact that shareholders have residual control rights in the form of voting on major matters. As we have seen today, this is the legal basis on which managers' fiduciary duties to shareholders are protected by the law. Compared with the original intention of the incomplete contract theory developed by Hart, the reason why the shareholders' rights are protected by law and the logical starting point of residual control rights that shareholders actually enjoy comes from the incompleteness of the contract signed by shareholders and managers. This means that what is explicitly stated in the contract does not need and should not be realized by shareholders in the form of residual control. Equally important, the reason why shareholders have the right (protected by law) to make final decisions on major matters also lies in their ability to assume responsibility as contributors. These two elements determine that the matters that need to be submitted to the general meeting of shareholders for deliberation as stipulated in the Company Law and the Articles of Association should have the following basic characteristics. First, it involves major asset restructuring, business strategy adjustment and other matters that could not have been anticipated at the time of incorporation. This is consistent with the view that the incomplete contract is the logical starting point of modern property rights arrangement. Second, shareholders have the capacity liability for the matters on which they vote.

It is easy to understand that shareholders should have the capacity liability for their votes at the general meeting. However, it is not easy to understand that shareholders can vote only on matters not specified in the incomplete contract and have no right to intervene in the matters that are already specified in the contract. This is also the source of the cognitive bias that many people believe that controlling shareholders act as they please. To further illustrate this point, let's take a real example. The shareholders of Gree Electric Appliances have the right to reject Dong Mingzhu's M&A proposal. Because her proposal is related to the incomplete contract (no such agreement was reached between Dong and the shareholders when the company was established), and the veto of the proposal has become the embodiment and representation of residual control enjoyed by Gree shareholders. However, as Dong Mingzhu has strictly fulfilled her contractual obligations, the shareholders' meeting of Gree did not refuse or limit her rights to pay the remuneration stipulated in the compensation contract, otherwise the shareholders would face a lawsuit filed by her according to the compensation contract.

Second, becoming a shareholder means limiting the exercise of residual control rights to matters not specified in the incomplete contract. At the same time, shareholders also need to strictly fulfill their obligations stipulated in the complete contracts signed in advance in accordance with the capacity liability reflected in the capital contribution. I believe that the reason why the local government trusted the high-speed railway project to the private company is precisely because the company made a solemn commitment to provide high-quality and low-cost railway transportation services to residents through its capacity liability reflected by the capital contribution. This is also a contractual obligation that the company needs to comply with in the future. The local government has the right to terminate the contract if the company fails to meet its obligations properly. A typical example is the acquisition of the Chicago Stock Exchange by private investors led by the Chongqing Casin Group in China. The acquisition was not only unanimously approved by the board of directors of the Chicago Stock Exchange but also welcomed by relevant US regulators. However, that doesn't mean Chongqing Casin Group, which bought shares in the Chicago Stock Exchange, can use its influence as a shareholder to open the door for enterprises from China to list on the Chicago Stock Exchange. The exchange needs to live up to its commitments to the US regulatory authorities and capital markets to provide fair and impartial intermediary services. Otherwise, it will not only face regulatory penalties but also penalties for breach of contract. This example tells us, to some extent, that the identity of controlling shareholder only shows the capital structure of a listed company, but a legal entity is required to strictly perform the complete contract signed in advance regardless of who the controlling shareholder is. Therefore, being a controlling shareholder is important, but not as important as you might think.

Third, according to anti-monopoly theories and practices, the Hangzhou-Shaoxing-Taizhou high-speed railway project has become the main regulatory target of the relevant anti-monopoly authorities due to its regional monopoly characteristics. For excessive pricing of high-speed railway tickets, the relevant regulatory authorities can conduct anti-monopoly investigations and impose penalties accordingly.

Fourth, even if the Hangzhou-Shaoxing-Taizhou high-speed railway project has shown some monopoly characteristics, there is still developed road, sea and air transportation in this area. These alternative modes of transportation are important reference factors for the pricing of the Hangzhou-Shaoxing-Taizhou high-speed railway project. And in theory, the excess monopoly profits obtained by the Hangzhou-Shaoxing-Taizhou high-speed railway project will attract new competitors to enter the market, thus breaking the monopoly situation of the project in the high-speed railway services in the region. Various practical and theoretical constraints show that even if private capital became the controlling shareholder of the Hangzhou-Shaoxing-Taizhou high-speed railway project, it has very limited pricing space in practice, so it cannot do as it pleases.

We can see that the Hangzhou-Shaoxing-Taizhou high-speed railway project, in which private capital is the controlling shareholder, is not as unconstrained as some people think. In fact, from the progress of the project so far, it has really brought convenience to residents in the Zhejiang area in terms of travel and economic development. The 269-kilometer Hangzhou-Shaoxing-Taizhou high-speed railway, which is designed for a speed of 350 kilometers per hour, connected three economically developed cities in Zhejiang Province, undoubtedly making a significant contribution to accelerating the construction of the economic belt in Zhejiang. However, if the railway is solely financed by China Railway Corporation, the national team of high-speed railway construction, it may take a long time. There is a very profound quote from Marx about railway construction:

> If it were necessary to wait for the accumulation of some individual capital to grow to the point where it can build railways, then I am afraid there are no railways in the world until today. However, it can be done in an instant through joint-stock companies.

The Hangzhou-Shaoxing-Taizhou high-speed railway project is a good illustration of Marx's idea that socialized mass production can only be realized through the socialization of capital. This is in line with the idea of China's SOE mixed-ownership reform, which can be achieved through the introduction of private capital in recent years. Since China Railway Corporation participated in the project as a shareholder, the Hangzhou-Shaoxing-Taizhou high-speed railway project has become a sample of SOE mixed-ownership reform.

Here comes a question worthy of our consideration. According to Wang Mengshu, an academician of the Chinese Academy of Engineering and a railway expert, as long as a railway is designed for both passenger and freight use, based on experience at home and abroad, it will make profits sooner or later; it is only a matter of time. But why is private capital more willing to participate in the mixed-ownership reform of the Hangzhou-Shaoxing-Taizhou high-speed railway project than in other projects? Obviously, this is mainly due to the fact that the private investment consortium participates as a controlling shareholder. Becoming a controlling shareholder undoubtedly gives private capital a relatively credible commitment to future investment returns, which is critical to solving the problem of investment incentives for private capital. This is also the reason why we once advocated that under the background of the transformation of SOEs from managing enterprises to managing capital, mixed-ownership reform can be achieved by converting state-owned capital into preferred shares with certain conditions attached. Preferred shares can be used to preserve and appreciate the state capital and promote the welfare of all people, while the private capital can see the sincerity and institutional commitment of the state capital in the mixed-ownership reform.

The Hangzhou-Shaoxing-Taizhou high-speed railway project has brought positive inspiration to the practice of corporate governance and SOE reform. To start with, the major issues that need shareholders' votes should be limited to asset restructuring and business strategy adjustment that were not explicitly stipulated in the incomplete contract when the company was established. Shareholders shall not discuss or decide matters specified in the contract but shall perform their respective obligations in accordance with the terms of the contract. Next, being the controlling shareholder means not only having influence on the matters not covered by the incomplete contract but also taking responsibility symmetrical to the amount of capital contribution for the decisions made. In addition, becoming a controlling shareholder gives private capital a relatively credible commitment to achieve investment returns, which helps solve the investment incentive of private capital. Finally, even if private capital becomes the controlling shareholder, it does not mean that it can act willfully.

3 Pitfalls With the Design of the State Special Management Share

It is reported that the Chinese government is piloting a state special management share system in two Internet media start-ups. The Internet regulatory department and People's Daily Online will hold less than 2% of the shares of the mobile news platforms Yidian Zixun and Beijing Tiexue Technology Co., Ltd. However, the Internet regulatory department and People's Daily Online will appoint a government official as a member of the company's board of directors and thus have a say in the operation and management.

The launch of China's state special management shares reminds people of the golden share, which was introduced in 1984 by the United Kingdom as part of the privatization of British Telecom (BT). BT sold 50% of its shares to the market and became a private company. In the process of three times divestment over a decade, the UK government gave up all its equity and earnings and retained only one golden share. The main right of the golden share is the veto right, rather than the beneficial right or other voting rights. Golden shares are usually only one share, which has little economic value. After privatization, BT has achieved great success in business and ranks among the world's top modern enterprises that have experienced SOE reforms.

Unlike the golden shares launched by the UK government to ensure the smooth privatization of BT, the state special management share system currently being piloted in China not only requires capital investment but also the appointment of government officials as board members and to have a say in the operation of the company.

China's relevant authorities introduced the measure in order to improve the effectiveness of regulation and to replace the rigid and inefficient traditional measures with the help of the modern corporate governance structure that seems to be more in line with the market principles. Despite the measure being well intentioned, if the equity design violates the basic principles, it may confuse the boundary between the government regulation and the equity exercise, blurring the fiduciary duties owed by directors to shareholders, which is contrary to the original intention.

In order to carry out the equity design, we first need to understand the legal basis of shareholder rights. We know that shareholders are the authority for the governance of modern joint-stock companies. The original meaning of corporate governance was thus understood by Coase as the distribution and enforcement of authority. Coase opened a long discussion on who should be the authority and how to distribute and enforce authority. It was Hart who proposed the theory of modern property rights in the 1990s and clarified that shareholders were the authority for corporate governance.

Unlike creditors, investors choose to hold shares that seem less credible. For example, equity financing does not have the underlying assets as collateral, nor does it have specific loan terms and interest rates, as bond indentures do. Modern joint-stock companies often threaten investors by not paying dividends in the event of poor performance, saying that dividend payments should not be an obligation of the company unless the board of directors make a commitment to do so.

But why do investors still want to buy such risky shares issued by joint-stock companies? This is the mystery of the modern joint-stock company.

Hart solved the mystery. Shareholders may be exposed to extortion by modern joint-stock companies after their investment. So Hart gave an important policy suggestion: make investors become owners and enjoy owner's equity through the property rights arrangement so that they are naturally willing to buy shares issued by listed companies. The owner's equity includes the following two meanings. One is the residual claim that the beneficial order of shareholders is ranked after creditors and employees. The other is residual control rights; that is, shareholders make the final decision on important matters by voting. This has become the basic and primary right that shareholders can enjoy as owners. Therefore, shareholders with residual control rights do not have to worry about rip-off behavior after the investment is done, because what is not stipulated in the incomplete contract is ultimately decided by shareholders.

Now we know why investors are willing to invest in stocks that look much less reliable than creditors' rights. Apparently, in order to encourage investors to invest, the modern joint-stock company makes a solemn commitment that investors will (collectively) enjoy owner's equity as shareholders.

Generally speaking, shareholders become the authority of corporate governance by, on the one hand, assuming limited liability for the final decisions made within the extent of their capital contributions and, on the other hand, collectively enjoying owner's equity through the shareholders' meeting. Modern property rights theory, which takes contractual incompleteness as a logical starting point, provides the legal and economic basis for shareholders to become the authority of corporate governance.

After understanding the legal principles of shareholder rights, next we will discuss the principles that should be followed in equity design. Starting from Hart's theory of modern property rights, a logical and seemingly natural corollary of the theory is that a tradition of shareholder primacy will be formed in the practice of corporate governance. Shareholders should follow the principle of one share–one vote in voting on important matters.

However, the emergence of corporate control with weighted voting rights has become more common. What constitutes the direct challenge to the one share–one vote is the dual-class or even multiple class share structure.

A typical example of Chinese companies issuing dual-class shares is JD.com, which went public on NASDAQ in 2014. JD.com issued two classes of shares simultaneously: Class A has one vote per share and Class B has 20 votes per share. Founder Liu Qiangdong, who contributed only 20% of the capital, gained 83.7% of the voting rights and absolute control over the company by holding Class B shares.

Snap, which went public on the New York Stock Exchange on March 2, 2017, issued triple-class shares: Class A shares have no voting rights, Class B shares have one vote per share and Class C shares have ten votes per share. Snap is firmly controlled by its two co-founders, who hold all Class C shares and together have 88.6% of the company's voting rights.

Alibaba, which went public on the New York Stock Exchange in 2014, is another example. Through the partnership system, Alibaba issued unequal-voting-rights stocks in a disguised form. At that time, SoftBank, the largest shareholder, and Yahoo, the second largest shareholder, held 31.8% and 15.3% of Alibaba shares, respectively. Alibaba's partners jointly hold 13%, of which Jack Ma holds only 7.6%. However, according to the provisions of Alibaba's Articles of Association, partners represented by Jack Ma have the right to appoint the majority of board of directors and become the actual controllers of the company. In Alibaba's

11-member board of directors, most of the executive directors and almost all of the key executives come from Alibaba partners. SoftBank, the largest shareholder with a 31.8% stake, appointed only one observer to the board of directors.

With the lowering of the capital constraint threshold and the value increase of human capital in the Internet era, both JD's dual-class share structure and Alibaba's partnership system are different from the one share–one vote rule, the optimal corporate governance model advocated by Hart. There seems to be an important change in the concept of equity design. However, it should be noted that the basic logic and principles of equity design have not changed. This is reflected in the following four aspects.

First, full respect for the wishes of shareholders. For the dual-class shares issued by JD.com, it is investors' behavior to decide whether and at what price they buy Class A shares, which have different voting rights from Class B shares. Due to different voting rights and different influence on control, Class B shares with higher voting rights are more expensive than Class A shares.

A typical example of the principle of full respect for the wishes of shareholders is the relinquishment of actual control of Alibaba by SoftBank, which holds 31.8%, and Yahoo, which holds 15.3%. Instead of appointing directors and candidates for the directorship, SoftBank appointed an observer to the board who would not participate in the voting. Yahoo did not even appoint an observer. By supporting the partnership system, SoftBank and Yahoo handed over the actual control of Alibaba to the Alibaba partners who hold only 13% of the shares, making Alibaba partners focus on business model innovation. At the same time, SoftBank and Yahoo have made a lot of money by giving up control.

Second, the deepening of the specialized division of labor. Both JD's dual-class share structure and Alibaba's partnership system are an extension of the logic of the specialized division of labor of modern joint-stock companies.

In Alibaba, the transformation from short-term employment contract to long-term partnership contract between Alibaba partners and major shareholders Soft-Bank and Yahoo has been achieved, resulting in the state of so-called constant managers and changing shareholders, or constant managers and constant share-holders. In this state, Alibaba partners focus on business model innovation, while shareholders such as SoftBank and Yahoo focus on risk sharing.

The objective advantage of deepening specialized division of labor is that it can effectively prevent barbarian invasion. While Vanke's management team led by the founder Wang Shi was plagued by barbarian incursions, Alibaba partners and Liu Qiangdong could devote to the business model innovations through the arrangement of control rights for listing. The dual-class structure of the weighted voting rights behind the seemingly unequal shares better realizes the equality of investors' rights and interests.

Third, the collective ownership of corporate property rights by shareholders. The practice of Company Law is that the general meeting of shareholders makes a final ruling on major matters of the company by voting, which usually requires the consent of more than two-thirds of the majority. In the practice of corporate governance in many countries, the protection of minority shareholders' interests in information disadvantages has not been neglected. One of the most important measures is the cumulative voting system. The cumulative voting system refers to a shareholder voting system that allows minority shareholders to elect directors who represent their interests by means of partially centralized voting, so as to avoid major shareholders monopolizing the election of all directors. The role of the cumulative voting system is to ensure fair protection of the rights and interests of different shareholders in a better way and at a higher level.

Fourth, the legal fiduciary duties between directors and shareholders. Since shareholders collectively enjoy the equity of the owner and make the final decision on major matters of the company by voting, they thus become the authority of corporate governance. Directors have a fiduciary duty to shareholders in law; that is, they need to fulfill the duty of loyalty and diligence to maximize the value of shareholders.

Therefore, when the state special management shares are launched in the name of regulation, part of the owner's equity of shareholders is handed over to third parties, thus blurring fiduciary duties. Shareholders who can bear the consequences of decision-making may not be able to make decisions, while third parties who cannot bear the consequences have the right to make decisions. The introduction of a third party can also place directors in a state of multiple accountability when the interests of shareholders and third parties conflict. Theoretically, directors may damage the legitimate interests of shareholders under the pretext of protecting the interests of a third party, or even pursue their personal interests in the name of protecting the interests of third party and shareholders, so as to damage the interests of both shareholders and third parties.

Contrast that the basic principles of equity design should be followed, we have seen, because no laws well reflect the deepening of specialized division of labor while changing the principle of collective sharing of owner's equity and respect for shareholders as the authority of corporate governance, the introduction of the state special management shares may face challenges at a general meeting of shareholders, and the shareholders may vote against it or even vote with their feet.

From the above discussion on the principles that should be followed in the design of equity, we have come to a basic conclusion that the equity exercise and the regulatory responsibilities are not interchangeable. Improving regulatory effectiveness through the introduction of state special management shares not only changes the basic principles that should be followed in the equity design but also confuses the boundary between the regulatory responsibilities and the equity exercise to a certain extent, and easily lead to offside, dislocation and absence of regulation.

The analysis shows that in modern joint-stock companies, shareholders become the authority of corporate governance as co-owners of corporate property, and directors have clear fiduciary duties to shareholders. Therefore, the legal and economic basis of the equity exercise is Hart's theory of modern property rights based on incomplete contracts.

In fact, the legal and economic basis of regulatory responsibility comes from the existence of negative externalities and the Coase theorem. According to the

Coase theorem, whether the upstream steel plant has the right to discharge pollution to the downstream fishery, or the downstream fishery has the right not to be polluted by the upstream steel plant, when the transaction cost between both sides is zero, an efficient amount of steel production and proper discharge can be achieved through reasonable compensation to the other party. Therefore, the initial allocation of property rights has nothing to do with the final efficiency of resource allocation. However, since the transaction cost of the performance of contract between the two sides is not zero in real economic life, the definition and protection of initial property rights become very important, so it is necessary to introduce third-party regulation to reduce negative externality. As watchman and referee in the market economy, the government naturally becomes the ideal third party to define and protect the initial property rights and reduce negative externalities. From this point of view, the irrelevance of property rights developed by the Coase theorem has become the legal and economic basis for the government's performance of regulatory duties caused by externalities in real economic life.

Table 4.1 shows the comparison of the differences between government regulation and equity exercise. It can be seen that there are significant differences between them in terms of legal basis, scope of exercise, implementation subject and implementation purpose. Therefore, the equity exercise cannot simply replace the government regulation.

Confusing the boundary between government regulation and equity exercise tends to lead to offside, dislocation and the absence of regulation. For example, some provinces in China have tried to solve the problem of coal mine safety production by merging state-owned mines with private ones. The transfer of regulatory responsibility for work safety from the government to SOEs directly led to the dislocation of regulation. The confusion of the roles of athlete and referee resulted in unfair competition between market participants, which led to the offside regulation. These integrated coal mines did not fundamentally solve the problem of production safety, resulting in the absence of regulation. The compulsory M&A

Table 4.1 Differences Between Government Regulation and Equity Exercise

	Legal Basis	*Scope of Exercise*	*Implementation Subject*	*Implementation Purpose*
Equity exercise	Hart's modern property rights theory based on incomplete contracts	Inside the company	Shareholders who are recognized by law as collective owners of equity	Encourage investors to invest
Government regulation	Existence of negative externalities and Coase theorem	Matters requiring property right definition and protection due to negative externalities	Third party (government)	Reduce negative externalities

to achieve regulatory purposes through property rights control has left some of the state-owned coal mines with operational difficulties.

Therefore, on the issue of state special management shares, my opinion is that equity belongs to shareholders, regulation belongs to the government, and each performs its own functions.

Regulation is not something that is imposed on enterprises through equity design, but how to improve the effectiveness of regulation. Taking the cultural and entertainment industry that is currently piloting the state special management share system as an example, the establishment and implementation of effective regulatory policies need three aspects: the transparency of rules before regulation, the fairness of procedures during regulation and the severity of penalties after regulation.

In the future, through the enactment of media-related laws and regulations, the government can clearly propose uniform regulatory standards to achieve the transparency of rules before regulation. The fairness of the procedures during the regulation involves three aspects. First, the objects of regulation, the press and the public have the right to know the regulatory information. Second, regulators carry out regulation independently in accordance with relevant laws and regulations to avoid power interference. The third is to severely punish corruption in the regulatory process. In addition to the construction of the legal system, in-process regulation can also be achieved through media exposure and social supervision. However, China is still facing a severe test of how to ensure the fairness and transparency of legal procedures and judicial decisions and avoid judicial corruption. In fact, this is an important reason for the frequent occurrence of food safety problems, coal mine accidents and even child abuse in kindergartens in China.

For special industries such as national defense and military industry, in addition to strictly enforcing the above regulations, special regulations can also be formulated according to the particularity of the industry.

4 Debt-to-Equity Swap: Soft Budget Constraint Under the Guise of Market Operation

Unlike debt financing, which is known as a hard constraint because it is subject to legal action and bankruptcy liquidation, equity financing faces a soft constraint. The company is not obliged to pay a dividend unless the board of directors makes a commitment. Debt-to-equity swaps have thus become one of the potential tools for companies to get out of financial difficulties and resolve the financial crisis. Even from the perspective of commercial banks, debt-to-equity swaps can be seen as a way for commercial banks to preserve their assets when certain problems occur in their loan objects. So can debt-to-equity swaps really become a panacea for enterprises to get out of the debt crisis and commercial banks to preserve their assets?

First of all, the complementary advantages of debt financing and equity financing are realized by choosing a reasonable capital structure rather than debt-to-equity swaps.

Debt financing and equity financing are often described in corporate finance textbooks as being at opposite ends of the continuum of financing tools. The typical feature of equity financing, that it is not the obligation of the company to pay dividends unless the board of directors makes a commitment, means that the board of directors will make the decision to pay dividends only when the benefits are good. Therefore, dividend payments will not become the external pressure that makes companies with operating difficulties and cash flow shortages worse. Unlike equity financing, debt financing requires repayment of the principal and interest within the term specified in the debt contract, or the debtor will face legal action and be forced into liquidation. This is why people usually say that debt financing is a hard constraint, while equity financing is a soft constraint.

For these two different types of financing tools, corporate financial practice can complement the advantages by choosing a reasonable capital structure. For example, information technology enterprises with high research and development (R&D) investment and market uncertainty should choose less debt with hard constraints and more equity that can be flexibly adjusted according to operating conditions. As a remedy for poor decisions of capital structure, a debt-to-equity swap is not as effective as a capital structure in complementing the advantages and avoiding the disadvantages of the two basic financing tools.

Second, Kornai attributed the reason for low efficiency and bad debts of state-owned banks in former socialist countries in Eastern Europe such as Hungary to soft budget constraints, and the debt-to-equity swap under the government intervention to some extent was a soft budget constraint disguised as market operation. Government agencies or state-owned banks that provide funds to SOEs often fail to adhere to their commercial agreement, allowing the enterprises to use the funds beyond the scope of current yield. However, under government intervention, instead of pushing inefficient firms that should be liquidated into bankruptcy, the banks softened the budget constraints by injecting new funds and repaying old debts with new ones. Due to the implicit guarantee provided by the government, SOEs under soft budget constraints lack the threat of bankruptcy and the incentive to reform and innovate, thus failing to change their inefficiency for a long time.

Kornai's theory of soft budget constraints explains why we still need to conduct a new round of SOE reform characterized by mixed ownership. When commenting on zombie enterprises and overcapacity, Professor Xu Chenggang pointed out that "These are actually very old problems, and the problem is completely expected."[1] The root cause of the problem is a very basic concept in economics, called soft budget constraints. This concept was first proposed by Professor Kornai in the 1970s during the reforms in Eastern Europe. Today, the debt-to-equity swap, which is used as a panacea by many enterprises in the debt crisis, disguised as a market operation that transforms the identity of banks issuing loans and the people holding corporate bonds from the creditors to shareholders. But in essence, it also transformed debt financing from hard constraints to soft constraints under government intervention.

Third, after the debt-to-equity swap, former creditors are not as relaxed as expected and have to invest a lot of new costs to fulfill their duties as shareholders.

In particular, participating in corporate governance and operation management in a specific industry is far from the comparative advantage of some commercial banks and ordinary creditors who are only good at asset management. Therefore, although the debt-to-equity swap seems to temporarily preserve the assets of creditors, if an effective governance framework is not truly established to urge the company to actually improve the management, it will merely postpone the debt that should be repaid, which cannot fundamentally resolve the debt crisis and the creditors' assets will remain at risk. In some cases, prolonged losses from bad loans are greater than immediate compensation from liquidation of residual value and can even drag down banks or creditors into the crisis of non-performing assets for a long time.

We have seen many painful lessons from domestic and foreign cases of debt-to-equity swaps to resolve debt crises. Countries such as Chile, Brazil, Argentina, Mexico, Bulgaria, Russia, Ukraine, Yugoslavia, Hungary and Poland once adopted debt-to-equity swaps. Except for a few successful cases carried out either because of short-term difficulties of capital turnover or based on market principles, most debt-to-equity swap projects with strong government intervention ended in failure.

It should be noted that the debt-to-equity swap plan did not appear for the first time in the history of Dongbei Special Steel Group. As early as 2000, one of the three largest special steel producers in China, Dalian Iron and Steel Group, the predecessor of Dongbei Special Steel, adopted the debt-to-equity model to resolve the crisis during the last round of SOE reform. In June of that year, after asset management companies of China Orient, Cinda and Huarong, SASAC of Liaoning Province and Heilongjiang Province and Fushun Special Steel Company made capital contributions, Dalian Special Steel's debt was converted into shares.

On March 24, 2016, Yang Hua, chairman of Dongbei Special Steel, committed suicide. On the third day after the unexpected event, the company announced that the 15 Dong Special Steel CP001 bond had constituted a material breach. This triggered a wave of defaults on Dongbei Special Steel bonds. The total amount of defaulted debts of different maturities (medium term, short term and ultra-short term) and issuance channels (public and non-public) exceeded 8.57 billion yuan. The new chairman proposed a debt-to-equity swap of 70% of the company's debt. When they realized that the finance department of Liaoning Province could no longer underwrite the debt-to-equity swap, the creditors unanimously refused to do so. As the creditors resolutely resisted the debt-to-equity swap plan at the shareholders' meeting and formally applied to Dalian Intermediate People's Court for the restructuring of Dongbei Special Steel on September 26, 2016, the company officially entered the bankruptcy restructuring procedure on October 10, 2016.

From the process of the debt-to-equity swap plan of Dongbei Special Steel, the three asset management companies agreed to the debt-to-equity swap largely because of the implicit guarantee and financial backing provided by the local government. Even after the debt-to-equity swaps, these asset management companies did not participate deeply in corporate governance as expected. When local finance is unable to buy back debt-to-equity swaps according to the contract, it will be the date of the outbreak of a new debt crisis that temporarily deferred by the swap. To a certain extent, the debt crisis of Dongbei Special Steel is a reappearance of what Kornai observed back then about state-owned bank loans turning into bad and doubtful debts step by step due to the softening of budget constraints. Therefore, Shen Wenrong's holding of Dongbei Special Steel, which was interpreted by the media as accidental privatization, was a desperate move taken by the local government to resolve the debt crisis of Dongbei Special Steel.

Finally, for the debts that are in temporary capital turnover difficulties and have the potential to be transformed into good assets in the future, other financing tools with lower costs can be used to resolve the crisis, rather than debt-to-equity swaps. If an asset management company believes that the debt-to-equity swap is indeed feasible after thorough value evaluation and asset analysis, the company shall make decisions independently based on market principles and bear the ultimate responsibility for its own decisions. Governments should never provide implicit guarantees in the form of financial backing, which may not only drag down the enterprise in the debt crisis and the creditors such as banks providing financial support but also affect the reputation and credibility of local governments.

In practice, debt-to-equity swaps are actively advocated not only by managers of enterprises in the debt crisis, but also by local governments who aim at solving the high debts of SOEs and implementing the de-leveraging policies of supply-side structural reform. However, the debt-to-equity swap cases of Latin American and Eastern European countries and Dongbei Special Steel show that the more the government intervenes, the less likely it is to succeed in resolving the debt crisis through a debt-to-equity swap. The implicit guarantee of the government can only delay the outbreak of the debt crisis, but not fundamentally eliminate it and resolve it. It is in this sense that we tend to think of debt-to-equity swaps under the government intervention as soft budget constraints in the guise of market operations.

5   How to Protect the Rights and Interests of Capital Participating in Subsidiaries

With the exception of a few cases such as China Unicom, which takes the listed company as the platform for SOE mixed-ownership reform, at present, it is more common to see mixed-ownership reform carried out at the subsidiary level by attracting social capital to form majority-owned subsidiaries. An example is the mixed-ownership reform case of Air China Cargo, a subsidiary of China National Aviation Corporation, and COFCO Capital, a specialized company in the financial sector under COFCO. These realization forms of mixed-ownership reform include the following realistic rationality. First, establish subsidiaries or transform branches into subsidiaries to provide physical platforms for the introduction and mixing of state-owned and private capitals. Second, the establishment of subsidiaries or the transformation of branches into subsidiaries helps change the regulatory concept of state-owned assets management system from managing enterprises to managing capital. Third, the state-owned capital can be concentrated in the main business.

However, from the current practice of mixed-ownership reform in some SOEs, some phenomena are worth noting. For example, capital inflow out of pressure and favor is interpreted by some enterprises as the completion of mixed-ownership reform. Some enterprises replace branches with subsidiaries and introduce corporate governance systems such as board of directors at subsidiaries, thinking that it has realized the transformation from managing enterprises to managing assets. The above phenomena shows to a certain extent that there are some misunderstandings in the current SOE mixed-ownership reform on how to establish and improve the arrangement of corporate governance system of the subsidiaries to ensure the rights and interests of other capitals participating in subsidiaries.

Before discussing the possible misunderstandings that exist in the realization of mixed-ownership reform by establishing subsidiaries, it is necessary for us to understand the differences in the organizational structure between branches and subsidiaries. Generally speaking, branches similar to the business division focus on the implementation of business tasks issued by the company's headquarters, so the principle of their establishment is based on whether they contribute to the efficiency of business management. In terms of organizational form, a branch company is not an independent legal entity, so there is no need to set up the board of directors, board of supervisors and other corporate governance structures. The general manager of a branch only needs to strictly carry out the business tasks assigned by the headquarters of the company, so the physical connection with the headquarters is the specific activities related to business management.

Different from branches, the capital needed for the development of a subsidiary company not only comes from the investment of the parent company but also from other sources, which are jointly financed to form a joint stock company. Take Vanke before Baoneng's shareholding as an example. China Resources Group, Vanke's largest shareholder, is its parent group. In other words, Vanke is a subsidiary of China Resources Group. Therefore, the physical connection between the subsidiary and the parent company is a capital chain. The basic principle of establishing a subsidiary is whether it is beneficial to improve the efficiency of investment management. As an independent legal entity, subsidiaries need to set up corporate governance structures such as the general meeting of shareholders, board of directors and supervisors to protect rights and interests of the parent company and other shareholders.

In Table 4.2, we summarize the differences between subsidiaries and branches in terms of principles of establishment, physical connections with parent companies and whether they are independent legal entities.

Due to the differences in the principles of establishment mentioned above, we can see that the authority of corporate governance varies between branches and subsidiaries. As a divisional subordinate organization, the main mission of a branch is to perform specific business tasks directly assigned by the headquarters of the company. Therefore, in the branch office, the authority of corporate governance is the headquarters. This means that the key management team members of the branch, including the general manager, are appointed directly from the headquarters. However, for subsidiaries, since the capital required for business activities sometimes

Table 4.2 Differences Between Functions of Subsidiaries and Branches

	Branch	Subsidiary
Principle of establishment	Efficiency of business activities	Efficiency of investment management
Physical connections with the parent company	Specific business management activities	Capital chain
Is it an independent legal entity?	No	Yes
Is there a board of directors and other corporate governance structures?	No	Yes
Corporate governance authority	Corporate headquarters	Shareholders' meeting and authorized board of directors of the subsidiary

does not come only from the parent company (an exception is the wholly owned subsidiary), but also from social capital, so how to protect the rights and interests of all shareholders and improve the efficiency of investment management becomes an important principle for subsidiaries. According to Hart's modern property rights theory, the reason shareholders are willing to invest in a modern joint-stock company is precisely because the solemn commitment of the modern joint-stock company to outside investors is that shareholders will be the owners of the company and have the final say on major matters. This is mainly reflected in the fact that shareholders have the right to make final decisions on important matters including asset restructuring, executive change and strategy adjustment by voting at the shareholders' meeting. Therefore, in a subsidiary, the authority of corporate governance is not the parent company but the general meeting of shareholders and its authorized board of directors. The rationale for this corporate governance authority is that the parent company is only one of the investors, and the company should protect the rights and interests of all shareholders, not some. This determines that the parent company's management intention can only be achieved through corporate governance platforms such as shareholders' meeting and the board organization, based on the physical connections of the capital chain.

After understanding the differences between branches and subsidiaries in terms of establishment principles and corporate governance authority, we now evaluate the misconceptions existing in the current SOE mixed-ownership reform in how to protect the rights and interests of other capitals participating in the subsidiaries.

First, before the mixed-ownership reform plan was put forward, some SOEs did not carefully distinguish whether the reform project was facing the problem of improving business management efficiency or the problem of financing constraints, and did not follow the establishment principle of subsidiaries and branches. Some enterprises mechanically introduced other capital and set up subsidiaries and corresponding corporate governance structures such as boards of directors and supervisors. It is easy to understand that the establishment and maintenance of the basic system of corporate governance, such as the board of directors and supervisors, requires ongoing costs. This may further hinder the improvement of business management efficiency, which is more important to the success of some SOEs.

Second, after introducing other capitals into subsidiaries, the parent company ignored the construction of the basic corporate governance system of subsidiaries and treated them as branches. This is mainly reflected in the following two aspects. First, the board of directors and the key management team of a subsidiary are appointed and dismissed by the parent company, not through consultation with other shareholders or by recommending directors according to their capital contribution and voting at the shareholders' meeting. The boards of directors of some subsidiaries are not selected from the professional manager market to perform supervisory and advisory functions. Instead, the parent company forcibly instructed its functional departments, such as financial planning and asset management, to form a board of directors for subsidiaries, which is similar in appearance but not in spirit. Part-time directors have no right to make actual decisions but must bear the risk of performing their duties, which makes it difficult to choose directors for subsidiaries. Second, the executive orders of the parent company directly replace the decisions made by the shareholders' meeting of the subsidiary and its authorized board of directors, so the corporate governance authority of the subsidiary is weakened, and the rights and interests of social capitals are not effectively guaranteed. It is conceivable that due to the above two reasons, even if corporate governance systems such as the board of directors and supervisors are established in the subsidiary company, it is difficult to substantially improve the efficiency of investment management.

Third, other capitals were forced to be involved in the reform for a short time due to goodwill or pressure, but waited for the right opportunity to withdraw, which made the seemingly achieved mixed-ownership reform weak and unsustainable.

The core problem behind all these phenomena is that some enterprises, due to the inertia of management thinking, have not completely come out of the branch management mindset of controlling subsidiaries by means of administrative orders and have not yet adapted to and completed the transformation of operation mode from managing enterprises to managing capital. Since the legitimate rights and interests of other capitals are not effectively guaranteed, the negative consequence of the above approach is that it will not only undermine the confidence of other capitals that have participated in the mixed-ownership reform to continue to pay attention to the development of the enterprise and improve the corporate governance structure, but also greatly discourage the enthusiasm of the strategic investors who are planning to participate in the reform.

So how can strategic investors be willing to participate in the mixed-ownership reform of subsidiaries of SOEs?

First, it is necessary to establish and improve corporate governance structures such as the general meeting of shareholders, board of directors and supervisors in the subsidiaries, so that the shareholders' meeting of subsidiaries and its authorized board of directors, rather than the parent company, becomes the authority of corporate governance to ensure the rights and interests of all shareholders. It can be improved in the following aspects in the future. First, directors and supervisors should be recommended in proportion to shareholders' capital contributions and elected by shareholders at the general meeting rather than appointed by the parent company. In order to protect the interests of minority shareholders, the cumulative voting system can be used in the election of directors. Second, a certain proportion of independent outside directors with neutral interests should be introduced. Third, decisions on major matters of the subsidiary, such as business strategy adjustment, need to be deliberated and discussed by the board of directors, and finally take effect by voting at the general meeting of shareholders. Fourth, the management team of the subsidiary is responsible to the board of directors of the subsidiary and strictly implements the major management decisions made by the board of directors. Fifth, the management intentions of the parent company should be reflected in the resolutions of the shareholders' meeting of the subsidiary and its authorized board of directors through proposals and consultations with shareholders.

Second, in the setting of shareholding structure, we should make flexible choices according to the nature of the project and the industrial layout of state-owned assets, not necessarily to take a controlling stake. In the mixed-ownership reform of Yunnan Baiyao, Yunnan SASAC and New Huadu Industrial Group each hold 50% shares of Baiyao Group, which has won praise from all walks of life and is known as the Baiyao model of SOE mixed-ownership reform. Equal shareholding or even no controlling shares is a very good expression of the credible commitment and institutional sincerity of state capital to introduce private capital. For some non-strategic competitive industries, we can even consider converting state-owned capital into preferred shares. By doing so, we can send a clear signal to society that we hope private capital will deeply participate in SOE corporate governance. On the other hand, it can better realize the purpose of preserving and increasing the value of state assets through preferential distribution of dividends.

Only by establishing and improving the corporate governance system that effectively protects the rights and interests of all shareholders participating in the subsidiaries, and by conveying a credible commitment and institutional sincerity to private capital through flexible and diverse options and arrangements for the shareholding structure, can private capital be motivated to substantially participate in SOE mixed-ownership reform. And this is the only way to achieve a real change in the regulatory concept and practice of SOEs from managing enterprises to managing capital.

Note

1 参见许成刚，中国经济这五年，第十期：对话许成钢，《凤凰财知道》，2017年10月25日。(China's economy in the past five years). *ifeng.com*. https://finance.ifeng.com/news/special/zhonggong19th10/.

5 Reform of the State-Owned Assets Management System

SOE reform is currently being carried out at two levels in parallel. In addition to the mixture of shareholding structure at the entity level, the new round of SOE reform is also reflected in changing the regulatory function of the state-owned asset management system from managing enterprises to managing capital through the interface between the government and the market by reorganizing and establishing new state-owned capital investment and operating companies.

The active transfer of control rights of listed companies since 2018, on the one hand, is related to the economic downturn, the stock market downturn and the capital shortage in that year. On the other hand, to a certain extent, it is still the continuation of the trend of M&A when China's capital market enters the era of dispersed ownership, or even a superposition of the two factors. Although interpreted by some media as the state sector advances while the private sector retreats, compared with the acquisition of private enterprises by state-owned enterprises in the same industry around 2008, the 2018 transformation of the nature of control rights from private capital to state-owned capital through the capital market has considerably smaller negative effects.

In early June 2019, as an important measure to promote the SOE mixed-ownership reform, the SASAC of the State Council issued the List of Authorization and Delegation of SASAC of the State Council (2019 Edition; hereinafter "List"). For how to avoid the vicious cycle whereby delegation leads to disorder while regulation leads to stagnation, the solution is to combine the delegation of power with mixed-ownership reform. On the one hand, through the issuance of the List, empower the central SOEs as shareholders actually responsible for managing capital, which better reflects the basic principles of power and responsibility distribution, information symmetry, and specialized division of labor in the modern enterprise system. On the other hand, as the major shareholder, central enterprise forms a mechanism of checks and balances and error correction through introducing strategic investors with private capital background, so as to avoid falling into the vicious cycle of delegation leads to disorder and regulation leads to stagnation.

DOI: 10.4324/9781003361404-6

1 Reform of the State-Owned Assets Management System in Exploration

SOE reform is currently being carried out at two levels in parallel. One is the reform of the management system of state-owned assets, through the capitalization of state-owned assets, to achieve the transformation of the regulatory function from managing enterprises to managing capital. The other is that, as operating entities of mixed-ownership, SOEs improve corporate governance and establish a modern enterprise system through the introduction of strategic investors.

In terms of the management system of state-owned assets, SASAC's role has changed from managing personnel, affairs and enterprises to capitalizing state-owned assets through establishing investment and operating institutions as the interface between the government and the market and transforming SOEs into corporations. Chen Qingtai, the former secretary of the Party Committee and the vice president of the Development Research Center of the State Council, pointed out that the so-called managing capital is to reform the implementation form of operational state-owned assets from a special value form of SOEs in physical form to state-owned capital that can be clearly defined in financial terms, has good liquidity and can enter the market operation. According to Chen Qingtai's vision, after the state-owned capital investment and operating institutions replace the entity enterprises as a new regulatory object of the SASAC, due to the state-owned capital investment and operating institutions invested in the entity enterprises, the SASAC no longer has a direct property relation with entity enterprises or has a right to intervene in its operation, thus it is natural to realize the separation of government from enterprise.

In 2016, the SASAC started to carry out pilot projects in eight enterprises (SDIC, COFCO, Shenhua, Baowu, Minmetals, China Merchants, CCCC and Poly) to delegate 18 powers originally belonging to SASAC to state-owned capital investment and operating companies, including asset allocation, salary distribution, market-oriented employment and structural reform. At the same time, the SASAC designated China Chengtong and China Reform Holdings as pilot companies of the state-owned capital operations.

Compared with the reform of the state-owned assets management system of central enterprises, which is still in the pilot phase, the reform practice in Shanxi and Tianjin is clearer. Let's take Tianjin as an example. Tianjin has set up three state-owned capital investment and operating companies according to industry categories: Jinlian (corresponding to the manufacturing industry), Jincheng (corresponding to the non-manufacturing industry) and Guoxing (corresponding to the high-tech industry). For example, in July 2017, Tianjin SASAC set up Tianjin Jincheng State-Owned Capital Investment and Operation Co., Ltd., a wholly state-owned company with a registered capital of 12 billion yuan, which is responsible for the investment and operation of non-manufacturing SOEs after capitalization of state-owned assets. On April 19, 2018, Tianjin SASAC decided to inject 100% of the shares held by Tianjin Real Estate Group into Tianjin Jincheng State Capital Investment and Operation Co., Ltd. As a result of the above institutional establishment and asset disposal, in theory, Tianjin SASAC takes state-owned capital investment and operating companies such as Jinlian, Jincheng and Guoxing as the supervision objects. On the other hand, Tianjin SASAC does not have property relations directly with the operating entity Tianjin Real Estate Group, thus realizing the transformation from managing personnel, affairs and enterprises to managing capital. As for Jincheng State-Owned Capital Investment and Operation Co., Ltd., it will participate in corporate governance as a shareholder together with the strategic investors introduced into Tianjin Real Estate Group through mixed-ownership reform. For Tianjin Real Estate Group, the capitalization of state-owned assets is realized through the reform of the corporate system, and effective corporate governance is realized through the general meeting of shareholders and the board of directors under the check and balance of rights and interests of multiple shareholders and stakeholders, thus forming a modern enterprise system.

At the Central Economic Work Conference held at the end of 2018, China's central government clearly stated that it would adhere to the principles of separating government administration from enterprise management, separating government administration from state assets management and fair competition, accelerate the transformation from managing enterprises to managing capital, reorganize, and establish a number of state-owned capital investment and operating companies to actively promote mixed-ownership reform. It is foreseeable that the reform of the state-owned assets management system will become the key task of the SOE reform in the future by establishing state-owned capital investment and operating companies to realize the transformation from managing personnel, affairs and enterprises to managing capital.

Theoretically, by setting up investment and operating companies, the SASAC is separated from the entity enterprises, and there will no longer be direct property relations between the entity enterprises and the SASAC. Just as Chen Qingtai said, the SASAC has no right to intervene in the companies in which the investment and operating institutions invest, so it is natural to realize the separation of government administration from enterprise management. The previous state of managing personnel, affairs and enterprises of the state-owned assets management system and the combination of government function and enterprise management will be restrained to a certain extent.

However, a potential problem with the establishment of state-owned capital investment and operating companies between the SASAC and the operating entities is that the already long principal-agent chain for state-owned assets management has been further extended. The SASAC used to hold the shares of listed subsidiaries indirectly through wholly owned holding companies, but now the SASAC owns state-owned capital investment and operating companies, which in turn hold the shares of holding companies, and then holding companies hold listed subsidiaries. In this way, the principle-agent chain of the state-owned assets management system has changed from three levels to at least four levels. As a typical shortcoming of SOEs, the extension of the principal-agent chain and the resulting absence of owners have long been criticized. In addition, the unresolved problem of horizontal competition between a holding company, which is also an operating entity, and its listed subsidiary arouses the concern of the capital market and regulatory authorities on the increased possibility of related party transactions between the two in the future.

In fact, this creates a dilemma for further reform of the state-owned assets management system. Investment and operating companies need to be introduced in order to realize the transformation from managing personnel, affairs and enterprises to managing capital. However, the introduction of investment and operating companies will inevitably extend the principal-agent chain. So how to realize the effective transformation from managing enterprises to managing capital in the state-owned assets management system?

On December 12, 2018, Yunnan Baiyao Group released the *Merger of Yunnan Baiyao Holdings Co., Ltd and the Related Party Transaction Report (Draft)*. Yunnan Baiyao Group merged with parent company Yunnan Baiyao Holdings to achieve the overall listing. According to the announcement, both parties ensured that Yunnan SASAC and New Huadu would hold the same proportion of shares after the transaction, continuing the basic principle of previous mixed-ownership reform of Yunnan Baiyao Holdings, that is, both the state capital and private capital as the largest shareholders. The practice of Yunnan Baiyao has thus accumulated valuable experience for the operating entities (such as Yunnan Baiyao Holdings) on how to complete the overall listing and the mixed-ownership reform with the help of the listed companies in which they hold shares.

Not only that, but it also inspired how the state-owned assets management system could effectively shorten the chain of the pyramidal holding structure. After Yunnan Baiyao merged with its parent company Baiyao Holdings to achieve the overall listing, Yunnan Baiyao's pyramidal holding structure changed from the original three-level Yunnan SASAC–Baiyao Holdings (holding company)–Yunnan Baiyao (listed company) to the current two-level Yunnan SASAC–Yunnan Baiyao. This brings new opportunities for Yunnan Baiyao to reduce management levels and governance costs and improve business efficiency. After merging with parent company Yunnan Baiyao Holdings, the state-owned listed company Yunnan Baiyao has solved the long-standing problem of horizontal competition between them.

According to the data of SASAC, as of the first half of 2018, there were 398 listed companies at home and abroad held by central enterprises, and 65.2% of the total assets and 61.7% of the net assets of state-owned assets had entered listed companies. Therefore, to some extent, it is feasible for central enterprises to take advantage of the listed companies in which holding companies hold shares to conduct overall listings, thus solving the problems of extended principal-agency and horizontal competition.

From the current stage of mixed-ownership reform of Yunnan Baiyao, the shareholder controlling Yunnan Baiyao together with New Huadu is still the Yunnan SASAC. In the case of Yunnan SASAC and Yunnan Baiyao, there is no interface between the government and the market or an isolation layer between the government and enterprises. According to the reform of Tianjin's state-owned assets management system, it seems that this kind of approach is not conducive to the transformation of Tianjin's state-owned assets management system from managing personnel, affairs and enterprises to managing capital.

Combining the reform idea of Tianjin's state-owned assets management system with the idea of overall listing of Yunnan Baiyao's merger with its holding company may solve the problems faced by the current SOE reform. On the one hand, we can learn from the Yunnan Baiyao model to complete the mixed-ownership reform of the holding company and shorten the principal-agent chain. On the other hand, we can draw lessons from the mixed-ownership reform of Tianjin's state-owned assets management system to realize the transformation of the state-owned assets management system from managing personnel, affairs and enterprises to managing capital by establishing state-owned capital investment and operating companies.

2 How Can Investment and Operating Companies Act as an Isolation Layer Between the Government and Enterprises

At the Central Economic Work Conference held at the end of 2018, it was proposed to adhere to the principles of separating the government administration from enterprise management, separating the government administration from state assets management and fair competition, accelerate the transformation from managing enterprises to managing capital, reorganize and establish a number of state-owned capital investment and operating companies, and actively promote the mixed-ownership reform. Reorganizing and establishing state-owned capital investment and operating companies to realize the transformation of the state-owned assets management system from managing personnel, affairs and enterprises to managing capital will undoubtedly become the focus of promoting SOE reform in 2019. In theory, by setting up a state-owned capital investment and operating company, the SASAC is separated from the entity enterprises, and the two no longer have property relations, so the SASAC has no right to intervene in the business of entity enterprises beyond the investment and operating companies, so that the separation of the government administration from enterprise management is naturally achieved. The situation of managing personnel, affairs and enterprises, combining the government function with enterprise management, and with state assets management in the previous state-owned assets management system has been curbed to a certain extent. Therefore, it is a common practice to reorganize or establish state-owned assets investment and operating companies as the interface between the government and the market or the isolation layer between the government and enterprises in the new round of SOE mixed-ownership reform, regardless of the central or local state-owned assets management system.

At the end of 2018, the SASAC further identified 11 central enterprises, including Aviation Industry Corporation of China and State Power Investment Corporation Limited, as new pilot enterprises of state-owned capital investment companies. So far, among 96 central SOEs, nearly 20 companies have been reorganized and established in three batches into state-owned capital investment companies on a trial basis. In addition to the reorganization and establishment of the state-owned capital investment company, in 2014 the SASAC also appointed China Chengtong Group and China Reform Holdings as pilot state-owned capital operating companies.

So how can state-owned capital investment and operating companies act as an isolation layer between the government and enterprises? In our view, from the current interpretation of relevant policies and the limited pilot practice, the following issues are worthy for the theoretical, practical and policy circles to pay attention and consider.

First, how to strike a balance between reorganizing or establishing state-owned capital investment and operating companies and avoiding the extension of principal-agency of the state-owned assets management system?

The extended principal-agent chain and the resulting owner absence have long been criticized as typical disadvantages of SOEs (see Chapter 1, section 1 of this book), so that some scholars have borrowed Friedman's statement "when a man spends someone else's money on someone else, he doesn't care how much he spends or what he spends it on" to evaluate SOEs with the problems of long principal-agent chain and owner absence. The opposite is true in private enterprises: Friedman stated, "when a man spends his own money to buy something for himself, he is very careful about how much he spends and how he spends it."

The current practice of forming an isolation layer between the government and enterprises through the reorganization and establishment of state-owned capital investment and operating companies, which is widely used in the reform of the state-owned asset management system, is bound to further extend the already long principal-agent chain.

In addition, the problem of horizontal competition between holding companies, which are also operating entities, and listed subsidiaries that they control or hold shares has not been solved. This situation has caused concern among the capital market and regulatory authorities about the possibility of related party transactions between the two.

Therefore, it is important to strike a balance between restructuring and establishing state-owned investment and operating companies to form an isolation layer between the government and enterprises and avoiding the problem of extension of principal agency in the state-owned assets management system.

Second, how to achieve a balance among the demands for equal rights after introducing strategic investors in the mixed-ownership reform of operating entities and the quest of control after reorganizing holding companies into state-owned capital investment companies?

After introducing strategic investors to the mixed-ownership reforms of operating entities, the original state-controlled operating entities will be transformed into public companies under the socialization of capital. The reason why private capital is willing to participate in the mixed-ownership reform as a strategic investor is that SOEs have made the commitment of ownership rights to private capital, which makes it incentive compatible to a certain extent. The institutional basis for such a credible commitment is either the private capital directly acquires actual controlling position as the Tianjin Northern Trust model, or state-owned capital dominates in the equity structure and strategic investors dominate in the board organization as the China Unicom model (see Chapter 3, section 4 of this book).

Therefore, the basic corporate governance structure of operating entities after the completion of the mixed-ownership reform is equal consultation between state-owned capital investment and operating companies and major strategic investors. At this point, as shareholders, state-owned capital investment and operating companies participate in relevant corporate governance on an equal footing with other strategic investors and dispersed outside shareholders. For example, in the case of basic and strategic industries, according to the agreement with other shareholders, the state-owned capital investment and operating companies have the right to nominate directors (chairmen), but the final decision needs to be voted with other strategic investors and dispersed shareholders at the general meeting of shareholders according to the one share–one vote rule. I have noticed that when predicting the policy of a new round of state-owned assets reform, some media emphasized that the investors rights exercised by the state-owned asset supervisory and management authorities, such as investment plans, property rights management and decision-making on major matters, should be delegated to state-owned capital investment and operating companies and other enterprises directly supervised.

From the above example, we can see that it is obviously not a simple matter of authorizing the state-owned capital investment and operating companies to perform the responsibilities of the SASAC and directly appoint the chairman. Therefore, in my opinion, in order to truly achieve the purpose of preserving and increasing the value of state-owned assets, it is not enough for the new round of state-owned asset reform to only focus on the improvement of the authorization system, but also recognize and respect other strategic investors and dispersed shareholders as the basic rights of investors. Because this is the basic right that investors should have when assuming limited liability to the extent of their capital contributions. What we need is a return from a commanding person to an equal negotiator with the same rights and shares.

In fact, since the mid-1990s, in order to promote the separation of government administration from enterprise management and establish a modern enterprise system, China has successively removed the specialized ministries that were highly fragmented and combined the government function with enterprise management and had a strong feature of planned economy, and established market-oriented group companies. For example, in 1993, the Ministry of Aerospace Industry was abolished and AVIC I and AVIC II were established. After the establishment of the SASAC in 2003, the SASAC, as an agency of the State Council, took full control of these wholly state-owned group companies. For example, on November 6, 2008, AVIC I and AVIC II were reorganized and integrated to form the Aviation Industry Corporation of China (AVIC), a state-owned mega-enterprise group wholly owned by SASAC. AVIC has successively controlled or held shares in more than 20 listed companies, such as AVIC Capital, AVIC Real Estate, FIYTA, Tianma and Rainbow Shopping Mall, and has become the prestigious AVIC

System in the Chinese capital market. As we see from specialized ministries to market-oriented group companies and then to the SASAC performing the role of capital contributor on behalf of the State Council, SOE reform has undergone a transformation from the continuation of government administrative system to a market player based on capital ties.

However, today we still need to promote mixed-ownership reform. The fundamental reason is that although the capital connection was established in the past, it was still managing personnel, affairs and enterprises in practice. It continues the strong administrative thinking of planned economy, fails to achieve the separation of government administration from enterprise management and separation of government administration from state assets management. At the same time, management rights and ownership cannot be effectively separated, and professional managers are unable to make timely and flexible management decisions according to the rapidly changing market.

Some media predicted that after reorganizing holding companies into state-owned capital investment companies. First, the enterprise assets can be disposed of at fair market prices through capital markets such as securities trading, property rights trading to realize the transformation of state-owned capital. Second, equity investment can be made in non-state-owned enterprises with great development potential and strong growth in high-tech, ecological and environmental protection, and strategic industries. Third, in the international market, it is conducive to give full play to international cooperation and brand advantages, actively and flexibly carry out the operation of the international capital market to form advantages of the combination of industry and finance on the global scale. We can see that these functions can also be performed in a holding company. It seems that the holding company does not need to change to a state-owned capital investment company in the SOE mixed-ownership reform.

According to media reports, a holding company is trying to build a three-level management and control structure to transform the type of group headquarters from functional operation to strategic control. Specific measures include that the headquarters adopts strategic operational control for its member units, and business units (member units) become the operation control subject of regional business segments. On the other hand are establishing a strategic control system of classified authorization of industrial subjects between the group headquarters and the secondary unit, and establishing a secondary control system focusing on the operation control between the secondary unit and the tertiary unit, so as to form a three-level structure of capital layer of the group headquarters–asset layer of professional platform–executive layer of production unit. What the holding company has done above is just a comprehensive reform aimed at improving the efficiency of operations and management by restructuring the internal organization of enterprise groups. This is an internal management problem that needs to be addressed at every stage of corporate development and has been done in the past. For example, CSR and CNR, two SOEs producing railway locomotives, merged into CRRC to avoid monopoly separation and improve international competitiveness. However, this approach does not seem to be the core and essence of the current round of SOE reform to achieve mixed ownership by introducing private capital strategic investors, and also certainly not the most expected goal of this round of reform.

Starting from the purpose of the current state-owned assets mixed-ownership reform, we need to recognize and respect the basic rights and interests of capital contributors and return the rights to investors, regardless of whether they are private capital strategic investors participating in the mixed-ownership reform or state-owned capital investment companies fulfilling the obligations of capital contributors on behalf of state-owned assets. Investors fulfill their obligations of managing capital and undertake their own responsibilities rather than some shareholders ignoring the other shareholders and excessively managing personnel, affairs and capital. From this point of view, it is obvious that simply reorganizing the holding companies into state-owned capital investment companies is not the real expectation of the new round of SOE mixed-ownership reform, which aims at transforming SOEs from managing personnel, affairs and enterprises to managing capital.

In some media reports on the reform of the state-owned asset management system, it is said that the future pilot reform of state-owned capital investment companies will support investment and operating companies to set up financial companies. For example,

> Standardize the operation of financial companies, encourage them to use internal funds to carry out capital operation, improve their ability of capital operation, and prevent various risks. Investment companies are allowed to apply for financial licenses reasonably based on their own conditions, taking into account the characteristics of their main businesses and the regulatory requirements of the industry, so as to better serve the real economy. However, it should also be emphasized that investment companies cannot engage in finance without their main business, nor can they simply circulating funds in the financial sector for the sake of arbitrage.

As we know, finance companies, as internal capital markets, are to some extent an alternative to the underdeveloped capital markets in early days which have existed in some enterprise groups for decades. In recent years, the internal capital market has been widely criticized for restricting the circulation of capital across society and for its inefficiency in resource allocation. It is absurd to consider the establishment of financial companies as an important step in the new reform of state-owned assets. What's more, once a financial company is established, the situation cannot be controlled simply by saying "we cannot engage in finance outside of our main business, let alone simply circulating funds in the financial sector for the sake of arbitrage."

Third, in the new round of state-owned assets management system reform, what is the relation between the state-owned capital investment companies that are considered to play a key role and need to be restructured and the newly established state-owned capital operating companies?

I believe that the foregoing discussion has given readers a general idea of the current state and possible structure of the holding companies reorganized into the state-owned capital investment companies. In addition to the pilot reorganization of a batch of state-owned capital investment companies, in 2014 the SASAC appointed two companies, China Chengtong Group and China Reform Holdings Corporation, as pilot state-owned capital operating companies. So what role will these state-owned capital operating companies play in the reform of the state-owned assets management system?

According to the media reports, China Chengtong Group and China Reform Holdings Corporation

> have gathered the central enterprises, local enterprises, financial enterprises, social capital and other parties in terms of the successful launch and actual operation of the fund, and provide new financing channels and the investment mechanism for the structural adjustment, transformation and upgrading of central enterprises. The two companies have also played a positive role in accelerating the supply side reform, leading the Belt and Road development, promoting SOE reform, and helping struggling enterprises out of trouble.

Both state-owned capital investment companies and operating companies are described by the media as the corporate enterprises authorized by the state to operate state-owned capital, and the professional platforms for the market operation of state-owned capital. The two types of companies exercise shareholder responsibility for the enterprises they have invested in, and effectively assume responsibility for preserving and increasing the value of state-owned assets in accordance with the principle of matching responsibility with power. The pilot investment and operating companies also face the main challenge of straightening out the relationship with the SASAC and the enterprises they have invested in. The similarities between the two are clearly introduced by the media, while the differences are somewhat vague and ambiguous. In terms of specific mission and function, state-owned capital investment companies focus on investment and financing and project construction and own equity through investment in industry. Instead of investing in industry, state-owned capital operating companies focus on capital operations, and their main battlefield is the capital market. In terms of operation mode, state-owned capital investment companies mainly aim to serve the national strategy, optimize the distribution of state-owned capital, and improve industrial competitiveness. State-owned capital investment companies hold strategic core businesses in important industries and key industries related to national security and the lifeline of the national economy. In contrast, state-owned capital operating companies mainly aim to improve operating efficiency and increase the return of state capital and focus on financial shareholding.

Does this mean for each enterprise that has completed mixed-ownership reform, in addition to the introduction of private strategic investors, there will also be two companies for state-owned capital investment and operating as shareholders? One of them is a state-owned capital investment company reorganized from a holding company, and the other is a newly established state-owned capital operating company such as China Chengtong Group and China Reform Holdings Corporation.

This is true, at least from the perspective of China Unicom, which has completed the mixed-ownership reform. In addition to China Unicom Group, a holding company that still holds 36.67% of the shares after the introduction of BATJ, China Structural Reform Fund Corporation, a subsidiary of the state-owned capital operating company China Chengtong Group, has been included in the shareholder list of China Unicom.

The question is, why can't state-owned capital investment companies implement the goal of improving the operation efficiency and increasing the return of state-owned capital set by state-owned capital operating companies? Conversely, why can't state-owned capital operating companies implement the goals of serving the national strategy, optimizing the layout of state-owned capital and enhancing industrial competitiveness set by state-owned capital investment companies? If the value of state-owned capital operating companies as financial investors lies in strengthening the strategic alliance of state-owned capital control, why must the state-owned capital operating companies fulfill this mission when there are other state-owned capitals in the capital market, such as insurance capital? For example, in the case of China Unicom's mixed-ownership reform, China Life Insurance, also from state-owned capital, held a 10% stake, becoming the largest strategic investor in the reform. As a financial investor, if the state-owned capital operating company does not participate in the corporate governance system such as the board organization, how will it achieve the purpose of improving the operation efficiency and increasing the return of state-owned capital? If the state-owned capital operating companies participate in corporate governance, we will see that state-owned capital investment companies and operating companies will double the construction cost of corporate governance systems such as the board organization. At least in terms of form, the obvious difference between the two is simply that the state-owned capital investment companies are strategic investors formed by the further restructuring of holding companies transformed from the specialized ministries, while the state-owned capital operating companies are financial investors newly established by the SASAC, the actual implementer of the reform of state-owned assets management system.

Of course, the fact that it is still in the pilot stage indicates to some extent that neither political nor theoretical circles have reached relatively mature judgments and conclusions on the relationship between the two types of companies. The media interpreted that we should define the boundary of authority and responsibility between state-owned asset supervisory and management authorities and state-owned capital investment and operating companies, as well as the authority and responsibility boundary between state-owned capital investment and operating companies and their shareholding enterprises. In our view, although the relationship between state-owned capital operating companies and investment companies needs to be further clarified, the two types of companies have clear positioning in the state-owned asset management system as an isolation layer between the government and enterprises. That is, a three-tier authorization structure should be formed in the whole state-owned assets regulation system, with the SASAC uniformly performing the regulation functions of operational state-owned assets, the state-owned capital investment and operating companies performing the responsibilities of capital contributors, while enterprises are the operators.

Fourth, from whom should China learn the experience of reforming state-owned assets and state-owned enterprises? What should be learned?

At the beginning of 2019, after 11 central enterprises including AVIC, SPIC, SINOMACH and CHINALCO were included in the pilot program, nearly 20 out of the 96 central enterprises were reorganized and established state-owned capital investment companies. Despite the officials repeatedly denying that China's reform of state-owned assets and state-owned enterprises learns from Singapore's Temasek model, the new round of pilot reform with the state-owned capital investment and operating companies as an isolation layer between the government and enterprises has left many observers the strong impression of the Temasek model. From the previous analysis, it is not difficult to see the difference between the Chinese model and the Temasek model. For example, in order to form an isolation layer between the government and enterprises, China reorganized and established two types of state-owned capital companies (one for investment and another for operation) between the SASAC and operating entities, rather than one type of companies in the Temasek model (if we count these as differences). China's state-owned capital investment companies have been reorganized from holding companies that originated from specialized ministries and have relatively clear main businesses. However, Temasek's model emphasizes mixed operation and diversification, so that the total value of subsidiaries managed by Temasek once accounted for more than half of the market value of all Singapore enterprises.

The reason why many observers have the above impression is that the current reform of China's state-owned asset management system, which introduced an isolation layer between the government and enterprises, is highly consistent with Temasek's strict adherence to separating the government administration from enterprise management and from state assets management, so as to effectively separate the management rights and ownership of operating entities. In fact, the specialized division of labor between the capital socialization and the professionalization of managers that results from the separation of ownership and management and the efficiency improvement achieved on this basis is the key to the success of all corporate governance structures. In this sense, there is no difference between the Temasek model and the Chinese model. Both are models of the specialized division of labor.

There is no doubt that China still has a lot to learn from the Temasek model in reform of state-owned assets and state-owned enterprises. For example, what effective institutional arrangements have Temasek's board of directors put in place to avoid administrative interference from Singapore's Ministry of Finance, its wholly owned controlling shareholder? What kind of corporate governance system (shareholders' meeting and board of directors) does Temasek adopt in the operating entities it holds or controls to ensure that the management decisions reflect the will of major shareholders and that the decision-making risks are shared by all shareholders?

In order to achieve long-term win-win cooperation, we should emphasize again that this problem cannot be solved by simple delegation of authority between management levels, but corporate governance system is needed with mutual checks and balances and a culture of equal consultation and communication among the strategic investors introduced in the mixed-ownership reform.

An unavoidable fact is that, if only delegating the management rights to an operating entity, as some media suggest, while the most important right of appointing and removing the chairman of the board remains in the state-owned capital investment company with a high or low shareholding (in normal corporate governance practice, it has only the nomination right of directors), then who should bear the consequences if the chairman makes a wrong decision due to his corruption, incompetence and willfulness? Is it a state-owned capital investment company that has the right to appoint and remove and to make such decisions? If it is expected that, on the one hand, it is impossible to challenge or veto the appointment or removal of the chairman, and on the other hand, it has to share responsibility within the limit of its capital contribution for chairman's wrong decisions, will the strategic investors participate unreservedly in the SOE mixed-ownership reform currently being actively promoted?

3 A New Round of M&A of SOEs From the Perspective of the History of SOE M&A

Since the beginning of 2018, many media have reported on the so-called M&A wave of SOEs in China's capital market. For example, according to a report by the *Economic Observer* in September 2018 titled "Frequent Transfer of Controlling Interests in Listed Companies", as of September 12, 2018, Shanghai and Shenzhen Stock Exchanges have publicized 73 announcements of controlling interests transfer in listed companies. Among them, there were 29 cases of backdoor behavior by SOEs acquiring controlling interests. Many acquirers are local state-owned capital operation platforms or SASAC, of which Shenzhen SASAC alone has strategic shareholding in four listed companies. At the China Economists 50 Forum held in December 2018, several economists mentioned the phenomenon whereby the state sector advances while the private sector retreats, reflected behind this wave of M&A. The argument that the private sector should be gradually phased out can also be understood in a sense as an endorsement of the new wave of SOE M&A. So how to interpret the new wave of SOE M&A?

First, as China's capital market entered the era of dispersed ownership in 2015, M&A of listed companies entered an active period, and the capital market began to show the functions of asset reorganization and resource allocation. Since 2015, the shareholding ratio of the largest shareholder in China's listed companies has dropped to 33.3% (which reflects the relative control of the one-vote veto), and China's capital market has entered the era of dispersed ownership from the previous single-shareholder dominance. This change is a long-term accumulation of quantitative changes since the completion of the split-share structure reform and the beginning of full circulation of stocks in 2007, and ushered in a qualitative change in 2015. The Vanke equity dispute occurred in the above context. Vanke is the epitome of corporate development since the reform and opening-up and plays an important role as a benchmark in China's business world. I think the Vanke equity dispute that occurred in 2015 is a symbol of China's capital market entering the era of dispersed ownership.

From historical experience, when performance is poor and valuations are low in listed companies, it is often an active period of capital market M&A and asset reorganization. In 2018, three years after the 2015 stock market crash, under the impact of exogenous events and short-term policies such as the trade friction between China and the United States, the introduction of de-leveraging policies and the implementation of new asset management regulations, investors' expected unicorns to return to A-shares and their dreams of sharing the dividends of new economic development have been dashed, and China's capital market has once again experienced a limit of a thousand shares falling. The listed companies that developed rapidly with the help of high leverage and capital operations generally faced the problem of cash flow shortage, and the risk of capital chain breakage intensified. At the same time, major shareholders in some companies previously pledged their equity faced the risk of liquidation under the double pressure of new asset management regulations and falling stock prices, so they had strong demand for the equity transfer and began to seek strong capital to take over.

We see that the control right transfer of listed companies has been active since 2018. On the one hand, it is related to the economic downturn, depressed stock prices and the tight funds of companies and shareholders in 2018. On the other hand, to a certain extent, it is the continuation of the trend of active M&A as China's capital market entering the era of dispersed ownership, or even the superposition of the above two factors.

From a positive perspective, the active M&A and frequent transfer of control in China's capital market indicate to a certain extent that listed companies are actively realizing asset reorganization and resource allocation optimization through the transfer of control rights. The capital market is performing its functions of asset reorganization and resource allocation.

Second, compared to the previous wave of M&A – SOEs acquired private enterprises in the same industry – implemented in some provinces around 2008 and interpreted as the state advances as the private sector retreats, this wave of M&A, although interpreted by some media as state advances as the private sector retreats as well, has a much smaller negative effect due to the change in the control from private capital to state-owned capital realized through the capital market. As for M&A and asset reorganization in China's capital market, the control rights are not only transfers from private capital to state capital, but also transfers from state capital to private capital, and of course transfers from private capital to private capital and from state capital to state capital. It should be noted that since 2010, the proportion of non-state-owned shareholders in China's listed companies has exceeded that of state-owned shareholders for the first time. The number of state-owned holding listed companies stabilized at about 1,000, while the number of non-state-owned holding listed companies soared from 1,036 in 2010 to 2,496 by the end of 2017, accounting for 70% of total listed companies in China, and its average annual growth rate exceeded 20%. At least from the perspective of the growth in the number of non-state-owned holding companies, China's capital market has ushered in a period of rapid growth of private capital listing since 2010. Logically, as listed companies controlled by private capital have become the majority of China's capital market, there will be more cases of the transfer of control of private capital, or even the transfer of control from private capital to state capital.

With the expansion of the scope of capital socialization in the capital market, in addition to the improvement of the efficiency of resource allocation in the whole society, we can equally feel that the distinction between the nature of capital source has become less important. Both state capital and private capital need to abide by the rules of the capital market and protect the rights and interests of every investor equally. At the Economists 50 Forum, Yang Weimin, former deputy director of the General Office of CPC Central Leading Group for Finance and Economics, put forward the view that the classification of ownership should be gradually abolished. The ownership classification of SOEs, private enterprises and foreign enterprises should be gradually diluted and abolished in the long run, and all enterprises registered within the territory of China should be treated equally in law and in policy according to the requirements of the 19th Party Congress. Chen Qingtai previously said that it is meaningless to strictly define state capital or private capital for mixed-ownership enterprises, and the government should weaken or even abolish the policy of differentiated treatment according to enterprise ownership, and promote equal rights, equal opportunities and equal rules for all enterprises. With the steady development of the resource allocation function of China's capital market, capital flow has created market conditions for the abolition of ownership classification.

Third, as Professor Li Yang pointed out at the Economists 50 Forum, although the change in the nature of control is normal in the era of dispersed ownership in China's capital market, it is obviously a retrogression of corporate governance if the new state capital controlling shareholders still manage personnel, affairs and enterprises like traditional SOEs. Therefore, in the so-called new round of state advances as the private sector retreats realized through M&A in the capital market, what we should really worry about is that, as Professor Li Yang pointed out, sending leaders to such enterprises is likely to stifle their original vitality.

It is necessary to remind the state capital that has just gained control through M&A that listed companies, as public companies, are a form of capital socialization, and there are other shareholders besides state capital. In terms of SOE mixed-ownership reform that is now actively promoted, listed companies can be understood as a natural mixture of different types of capital. The Company Law guarantees that all shareholders enjoy the equity of the owner collectively, not just some of them. In particular, the control rights of listed companies are obtained according to the rules of the capital market, which should continue to be followed in the future. Professor Fan Gang has suggested that state capital should enter private listed companies in the form of preferred shares, which may be an effective way for companies that issue preferred shares. As we have analyzed before, liquidity constraints are the problems faced by private enterprises, and corporate governance structure and the business model are not the important factors leading to the change of control, but rather the SOEs should learn from private enterprises in this round of mixed-ownership reform. In fact, the essence of the mixed-ownership reform lies precisely in the transformation from managing personnel, affairs and enterprises by the single-largest shareholder to managing capital in accordance with the rules of the capital market, with all shareholders enjoying owner's equity. This is reflected in the following aspects. On the one hand, the final decisions on major issues, including the composition of the board of directors, asset reorganization, strategic adjustment and so on, are made by means of the collective voting in general meeting of shareholders. On the other hand, the shareholders shall bear the economic consequences caused by collective decision-making errors within the limit of their capital contribution, to achieve symmetry of power and responsibility, and make the enterprise a true self-financing business entity.

Fourth, it is necessary to remind those state capital that have just gained control through M&A that there has been more than one wave of M&A initiated by state capital in history, but few succeeded. Whether SOEs can solve their own system and mechanism problems is the key to the ultimate success of M&A. Many SOEs have responded to the government's call to go global to carry out overseas M&A. At one time, Chinese SOE leaders frequently appeared in the global market for M&A with the momentum of buying up the entire Wall Street. Some SOEs even obtained control of some famous foreign companies, but in fact, many of them never came back after going global.

We hope that, just as it was a rational choice for private capital with financial difficulties to cede control in this wave of M&A, SOEs should also make rational choices in choosing to acquire private companies, especially in terms of corporate governance arrangements after gaining control. After all, solving its own system and mechanism is the key to the success of SOE M&A. Otherwise, the tragedies that have occurred several times in the history of SOE M&A will be repeated.

4 Delegation of Powers: The Return of Power Started by SOE Reform

In early June 2019, as an important initiative to promote SOE mixed-ownership reform, the SASAC of the State Council issued the List. It includes the approval of mixed-ownership reform plans and equity incentive plans by central enterprises in the scope of the power delegation, and supports market-oriented recruitment of professional managers by enterprises affiliated to central enterprises, and their compensation is determined by the board of directors of their respective subsidiaries.

Although formally this is only the delegation of power by SASAC to its direct subordinate central enterprises, in essence it returns shareholders and their entrusted board of directors part or all of the power originally belonging to them. Therefore, I tend to interpret the issuance of the List as the beginning of the return of power in the SOE reform. It has undoubtedly had a positive and far-reaching impact in promoting a new round of SOE mixed-ownership reform. So why is it that the issuance of the List has, to a certain extent, started the return of power in SOE reform?

First of all, the return of power to shareholders under power delegation highlights the principle of matching power and responsibility in the modern enterprise system. We know that the reason an investor is willing to invest in a company whose managers he is not familiar with is that the company has made a solemn commitment that investors enjoy the owner's equity as shareholders. According to Hart, as owners, shareholders have the right to make the final decision on major issues such as asset reorganization and strategic adjustment by means of collective voting at shareholders general meeting on the one hand. On the other hand, shareholders must bear limited liability for possible wrong decisions caused by collective decision-making within the limits of their capital contributions. The former is called residual control and the latter is called residual claim. The reason why shareholders can have the final say on major matters is apparently that their capital contributions can be held liable for the wrong decisions they participate in and may make. Therefore, the matching of power and responsibility has become the basic principle to be followed in property rights arrangement in a modern enterprise system, and the implementation and embodiment of this principle is that shareholders become the authority of corporate governance in modern joint-stock companies. The issuance of the List means that the approval of mixed-ownership reform plan and manager equity incentive plan, which was originally implemented by SASAC as the state-owned assets supervision authority, has been handed over to group companies (central enterprises directly under the SASAC) that have a certain responsibility bearing capacity and are the controlling shareholders of listed companies. In the future, group companies may be further authorized and return to their role as authoritative shareholders of corporate governance.

Second, the delegation of power to central enterprises by SASAC well reflects the information symmetry principle of the modern enterprise system. The List supports the market-oriented recruitment of professional managers by companies affiliated to central enterprises, stressing that their salaries should be determined by the board of directors of their respective subsidiaries. It is easy to understand that for different enterprises with different industry structures, different sizes and performance, the only result would be a one-size-fits-all salary limit if the managerial compensation is uniformly determined by the regulatory authorities. Years ago, this type of salary limit for SOE executives not only led to a brain drain but also became the institutional root of lazy and mediocre governance for SOEs. Formulating an effective and adequate salary for managers obviously gives the power of formulation to the board of directors with more symmetrical information, and lets the board of directors make scientific decisions according to the manager's performance and the market salary of the industry they work in. And neglecting the rational use of local information inevitably leads to a fatal conceit.

Finally, SASAC's delegation of power to central enterprises to some extent reflects the principle of specialized division of labor in the modern enterprise system, which is conducive to the transformation of state-owned asset management system from managing personnel, affairs and enterprises to managing capital. The rise of modern joint-stock companies, characterized by separation of ownership and management, has greatly improved the management efficiency and become one of the major reasons for the rapid growth of human wealth in the past few centuries (Butler) due to the realization of risk-sharing among shareholders in the social scope and the specialized division of labor of decision-making by professional managers. Although the separation of ownership and management leads to agency conflicts between shareholders and managers, the correct approach to the relationship between ownership and management is obvious to strive to achieve a balance between the efficiency improvement and agency cost reduction brought by the specialized division of labor between the socialization of capital and the professionalization of managers, so as to effectively separate ownership and management, rather than simply enforcing control. Thus, on the one hand, the List creates conditions for the central enterprises directly under the SASAC, as the major shareholder of subsidiaries, to work together with other shareholders to perform the function of managing capital through governance mechanisms such as the general meeting of shareholders. On the other hand, it frees the SASAC from a large number of cumbersome administrative approvals to focus on the supervision of state assets and the guidance of industrial layout, so as to achieve preservation and appreciation of state assets. Therefore, the delegation of power is conducive to the specialized division of labor between the SASAC and the central enterprises, and thus between the central enterprises and their subsidiaries, and helps the state-owned assets management system transform from managing personnel, affairs and enterprises to managing capital.

The delegation of power is not the first time in the past 40 years of SOE reform. The initial SOE contract system was promoted under the guiding ideology of delegating power and transferring profits. According to past experiences, the delegation of power often falls into the vicious circle of delegation leads to disorder and regulation leads to stagnation, and eventually has to retake the power because of chaotic and messy situations. We understand that this is indeed the concern of some SOE reform policy makers in promoting relevant policies.

So how can we really break the repetitive circle in the new round of power delegation? The approach of introducing private strategic investors to carry out mixed-ownership reform, which is currently being actively promoted, brings this possibility. The strategic investors with a private background introduced by the mixed-ownership reform are risk-sharers for possible decision-making mistakes. With the introduction of strategic investors, risks are shared among shareholders, including strategic investors, so as to avoid paying for decision-making mistakes by financial subsidies from taxpayers, and gradually harden the originally softened budget constraints. However, the implicit government guarantee and the soft budget constraint faced by SOEs under state paternalism have long been widely criticized by the theoretical circle and have even become the focus of the US-China trade war. Then, the checks and balances formed by strategic investors have become an error correction mechanism for decision-making. Strategic investors with clear profit motives and their appointed directors prevent major shareholders from making business decisions that may harm their interests. The above initiatives can, in turn, protect state-owned assets that also need to be protected.

The completed mixed-ownership reform of China Unicom provides a logical example for us to break out of the above-mentioned vicious circle by introducing strategic investors in the new round of power delegation. Different from the List authorizing China Unicom Group to examine and approve the equity incentive plan, the equity incentive plan of China Unicom – the holding company and the first central enterprise to complete the mixed-ownership reform – was actually launched under the guidance of SASAC through careful discussion and evaluation, and it was known as the last piece of the puzzle of mixed-ownership reform. A natural concern about the issuance of the List is whether the authorization of the equity incentive plan to China Unicom Group will lead to inappropriate equity incentives, or even to the excessive compensation of managers, hurting the interests of shareholders including China Unicom Group. If so, the delegation of power, which is intended to increase the vitality of SOEs, will once again fall into the doomed circle of delegation leads to disorder and regulation leads to stagnation.

Let's imagine what the result might have been if the above decision had been made jointly by China Unicom Group and the introduced strategic investor BATJ after the completion of mixed-ownership reform. We would see that BATJ, the four Internet giants, which have a clear profit motive, would support rather than oppose the equity incentive plan launched by China Unicom Group for motivating the management and key employees. This is because they can easily understand that while it seems the management and key employees are paid high compensations, fully motivated management and employees will create greater value for the company and bring more returns to investors. And these will far exceed the salary expenses paid. In addition, BATJ and their appointed directors prevent China Unicom Group from proposing unreasonable equity incentive plans. This is not because the plan will harm the interests of China Unicom Group and thus the state-owned assets, but because it will harm the interests of BATJ. Even though there is a complex relationship of rivalry and sympathy among BATJ, they will stand firmly together on the issue of opposing the equity incentive plan that China Unicom Group may launch that leads to excessive executive pay.

Therefore, as to how to avoid falling into the circle of delegation leads to disorder and regulation leads to stagnation, based on the previous analysis, a possible idea is to combine delegation of power with mixed-ownership reform. On the one hand, central enterprises as the actual responsible person for managing capital, gain the rights of shareholders through the issuance of the List and better reflect the basic principles of modern enterprise system, such as matching power and responsibility, information symmetry and specialized division of labor. On the other hand, through introducing private strategic investors to mixed-ownership reform, check and balance the power of central enterprises as the main shareholders, so as to avoid falling into the repetitive circle of delegation leads to disorder and regulation leads to stagnation.

We can see that, of the current practical and theoretical controversy of the relationship between mixing and reform of SOEs, the issuance of the List of power delegation helps us understand the relationship from a new perspective. That is, only by mixing can reform rest assured. The mixing is the only way to achieve the real reform of SOEs.

6 Reform of Executive Compensation and Incentive System in SOEs

In 2014, the Chinese government imposed a new round of salary restrictions on SOE executives in response to the prominent problem of excessive pay. In addition to the compensation of managers' human capital, managerial compensation also includes the incentive factor of paying information rent, which is also an embodiment of entrepreneurship. Therefore, the one-size-fits-all salary limit is not the right choice. In evaluating whether the manager's compensation is reasonable, the benchmark is how much value the manager creates for the company and if the party with the information advantage leads the design and implementation of incentive contracts.

In just three years, SOEs are again facing the urgency of reforming executive compensation design. It shows that the top-down salary limit of the administration cannot solve the long-standing problem of executive compensation in SOEs. Only returning to the path of market-oriented reform and considering how to set executive compensation in accordance with the market law is the basic way out.

As an important means of SOE mixed-ownership reform, the employee stock ownership plan (ESOP) is frequently adopted in mixed-ownership reform plans from central to local SOEs. Because of the nature of incremental reform and the fact that it does not significantly change the previous pattern of interests, many SOEs are willing to adopt the employee stock ownership plan, which is easier to be accepted by different stakeholders in the practice of mixed-ownership reform. So what kind of employee stock ownership plan should be expected as an important support measure for SOE mixed-ownership reform?

Even listed companies are difficult to convince employees that the actual controller of the company will distribute "real money" to them. However, two unlisted private companies from the province of Hebei unexpectedly pulled off employee stock ownership plans. So what did the two private companies do right in implementing the employee stock ownership plan? What is the inspiration for the employee stock ownership plan that has been actively promoted in the SOE reform process in China?

DOI: 10.4324/9781003361404-7

1   Information Problems With the Design of Salary Limits and Compensation Contracts for SOE Executives

Against the background of the 2008 international financial crisis and the prominent issue of excessive compensation for SOE executives, the Chinese government has repeatedly imposed salary restrictions. The new policy of executive salary limit is stipulated in the *Opinions on Deepening the Reform of the Compensation System for the Heads of Centrally Administered Enterprises* (Doc. 12 [2014] released by the General Office of the CPC Central Committee) issued in November 2014.

The remarkable features of the new salary limit policy for SOE executives can be summarized as two aspects: the average annual salary of employees of central enterprises in the previous year as the reference system, and the top-down implementation of salary limit by issuing documents in the name of the General Office of the CPC Central Committee. Although the policy of the salary limit mainly aimed at the central SOE directors appointed by organization departments, due to the fuzzy boundary between the appointed directors and professional managers and the related spillover effect, the above-mentioned practice will undoubtedly have an important impact on the practice of salary design for SOE managers in China.

In fact, since the era of Taylor's scientific management, the problem that has always plagued people in formulating reasonable managerial (functional foremen) compensation is that only the managers themselves know how hard they work, while shareholders are legally unable to verify even unable to observe the effort level of managers. Therefore, the distribution of information between managers and shareholders about the extent of managers' efforts is asymmetric. Because of the private information characteristic of managers' effort, Taylor could not really achieve scientific quotas and standardization, otherwise Taylor's scientific quotas would not have been accused by Marx as the "exploitation of workers by capitalists". For the same reason, it is impossible to accurately define the value of labor as a special commodity based on abstract concepts such as socially necessary labor time. After all, the "existing social normal production conditions" and "social average labor proficiency and the labor intensity"[1] on which this concept depends on cannot form a consistent understanding between capitalists and workers based on sufficient information. Therefore, neither scientific management theory nor surplus value theory can complete the scientific formulation of managerial compensation contracts.

This problem did not change significantly until the 1970s, when information economics based on modern game theory developed and matured. As mentioned above, shareholders are usually unable to identify whether a company's poor performance is due to a bad external business environment or management laziness. So there is an information asymmetry between managers who privately know their efforts and outside shareholders. The economic consequence of information asymmetry is that managers are prone to moral hazard. Since shareholders cannot verify or even observe managers' efforts, managers will choose to be lazy to reduce their negative utility in the case of a given (average) compensation level. It should be noted that unlike Marx's concern about the exploitation of workers by capitalists, information economics is concerned with the laziness of managers with private information.

Then, how to motivate a manager whose efforts we cannot verify or even observe? In the view of information economics, although the effort level of managers cannot be verified or even observed, managers' compensation can be linked to a direct mechanism that is verifiable (such as corporate performance). Managers are expected to get high pay only when corporate performance is good. In order to perform well, managers need to work hard rather than slack off. By directly linking the design of managers' compensation with verifiable corporate performance, the economics of information solves to some extent the problem of information asymmetry between managers and shareholders concerning the effort level of managers. Since the reform and opening-up, China's farmers have followed the above logic from the people's commune to the household contract responsibility system, and workers from indiscriminate egalitarianism to merit pay.

In addition to being linked to corporate performance, a scientific managerial compensation contract needs to meet two basic constraints. The first is the participation constraint, that is, the salary a manager can get should not be less than what other jobs will bring. This condition considers the opportunity cost for the manager to accept the company's employment. The second is the incentive compatibility constraint, that is, by paying managers incentive compensation to reconcile the conflict of interest with shareholders and be optimal for both parties. In other words, shareholders pay higher incentive compensation to managers, but the hard work of motivated managers eventually creates the greater value for shareholders. Shareholders maximize shareholder value by balancing the return on investment with the compensation paid to managers, while managers maximize the managerial utility by balancing high incentive compensation with the negative utility of effort. Both parties achieve a win-win situation (Nash equilibrium) through the design of the managerial compensation contract: shareholders create wealth with the help of the manager's professional knowledge, while managers realize the value of life through the career platform provided by shareholders. Because managers have the advantage of controlling private information, in order to keep them loyal to the company, shareholders need to pay managers higher wages (compared to the opportunity cost). Information economics refers to the above unproductive premiums associated with the information control as information rents.

By briefly comparing the differences between neoclassical economics and information economics, we can see that neoclassical economics based on information symmetry considers wages as the compensation for the price of labor and human capital (managers), while information economics based on information asymmetry emphasizes that managerial compensation should not only compensate human capital (the manifestation of participation constraint) but also include information rent (the manifestation of incentive compatibility constraint) to encourage managers telling the truth. Therefore, a new function of managerial compensation contract design is to provide incentives for managers, not just compensation for human capital. The direct inspiration from the idea of managerial compensation design based on information economics is as follows.

First, in assessing whether a manager's compensation is reasonable, the benchmark is how much value the manager creates for the company. The reason is that incomplete information from shareholders about the manager's effort level is the logical and factual starting point for designing managerial compensation contracts. If the performance of one company differs from that of another, the managerial compensation of that company has reasons to be different from that of another. In addition to corporate performance, managers' attitude to risk, the uncertainty of external business environment, the size of the firm and the degree of competition in the industry can significantly affect the level and structure of managerial compensation. If a company is in a different industry than another, it makes sense for its managers to be paid differently. In practice, the strength of the manager's incentives is judged based on the sensitivity of the manager's compensation performance. Research shows that the sensitivity between corporate performance and CEO compensation in the US enterprises is 1,000:6, that is, the CEO can get $6 incentive compensation for every $1,000 increase in shareholder's equity. However, the sensitivity between CEO compensation and corporate performance in the US banking industry is only 1,000:4.7. This is because the high risk and highly regulated nature of the banking industry make the sensitivity of compensation performance usually lower than that of other industries such as manufacturing.

This fact reminds the theorists and practitioners to reconsider the rationality of the new policy of executive salary limit – taking the average annual salary of employees in central enterprises in the previous year as the reference system. After all, the relationship between executives and employees is different from that between functional foremen and workers in Taylor's scientific management era. In addition, the development of information economics tells us that the core problem to be solved in the design of managerial compensation contracts is the incomplete information about the efforts of managers. Therefore, it is questionable whether the average annual salary of employees in central enterprises can replace corporate performance as a benchmark for evaluating the rationality of management compensation. It is even more perplexing what kind of benchmarks or factors are used to determine the average annual salary of employees in central enterprises, and what are the theoretical and practical bases for it.

Second, another important idea contained in the design of managerial compensation contracts based on information economics is that when information is incomplete, the party with information advantages should lead the design and implementation of the contract. For example, as the core management of corporate governance, the board of directors has information advantages in evaluating corporate performance, so the design and implementation of managerial compensation are usually done by the board of directors (compensation committee). This fully reflects the principle of matching the authorization structure of modern organizations with the information structure. However, it is a clear violation of this principle that the government, which lacks information advantages, is leading the current policy on executive pay limits.

The above two inspirations constitute the basic principles that should be followed in the design of compensation contracts for managers in modern companies.

In the process of promoting executive salary limits, theoretical and practical circles should also pay special attention to the following issues.

First, restricting explicit compensation will make managers pursue implicit compensation. The one-size-fits-all salary limit not only inevitably leads to the loss of management talent, but also makes managers seek implicit compensation. In some cases, the significant increase in agency costs far outweighs the savings achieved through executive pay limits, which in turn is more harmful to shareholders' interests. If implicit compensation is not available due to the government's strong anti-corruption efforts, SOE executives will become lazy and mediocre at work. Therefore, we need to be clearly aware that in some cases, although paying high salaries to managers increases the administrative cost of the company, it is totally worthwhile if the company achieves the greater value through the increase of managers' salaries.

Second, how to consider efficiency and fairness in the design of management compensation. It is not difficult to find that there are considerations of fairness behind the reason why the average annual salary of employees in central enterprises is used as the reference system for executive compensation in the new round of salary limits. The previous analysis shows that in addition to the compensation of the human capital of the manager, the managers' salary also includes the incentive to pay information rent and the embodiment of entrepreneurship. Therefore, fairness cannot be simply reflected by comparing the average salary of ordinary employees. When it comes to efficiency and fairness, achieving limited fairness at the expense of too much efficiency often creates more problems than it solves. In fact, salary limits are not the only way to achieve fairness, and it seems that tax regulations are more effective.

Third, how to solve the problem of excessive compensation for managers in some listed companies. Research shows that some listed companies in China do have the phenomenon of managerial overcompensation. However, the right way to solve the managerial overcompensation is not through the one-size-fits-all salary limit from government departments, but through the self-review of executive compensation by the board of directors (compensation committee) of listed companies with more local information under the requirement of regulatory authorities. In the process of self-review, the board of directors should use the pay-performance sensitivity of managers as a benchmark for evaluation. If corporate performance declines while the managerial compensation increases, it is obviously an unreasonable compensation design that should be corrected.

In fact, the managerial overcompensation is precise evidence of the unreasonable corporate governance structure, which needs to be corrected by reforming the corporate governance structure instead of simply limiting the salary.

2 Compensation Reform of SOE Executives at Different Stages

Economic Information Daily reported in September 2017 on the new trend of SOE executive compensation reform under the title "Carrying Out Detailed Plans for

SOE Reform to Accelerate Market-Oriented Compensation Reform in Local SOEs". Since the top leaders of central and local SOEs are more often recruited from the market, salary reform has begun. The newspaper predicted that there are signs that market-oriented compensation reform will speed up in the next stage of SOE reform.

In November 2014, the CPC Central Committee and the State Council issued the *Opinions on Deepening the Reform of the Compensation System for the Heads of Centrally Administered Enterprises*, known as the strictest pay limit in history. The opinion divides the compensation of heads appointed by organization departments into three parts: annual base salary, annual performance-related pay and tenure incentive income. The salary of each part is limited according to a certain multiple of the average salary of employees in central enterprises in the previous year. For example, the base salary cannot exceed two times the average annual salary of the employees of central enterprises in the previous year, and the performance-related pay cannot exceed six times. The tenure incentive income cannot exceed 30% of the total annual salary of the person in charge during his tenure (about 2.4 times of the average annual salary of employees in central enterprises in the previous year). Through the above-mentioned salary limit policy, the gap between the salary of central SOE executives appointed by organization departments and the average annual salary of central SOE employees will be controlled within 10.4 times.

In section 1 of this chapter, we clearly pointed out the two basic principles that should be followed in the formulation of SOE executive compensation. First, when it comes to assessing whether managerial compensation is reasonable, the benchmark is how much value the manager creates for the company, not the average annual salary of employees in central enterprises in the previous year. After all, if the performance of one company is different from that of another, it is reasonable to pay the executives of the two companies differently. In addition to corporate performance, managers' attitude to risk, the uncertainty of external business environment, the size of the firm and the degree of competition in the industry can significantly affect the level and structure of managerial compensation. Second, the board of directors of the company, which has information advantages in evaluating corporate performance, rather than the superior government departments, should participate in the design and formulation of executive compensation. Although there is no way to know the reason why SOE executive compensation reform shifts from the salary limit launched three years ago to the market-oriented compensation reform emphasized today, we suspect that this is partly related to the one-size-fits-all salary limit which inevitably leads to the loss of management talent and induces managers to seek implicit compensation. If implicit compensation is not available due to the government's strong anti-corruption efforts, SOE executives will become lazy and mediocre at work.

Given today's market-oriented SOE executive compensation reform, we believe many market observers will feel the change of time. As a new round of SOE executive compensation reform is launched, we hope the policy makers of the reform will draw lessons from the following issues and avoid repeating the mistakes.

First, instead of top-down promotion of the market-oriented compensation reform for SOE executives as in the past, it is better to streamline administration and delegate power, and return the formulation right of executive compensation that should belong to the enterprise to the enterprise. Some readers worry that if the board of directors of a company is entrusted with determining the executive compensation, will this exacerbate the problem of managerial overcompensation? There is no denying the fact that some Chinese companies have overcompensation in management. However, the right way to solve the problem of excessive managerial compensation is not through a one-size-fits-all salary limit by the government but through a self-review of managerial compensation by the board of directors (especially the compensation committee) of listed companies with more local information under the requirement of regulatory authorities. If the problem of managerial overcompensation still exists after the self-review, it must be dereliction of duty of board of directors, and shareholders should hold them responsible for their violation of fiduciary duty.

Second, outside strategic investors introduced in the mixed-ownership reform will play an important role in curbing the problem of managerial overcompensation and become one of the most significant forces of SOEs that have partially completed the mixed-ownership reform. Let's take China Unicom, which has just completed its mixed-ownership reform. When the China Unicom Group held more than 60% of shares and the chairman and general manager of China Unicom were appointed by the relevant organizational departments, it was unrealistic to rely on the board of directors to curb excessive compensation. However, after the completion of the mixed-ownership reform, China Unicom Group's shareholding has dropped to 36%, and the newly introduced four Internet giants, BATJ, may jointly question the board of directors about possible malfeasance in self-reviewing managerial overcompensation. Although the four giants have a competitive relationship in business, they may come together on this issue. As the capital market enters the era of dispersed ownership, decentralized control will become the basic governance structure of many listed companies. The checks and balances formed by different shareholders on managerial overcompensation will be more effective than the one-size-fits-all salary limits of government departments with asymmetric information. Therefore, the solution to the problem of excessive managerial compensation, which is the reason for the salary restriction three years ago, essentially needs to rely on the improvement of the governance structure, rather than top-down enforcement of salary limit.

Third, market-oriented compensation reform of SOE executives should be carried out together with market-oriented selection and engagement mechanism reform of SOE executives. The reason China adopted top-down salary limits for SOE executives was partly related to the top-down personnel appointment and removal system of major SOE leaders. Due to the rigid top-down enforcement of administrative orders and the lack of flexible disposal of local information, the salary limits inevitably hurt many "innocent" managers who were selected and hired by the market. After the completion of mixed-ownership reform, in line with the concept of win-win cooperation, the shareholders with state-owned background and other strategic investors will select and hire professional managers in accordance with the market procedures, so as to promote the formation of China's professional manager market. This in turn provides a good frame of reference for the formulation of executive compensation and better promotes the market-oriented reform of SOE executive compensation.

In the practice of SOE executive compensation, we should gradually form a diversified compensation structure to avoid uniformly adopting high-efficiency incentive methods. Experiencing the lack of incentives in egalitarianism in the era of planned economy, since the reform and opening-up, many enterprises and social organizations have blindly emphasized the importance of incentive compensation and stressed that compensation should be linked to observable and verifiable performance.

A typical example is an assessment method of "100,000+ online reprints is equal to publishing papers in academic journal" proposed by a university,[2] which reflects the quantitative management thinking under administrative leadership, ignoring the boundary between scholarship and propaganda and the rules of the academic circle. After 40 years of reform and opening-up, it is time to carry out scientific and reasonable salary design according to the nature and development stage of incentive objects, so as to form a diversified salary structure.

Take the compensation of independent directors. Similar to scholars in universities, the fact that economic consequences are difficult to directly observe determines that the reputation incentive should be the main factor in the design of independent directors' compensation. This means that for the compensation contract of independent directors, the salary offered by listed companies is only part of the various implicit and explicit income they receive. Independent directors hope to gain a good reputation for strictly performing supervision and strategic consulting functions in companies with low monetary compensation, so as to be employed by more companies in the future. Therefore, they may not need to emphasize the sensitivity of compensation performance as well as managers. This is also an important reason why world-class universities tend to adopt a tenure system with a fixed salary after young scholars have proven their research ability. This is because scholars value the accumulation of reputation based on academic freedom rather than incentive pay systems tied to various awards, titles and the number of papers published. The latter will only aggravate the administerization and academic fickleness of universities.

Fourth, when it comes to diversified compensation structure, we have to consider employee stock ownership plans (ESOP) that have been frequently adopted in the SOE mixed-ownership reform. As an important means of mixed-ownership reform, the employee stock ownership plan is often seen in mixed-ownership reform plans from central to local SOEs. Since the reform is incremental in nature and does not cause significant changes in the previous pattern of interests, many SOEs are willing to adopt this reform plan in the practice of mixed-ownership reform, which is more acceptable to different stakeholders and does not attract more opposition. However, from the perspective of the employee joint-stock cooperative system implemented in China and the practice of employee stock ownership plan in some enterprises, due to the lack of a transferable exit mechanism and basic corporate governance system for the protection of shareholder rights has often made employee shareholders – who are both shareholders and employees – potential obstacles to the future process of market-oriented reform. Many high-profile equity disputes have to do with the aftermath of the seemingly easy-to-solve employee stock ownership plan implemented then.

Even in the practice of corporate governance in the United States, Jensen, a financier who once advocated giving equity incentives to managers, changed his view after realizing that it could easily lead to incentive distortion and managerial entrenchment effect, and pointed out that equity incentives have become the "opium" of managerial incentives. Therefore, if there is an alternative to traditional incentive compensation, ESOP should be used as little as possible in principle to promote SOE mixed-ownership reform so as to avoid hidden dangers for the subsequent reform. More importantly, we should not emphasize the introduction of employee stock ownership plans to achieve mixed-ownership reform. The inefficiency of many SOEs undergoing mixed-ownership reform is not due to the lack of employee stock ownership plan to motivate employees, but rather to the lack of scientific design and effective implementation of traditional incentive compensation.

In just three years, SOEs are again facing the urgency of reforming executive compensation design. It shows that the top-down salary limit of the administration is unrealistic to solve the long-standing problem of executive compensation in SOE reforms. The result is that we must return to the market-oriented reform path and consider how to formulate the corporate executive compensation system according to the market law.

A lesson from the past should enlighten us in the future. I hope that policy makers will respect the rules of market economy in the formulation of a new round of SOE reform policies, so as to ensure that SOE executive compensation reform can go further and better.

3 Why Do State-Owned Holding Listed Companies Lack Incentives to Implement Employee Stock Ownership Plans

Starting from the classic paper published by Jensen and Meckling in 1976, which marked the beginning of modern corporate governance study, it has become a consensus among the theoretical and practical circles of corporate governance that equity incentives will help to coordinate the interests between managers and shareholders and reduce agency costs. The China Securities Regulatory Commission (CSRC) issued the *Measures for the Administration of Equity Incentives for Listed Companies (Trial)* on December 31, 2005, and the SASAC and the Ministry of Finance (MOF) jointly issued the *Trial Measures for the Implementation of Equity Incentives for State-Owned Holding Listed Companies (Domestic)* in September 2006, which were used to regulate the practice of equity incentive plans introduced for executives of state-owned holding listed companies. In June 2014, the CSRC issued the *Guiding Opinions on the Pilot Project of Employee Stock Ownership Plans for Listed Companies*, and in August 2016, the SASAC, the Ministry of Finance and the CSRC jointly issued the *Opinions on the Pilot Project of ESOP for State-Owned Holding Enterprises With Mixed Ownership* for regulating the practice of employee stock ownership plans for state-owned listed companies.

However, in terms of the implementation of equity incentive plans for managers, from the beginning of 2006 to the end of 2011, there were about 351 equity incentive plans proposed by 301 listed companies in China. Of these, 286 were from private companies and 65 were from state-owned listed companies. By contrast, by the end of 1997, before the Asian financial crisis, 45% of listed companies in the United States granted stock options to their managers.

Since the implementation of the employee stock ownership plan, a total of 486 listed companies have implemented the plan from 2014 to 2017. Among them, only 55 state-owned listed companies have implemented employee stock ownership plans, accounting for only 6.37% of all state-owned listed companies in China. By comparison, up to 29.6% of non-state-owned listed companies have implemented employee stock ownership plans.

It is easy to understand that compared with SOEs that have not yet been listed, state-owned listed companies that have completed capital socialization and become public companies obviously have institutional convenience and advantages in public opinion in implementing incentive plans. However, in the state-owned holding listed companies, why is it that neither the executive equity incentive plan nor the employee stock ownership plan is widely implemented as expected by theorists and practitioners?

First of all, from the perspective of the selection of incentive targets, the chairman and general manager of the state-owned holding listed company, the main promoter of the plan, cannot be the objects of the incentive plan according to the regulations because they are appointed by the superior organization department or the SASAC. For example, in the case of China Unicom's mixed-ownership reform, which is the benchmark of SOE reform, Wang Xiaochu, the chairman of the board appointed by the superior organization, cannot be the beneficiary of the incentive plan. This makes the launch of incentive plan an awkward situation: the senior executives who have the right to promote the incentive plan are ineligible to be the beneficiaries, while the ordinary managers and employees who are qualified to be the beneficiaries have no right to interfere with the promotion of the plan. Therefore, whether to actively promote the incentive plan has become to some extent a test of the personal responsibility and dedication of the chairman and general manager. However, in the face of the potential risk of punishment brought by non-compliance due to the rigorous approval procedures and the personal stress caused by complex interest pattern, inaction has become the rational choice for many senior executives who have the authority to promote incentive plans.

Second, from the perspective of the incentive range, the plans are subject to many restrictions that do not fully reflect the proper impact of incentive plans related to shares. For example, according to relevant regulations, for the first implementation of the equity incentive plan, the amount of equity granted shall not exceed 1% of the total share capital of the listed company in principle; the total number of underlying shares involved in all effective equity incentive plans of the company should be controlled within 10% of the total share capital of the listed company; and the expected income of the individual equity incentive for SOE executives should not exceed 30% of their total salary. Since the incentive range was limited, executives of state-owned listed companies were not enthusiastic about adopting the equity incentive. We have noted that in the employee stock ownership plan launched by China Unicom, China Unicom granted 847.88 million restricted shares to employees as equity incentives at a price of 3.79 yuan per share (about 50% of 7.74 yuan) before the trade suspension, accounting for about 4% of the total share capital of the company at that time, which has far exceeded the upper limit of 1% stipulated in the regulations.

Finally, from the approval procedure of incentive plans, according to the relevant opinions, in addition to voting at the general meeting of shareholders, it used to need to be reported to the state-owned holding group companies and the SASAC for approval. The red tape of official documents and the bureaucratic mentality of income and responsibility asymmetry thus become one of the institutional costs that some state-owned holding listed companies have to consider when launching their incentive plans. The pace of approval is often inconsistent with the issuance of incentive plans by listed companies based on market conditions. This further increases the implementation cost of incentive plans. For state-owned holding listed companies, the good news is that, according to the List, the approval of employee stock ownership plan will no longer be carried out by the SASAC, but will be delegated to the group company that is the controlling shareholder. This has reduced the approval process, at least for SASAC.

If the current opinions only inhibit the internal enthusiasm of the state-owned holding listed companies to launch incentive plans due to some deficiencies of incentive objects, incentive ranges and approval procedures, then the once-launched one-size-fits-all salary limit for executives of central enterprises has somewhat dissuaded state-owned listed companies from perfecting their incentive plans.

In order to address the fairness concerns and public opinion caused by managerial overcompensation in some enterprises, in November 2014, the CPC Central Committee and the State Council issued the *Opinions on Deepening the Reform of the Compensation System for the Heads of Centrally Administered Enterprises*. The opinion divides the compensation of executives appointed by the superior organization department into three parts: annual base salary, annual performance-related pay and tenure incentive income. The compensation of each part is limited according to a certain multiple of the average salary of employees in central enterprises in the previous year. For example, the base salary shall not exceed two times of the average annual salary of the employees in central enterprises in the previous year, and the performance-related pay shall not exceed six times. The tenure incentive income shall not exceed 30% of the total annual salary of the person in charge during his tenure (about 2.4 times the average annual salary of employees in central enterprises in the previous year). Through the above-mentioned salary limit policy, the gap between the salary of central SOE executives appointed by organization departments and the average annual salary of central SOE employees will be controlled within 10.4 times.

Although the policy of salary limits mainly aimed at central SOE directors appointed by organization departments, due to the fuzzy boundary between the appointed directors and professional managers and the related spillover effect, the above practice will undoubtedly have an important impact on the salary design for SOE managers in China.

The above practice will undoubtedly have an important impact on the practice of managerial compensation design in SOEs in China. In addition to inevitably leading to the brain drain of some SOEs, the one-size-fits-all salary limit will also induce SOE executives to seek implicit income, corruption and rent-seeking. If implicit compensation is not available due to the government's strong anti-corruption efforts, SOE executives will become lazy and mediocre at work.

We have noted that the List issued by the SASAC supports the selection and engagement of professional managers by the companies affiliated to the central enterprises on a market base, and their compensation will be determined by the board of directors of the corresponding subsidiaries, so that the formulation right of the compensation for managers returns to the board of directors. This may provide an institutional guarantee for state-owned holding companies to change the situation of insufficient incentives and improve incentive plans.

So how to improve the incentives of state-owned holding listed companies?

The first is that a decentralized control pattern is formed in which the major shareholders check and balance each other, so that institutions and strategic investors with clear profit motives become an active force to promote the implementation of incentive plans. Institutions and strategic investors with clear profit motives tend to actively support and promote the launch of employee stock ownership plans that motivate management and key employees. Although it seems that companies have issued more shares to management and key employees, or even diluted their equity, adequately motivated management and employees will create the greater value for the business and bring more returns to investors. Our research also found that companies with more dispersed ownership and facing external takeover threats are more likely to launch employee stock ownership plans. In this sense, mixed ownership will help reform the incentives of state-owned holding listed companies.

The second is that the board of directors with more symmetric information should be the leading force in the formulation of management incentive plans. As we all know, if managerial compensation is formulated by regulatory authorities, the only result will be a one-size-fits-all salary limit for companies with different industrial structures, different sizes and performance. Obviously, an effective incentive plan is made by a more information-symmetrical board of directors, based on the assessment and evaluation of the design scheme of the consulting agency, and according to the performance of managers and the salary marketization of the industry. The incentive plan formulated by the board of directors will undoubtedly be implemented after voting at the general meeting of shareholders.

In the end, the managerial overcompensation may be brought by incentive plans that have already existed in some enterprises or will be implemented in the future. The board of directors (especially the compensation committee) of listed companies with more local information should conduct self-review on managerial compensation and incentive status at the request of the relevant regulatory authorities and shareholders, rather than through the one-size-fits-all pay limits. The board of directors should use the sensitivity of managerial compensation performance as a benchmark when evaluating management incentive plans. If the managerial compensation increases while corporate performance declines, it is obviously an unreasonable design of compensation and incentive plans that should be adjusted and corrected.

It should be noted that a decentralized control structure with mutual checks and balances formed among shareholders will also help to discourage the introduction of incentive schemes that might lead to managerial overcompensation. The reason for doing so may not be that this plan will harm the interests of state-owned assets but that it will harm their own interests.

4 What Kind of Employee Stock Ownership Plan Should We Expect in SOE Mixed-Ownership Reform

In 2016, the SASAC, the Ministry of Finance and the China Securities Regulatory Commission (CSRC) jointly issued the *Opinions on the Pilot Project of ESOP for State-Owned Holding Enterprises With Mixed Ownership* (hereinafter *Pilot Opinions*). As an important support measure for SOE mixed-ownership reform, theorists and practitioners are full of expectations for the *Pilot Opinions*. So what kind of employee stock ownership plan should we expect?

First, employee stock ownership plans should encourage shareholding employees to become true owners of the company through appropriate institutional arrangements of corporate governance. Compared with traditional compensation incentives such as merit pay, the advantage of an employee stock ownership plan is to bind the rewards of employees to the long-term development of the company so that employees can pay more attention to the long-term performance of the company and avoid the pursuit of short-term interests at the expense of the long-term interests of the company. The extent to which an employee can decide his future contribution to the company's long-term performance is largely related to the institutional arrangements of corporate governance. For example, can employees have the right to recommend directors when their shareholding reaches a certain proportion? In particular, is it permissible to elect directors who represent their interests through cumulative voting rights? If the director they recommended fails to protect the interests of shareholding employees, how do they remove the director and elect a new one? As far as the current plan is concerned, the *Pilot Opinions* are vague on these crucial issues. In particular, management is often appointed by superior departments, which is not a target of the employee stock ownership plan according to the *Pilot Opinions*, while employees who are allowed to hold shares do not have corresponding corporate governance system arrangements to protect their rights and interests. Lack of clarity in the corporate governance system may go against the original intent and purpose of the employee stock ownership plan.

Second, the employee stock ownership plan should encourage private capital to participate in SOE mixed-ownership reform. Employees who are highly motivated by (employee stock ownership plan) are certainly one of the reasons to attract private capital to participate in the SOE mixed-ownership reform. However, there is no doubt that employee stock ownership will greatly increase the number of shareholders that private capital must face. These shareholders are not ordinary financial investors, but very important stakeholders. The question is whether the employee stock ownership plan should be launched after the mixed-ownership reform has been implemented by the board of directors representing different shareholders' interests based on needs of employee incentives (the board of directors believes that traditional base salary + performance-related pay is not enough to provide sufficient incentives to employees after scientific assessment), or it should be launched first and then introduce social capital to carry out the reform. One possible outcome is that the implementation of an employee stock ownership plan has discouraged social capital who were ready to participate in SOE reforms, unless the shareholding employees are the ideal object of mixed-ownership reform in the minds of the reform plan designers.

Third, the goal of the employee stock ownership plan should be to focus on the stock funds of state-owned enterprises. As we all know, the attraction and potential problems of SOEs are mainly concentrated in stock funds. On the one hand, the *Pilot Opinions* emphasize the introduction of incremental funds, and advocates the implementation of employee stock ownership by means of capital increase and share expansion and new investment. On the other hand, it emphasizes that employee stock ownership is not obtained free of charge, and the employee should mainly contribute in currency and pay according to the agreed time. At the same time, pilot companies are not allowed to provide financial assistance, such as advances, guarantees or loans, to shareholding employees. In fact, a new project that needs to be funded is not necessarily a project that employees are interested in. Equally important, it is debatable whether it is necessary to bind the interests of employees who are not project implementers and shareholders of the new investment projects through employee stock ownership, because if employees are interested in a certain project, they can buy shares directly through the capital market. We are also concerned that if the plan is implemented, the final result may be that the targets in which employees are interested in (such as the stock funds of SOEs) are not allowed to be held, while the targets allowing employees to hold shares may not appeal to them. This may make employee stock ownership the wishful thinking of the designers of SOE mixed-ownership plan.

Fourth, employee stock ownership plans should improve the incentive effect of traditional compensation programs. In theory, an employee stock ownership plan could be either a supplement to a traditional compensation program or an alternative program. This means that current employee compensation programs need to be carefully evaluated before introducing employee stock ownership plans. For example, has current employee salary been closely related to performance, and has it realized more pay for more work, less pay for less work, and no pay for no work? If the current poor performance is simply due to the improperly designed traditional incentive plans and redundant employees, this is obviously not a sufficient reason to implement an employee stock ownership plan.

Fifth, employee stock ownership plans should have a reasonable exit mechanism. The employee joint-stock cooperative system introduced during the SOE reform process ended because it could not establish a reasonable exit mechanism. In addition to allowing incentive objects to purchase shares at a specified price, the standard equity incentive plan often stipulates that incentive objects have a right to sell the shares in the market after the lock-up period ends. Employees are willing to hold a company's stock because they will get dividends, especially after the lock-up period. This makes public companies with good stock liquidity the subject of employee stock ownership plans. The *Pilot Opinions* provide that

> If a shareholding employee leaves the company for reasons such as resignation, transfer, retirement, death or dismissal, the shares held shall be internally transferred within twelve months. In the case of transfer to the shareholding platform, eligible employees or non-public capital shareholders, the transfer price shall be determined by mutual agreement.

It also stipulates that "the transfer price shall not be higher than the audited net asset value per share of the previous year." This means that employees who hold shares may transfer their shares to a given market with little room for bargaining. This makes stock ownership less attractive to employees who have to change jobs. To make matters worse, the implementation of this policy may even lead to an adverse selection effect: those who are truly capable are reluctant to accept employee stock ownership plans for fear of being tied down, while those who accept employee stock ownership plans are often those who are less capable.

The controversy over the *Pilot Opinions* should be expected by policy makers. We believe that the policy makers' emphasis on the pilot phase before formal policies is intended to identify problems as early as possible, to summarize experiences and lessons in a timely manner, and to avoid large-scale outbreak of problems. It is hoped that our expectations and concerns about the *Pilot Opinions* will help policy makers find out problems in time and launch effective and feasible employee stock ownership plans to solidly promote the SOE mixed-ownership reform in China.

Notes

1 卡尔·马克思,《资本论》, 第一卷, 第一篇商品和货币, 第一章商品P53。
2 In 2017, Zhejiang University issued the *Implementation Measures for the Recognition of Outstanding Network Cultural Achievements*, which stipulates that excellent online articles can be identified as domestic authoritative, first-class and core academic journal papers according to the publishing platform and dissemination level.

7 Outlook for SOE Mixed-Ownership Reform

Some practitioners argue that mixed ownership cannot fundamentally solve the problems of SOE reform in China in view of the actual difficulties faced by SOE reform. This chapter looks into the future of SOE mixed-ownership reform by responding to why it is necessary to introduce strategic investors with private capital background to realize mixed ownership in the practice of SOE reform. We emphasize that, just as the reform can be promoted in a sustained and in-depth manner by maintaining the continuous opening-up to the outside world and providing a steady stream of external pressure and internal impetus for reform, only the mixing of different ownership can realize the reform of management mechanism.

In the practice of SOE reform, based on the idea of reorganization of state-owned resources and optimization of the layout of state-owned industries through M&A which is parallel to the mixed-ownership reform, we believe that the high profits brought by the temporary or partial monopoly industrial structure formed by the merger will cover up the real problems faced by SOEs in the transformation of operation mechanism. The final solution to this problem still needs to be achieved through mixing. Therefore, in the choice of SOE reform path, we emphasize that it is better to mix rather than merge.

1 SOE Mixed-Ownership Reform: Only Mixing Can Lead to Reform

State-owned enterprises have a unique position and extensive influence in China's national economy. SOE reform has always been the central link and core content of China's economic system reform. The current SOE mixed-ownership reform, which is typically characterized by mixed ownership, can be interpreted to a certain extent as the continuation of the traditional logic of capital socialization that was indistinct in SOE reform over the past decades. SOEs have undergone restructuring in the form of the employee joint-stock cooperative system and the listing of some holding companies of enterprise groups. After several years of pilot exploration and practice, the new round of SOE mixed-ownership reform was initially formed. In the state-owned asset management system, the state-owned capital investment and operating company has been reorganized or newly established as

DOI: 10.4324/9781003361404-8

the interface between the government and the market to isolate the SASAC and entity enterprises, thus realizing the transformation from managing personnel, affairs and enterprises to managing capital. As for the operating entities, the reform direction, such as the decentralized control pattern among major shareholders, is formed by introducing strategic investors with a private capital background. Like the reform in any field, when SOE mixed-ownership reform enters the deep-water area, it will inevitably encounter various practical difficulties and potential resistance, and there will be various rational speculation and even public doubts. For example, in response to the fact that some SOEs have only introduced strategic investors as the goal of mixed-ownership reform, some scholars suggest that mixed ownership is not the only way and last form to realize the SOE reform. In view of the practical difficulties of introducing strategic investors in specific industries, some scholars pointed out that mixed ownership cannot fundamentally solve the problem of SOE reform in China, and that the key to SOE reform is to let the market play a decisive role in the resource allocation. If we observe and understand the above views in the context of some specific SOE reform scenarios, they undoubtedly have a certain realistic rationality. So how should we correctly understand the relationship between mixing and reform in the new round of SOE reform?

Before answering this question, we need to first understand the main problems facing the development of SOEs. Generally speaking, the problems faced by SOE development are mainly focused on the following two aspects. The first is the problem of excessive supervision resulting from the failure to effectively separate ownership from management. For example, instead of self-review by the board of directors of the company in problem, the state-owned assets management system tries to solve the problem of excessive executive salaries which exist only in some SOEs by imposing a one-size-fits-all administrative salary limit. However, the consequences of the one-size-fits-all administrative salary limit is that some SOEs have experienced a serious lack of executive incentives and a brain drain, so they have to turn to the establishment and improvement of a market-oriented professional manager compensation system.

Second, due to owner absence and the complex principal-agent in SOEs, no one is willing to or dares to take charge of management compensation design, which should be performed by the board of directors in theory, resulting in insufficient or even distorted incentives for management. For example, executive equity incentive plans, which have been widely proven to be effective, have not been promoted vigorously in SOEs. Even in some companies that have introduced incentive plans, there are strict restrictions on the design of the plans. If we use a popular language to interpret the main problems faced by the development of SOEs in China, it is that "absent for what should be managed and intervening in what should not be managed". An effective SOE reform plan undoubtedly needs to address the above-mentioned problems in the development of SOEs and apply the right medicine to the case in order to achieve the goal. As we can see, the introduction of strategic investors with private capital backgrounds to form a mixed-ownership system has a very important practical significance for SOEs to solve the problem of absent for what should be managed and intervening in what should not be managed.

First, by introducing strategic investors with private capital background as a new counterbalance force and establishing competitive relationships among major shareholders, SOEs completing mixed ownership will establish an automatic error correction mechanism, which can alleviate the problem of excessive supervision caused by ineffective separation of the ownership and management rights of SOEs to a certain extent. Faced with the strong demand for rights and interests from strategic investors with clear profit motive and private capital background, SOEs will be forced to return to a modern corporate governance framework in which all shareholders collectively enjoy the owner's equity after the completion of mixed-ownership reform. This is reflected in major issues such as asset reorganization, strategic adjustment and board composition. All shareholders, including strategic investors, make the final decision through one share–one vote voting at the general meeting of shareholders. If the proposal is harmful to the interests of strategic investors, it will undoubtedly be abandoned due to the opposition of strategic investors. Previous studies have shown that when a company has multiple shareholders who check and balance each other, the compromise resolution formed by negotiating among the parties can often prevent possible deviations and distortion in the use of funds. Thus, the competitive relationship between the major shareholders established through the introduction of strategic investors in the SOE mixed-ownership reform will become an automatic error correction mechanism, which to some extent avoids the problem of excessive supervision that existed in SOEs and achieves an effective separation of ownership and management rights.

Second, by introducing private investors with clear profit motive, the mixed-ownership reform will organically unify the profit goal of private investors and the goal of preserving and increasing the value of SOEs, and form a consensus among different shareholders that only cooperation can lead to a win-win situation. Therefore, it is motivated to establish a long-term incentive mechanism based on the actual situation of the company, so as to solve the problem of insufficient incentive for managers under the agency conflict and the distortion of absent for what should be managed. As for the formulation of executive compensation, a thorny issue in SOE reform, private capital investors with clear profit motive will try to convince other shareholders (including state-owned capital investors) that although they pay high salaries to managers, fully motivated managers can earn more money for them. Thus, the newly formed board of directors after the completion of mixed-ownership reform will be motivated to rebuild the management system according to market-based principles, thus naturally solving the long-term incentive mechanism of selecting professional managers according to market-based principles and designing compensation for the managers – which is repeatedly mentioned in the reports of SOE reforms.

At present, many SOEs are actively promoting the SOE mixed-ownership reform, which is characterized by introducing strategic investors with private capital background and realizing mixed ownership. If we want to find a theoretical basis for the new round of SOE mixed-ownership reform, we can take the theory of decentralized control developed by Bolton, Müller and Bennedson. The core of this theory is to form a decentralized control pattern among major shareholders by introducing new major shareholders, creating a compromise effect and reducing the distortion in the fund use so as to avoid the problem of excessive supervision under the dominance of a single shareholder. Hart's theory of modern property rights revealed how authority is distributed in enterprises and responded to the mystery of the modern joint-stock company of why investors are willing to buy shares issued by joint-stock companies. Just as modern property rights theory is considered by Chinese scholars as the theoretical basis of SOE reform, the decentralized control theory initially used to solve the problem of excessive intervention may become the theoretical basis for the new round of SOE mixed-ownership reform.

If the theory of decentralized control only theoretically discussed the possibility of introducing strategic investors with private capital background to establish a mixed-ownership to help solve the problem of absent for what should be managed and intervening in what should not be managed, the case of China Unicom, which has completed its mixed-ownership reform, has proved that the mixed-ownership reform really helps SOEs overcome the above problem. After the introduction of BATJ and other capital to complete the mixed-ownership reform, in addition to the fact that the shareholding ratio of the original controlling shareholder China Unicom Group decreased, several major strategic investors appointed directors representing their own interests in the board of directors of China Unicom. Compared with the dominant state of China Unicom Group in the past, after the completion of mixed-ownership reform, if the majority shareholder China Unicom Group proposes a motion that is detrimental to the interests of outside shareholders, it may be unanimously opposed by major strategic investors. As a result, China Unicom has developed an automatic error correction mechanism based on competition and counterbalance among shareholders, which to a certain extent avoids the excessive supervision problem that might have existed under the dominance of the single-largest shareholder China Unicom Group. At the same time, after the introduction of BATJ, the major shareholders of China Unicom, who aim at win-win cooperation, can easily reach a consensus on how to effectively motivate the management and technical backbone. Therefore, the employee stock ownership plan was naturally launched as part of China Unicom's mixed-ownership reform plan.

In addition to the cases of China Unicom, which has completed its mixed-ownership reform through the introduction of strategic investors, the actual performance of some SOEs that completed mixed-ownership reform through listing and social capitalization can also provide indirect evidence in the sense of large sample statistics that mixed-ownership reform can help solve the problem of absent for what should be managed and intervening in what should not be managed. On December 12, 2018, at the 2018 CCTV Financial Forum Chinese Listed Companies Summit, relevant personnel from the SASAC revealed that 65.2% of its total assets and 61.7% of the net assets have been invested into listed companies, and 61.2% of the operating revenue and 87.6% of the total profit came from listed companies.

So why can state-owned listed companies generate 87.6% of profits with 61.7% of net assets? It is easy to see that this is directly related to the modern corporate governance structure established through the socialization of capital. Among the shareholders of state-owned listed companies, private investors with clear profit motive and other institutional investors will request listed companies to vote at the general meeting of shareholders around major issues such as asset reorganization in accordance with the relevant provisions of the Company Law to protect investors' rights and interests. They also choose representatives to form the board of directors to supervise and restrain managers' possible acts of seeking private interests to the detriment of shareholders' interests. In order to improve the quality of supervision, the listed companies need to bring talents from outside, who are interest-neutral, reputation-oriented and have expertise in law, accounting and finance, as independent directors for supervision and strategic consultation. We have seen that after completing the mixed-ownership reform through listing and capital socialization, state-owned companies have gradually established and improved the basic corporate governance structure, effectively separated the management rights in the hands of professional managers from the control rights in the hands of shareholders and stimulated the creativity of managers, thus generating 87.6% of the profit with 61.7% of net assets.

The relationship between the mixing of introducing strategic investors to form a mixed-ownership system and the reform of establishing a sound corporate governance system and an efficient management mechanism is similar to the relationship between opening-up and reform. Only by maintaining the continuous opening-up to the outside world and providing steady external pressure and internal motivation can we continue to deepen reform. Opening-up plays a crucial role in reform, as does the role of strategic investors with obvious profit motives and private capital background in SOE reform. Just as reform and opening-up are inseparable, in the practice of SOE reform, the mixing of different ownership and the reform of establishing effective management mechanisms are also inseparable. Only mixing can bring real reform. Some practitioners of SOE reform have observed that "as long as private enterprises are allowed in, SOE mechanisms will be liberalized", and that "[even though] SOEs know [they should] liberalize and revitalize, they do not do so."[1] This is actually the root cause. In other words, in the absence of strategic investors with a private capital background and clear profit motive, it is difficult for SOEs to avoid paternalistic intervention and establish long-term incentive mechanisms.

To a certain extent, these analyses show the importance of mixing to the completion of reform in the practice of SOE mixed-ownership reform. So in addition to the mixing of strategic investors with private capital background, is there any other fundamental and important way to resolve difficulties in SOE reform? Is it true that mixed ownership cannot fundamentally solve the problem of China's SOE reform, as some scholars have pointed out? Is the only solution to SOE reform to enable the market to play a decisive role in the resource allocation?

In fact, during the 40-year history of SOE reform in China, there have been debates in theoretical and practical circles on whether property rights or competitive market environment is more important. The most famous one is the debate in the mid-1990s about whether SOE reform should start with the reform of property rights or the improvement of the competitive market environment. While the improvement of the competitive market environment is undoubtedly important, the breakthrough of SOE reform is to transform SOEs into vibrant organizations with intrinsic motivation to establish the long-term management mechanisms through introducing strategic investors to form mixed ownership. Only when enterprises have strong internal market demand for government agencies to streamline administration and delegate power, for the market to play a decisive role in the resource allocation, can relevant departments introduce reform measures to comply with the above changes. Otherwise, SOEs can only wait passively or even sit on the sidelines amid calls for market-oriented reforms. Especially for SOEs in the competitive fields, since the reform and opening-up, the development of the private economy has created a competitive external management environment, which constitutes a strong pressure and sustainable impetus for SOE reform.

More importantly, the mixed-ownership reform achieved by introducing strategic investors with private capital background will create a spontaneous order among competing shareholders that actively seeks to build a corporate governance system that reflects and protects the interests of shareholders. For example, in order to avoid related party transactions and tunneling by major shareholders and protect their own interests, the strategic investors with private capital background emphasize that major issues need to be voted on and approved by the general meeting of shareholders before finally translated into the corporate will. As a result, a basic corporate governance system that balances the interests of all parties and protects the equity of shareholders, as well as various effective management mechanisms that provide sufficient incentives to management will gradually be formed, instead of relying solely on the limited experience and self-restraint of the SOE executives to establish so-called dynamic management mechanisms that adapt to market changes after the government has delegated power. One-sidedly emphasizing that only the market plays a decisive role in the resource allocation is the key to SOE reform, and advocating that mixed ownership cannot fundamentally solve the problems of SOE reform may mislead the initial formation of the correct direction of SOE reform by mixing to promote reform.

As for the practical difficulties of introducing strategic investors into specific industries, it should be emphasized that the introduction of strategic investors does not focus on its industry experience but on the intrinsic motivation formed by clear profit motive to alleviate the excessive supervision under the dominance of single shareholder and to launch the long-term incentive mechanism from the perspective of win-win cooperation. The formulation and efficient implementation of industry development strategies can be fully realized through the selection of management teams under market-oriented compensation incentives.

For the practical difficulties of introducing strategic investors to realize the mixed-ownership reform, we should not consider this problem from the perspective that private capital of the same industry is not strong enough to mix and reform, but from the perspective of why strategic investors with private capital background are reluctant to participate in SOE mixed-ownership reform.

Making strategic investors with private capital backgrounds willing to participate in mixed-ownership reform is a basic incentive compatibility problem in economics. Specifically, in the practice of SOE mixed-ownership reform, it is how to protect the interests of strategic investors while meeting the purpose of preserving and increasing the value of state-owned assets through mixed-ownership reform. Only when there is a credible way and mechanism to prevent the major shareholders from damaging the interests of strategic investors with private capital background will the strategic investors have the motivation to participate in the mixed-ownership reform.

Then, how can we realize the incentive compatibility of strategic investors with private capital background to mixed-ownership reform? From the practice of SOE mixed-ownership reform so far, there are at least the following two models. One is the Tianjin Northern Trust model. Northern Trust successfully introduced three new shareholders of private enterprises, including Rizhao Steel Holding Group Co. Ltd., and transferred a total of 50.07% of the equity. Among them, Rizhao Steel, which holds 18.30% of the shares, became the largest shareholder and was given the right to recommend the chairman of the board. The state-owned TEDA Investment Holding, the former largest shareholder, saw its stake diluted to 17.94%, making it the second largest shareholder. The other is the China Unicom model. In order to retain the relative control of state-owned assets in China Unicom, which is in a basic and strategic industry, China Unicom Group still holds 36.67% of its shares after the completion of mixed-ownership reform. China Unicom was forced to choose the model of state-owned capital dominating in the equity structure and strategic investors dominate in the board organization to achieve incentive compatibility of strategic investors. In the newly formed board of directors after the mixed-ownership reform, five directors from strategic investors such as Baidu, Alibaba, Tencent and JD.com accounted for the majority of all eight non-independent directors. In both models, strategic investors expect their rights and interests to be guaranteed, so they become incentive compatible and willing to participate in mixed-ownership reform. It is important to remind readers that BATJ, which is mixed into China Unicom, is not from the communication industry; and Rizhao Steel, which is mixed into Northern Trust, is not from the financial industry. Therefore, whether strategic investors with private capital backgrounds are willing to participate in the mixed-ownership reform is not a question of whether strategic investors from the same industry are powerful enough but rather how to make their rights and interests protected by incentive compatibility.

The success or failure of the new round of SOE reform is undoubtedly crucial to the ultimate realization of China's market-oriented economic transformation. The success of SOE reform largely depends on whether we can adhere to the established direction of mixing to promote reform in the practice of SOE reform. Just as only opening-up can promote reform, in the practice of SOE mixed-ownership reform, only mixing can truly achieve reform.

2   SOE Mixed-Ownership Reform: Mixing Is Better Than Merger

Observers of SOE reform can easily find that while SOE reform is advancing along the line of introducing strategic investors with a private capital background to achieve mixed ownership, it seems that there is another idea of SOE reform, which is to realize the recombination of state-owned resources and the optimization of the layout of state-owned industries through merger, acquisition and reorganization. For example, CSR and CNR merged into CRRC in 2015, Baosteel and WISCO (Wuhan Iron and Steel) merged into Baowu in 2017, CNNC and CNEC merged into the new CNNC in 2018, and so on. The latest buzz is the merger of CSSG (China State Shipbuilding Corporation) and CSIC (China Shipbuilding Industry Corporation). If we call the previous thoughts on SOE reform mixing, we can call another idea just mentioned "merger".

In the completed cases of M&A and restructuring of SOEs, it is easy to observe that merger has played a positive role in reducing vicious competition among SOEs and eliminating excess capacity. For example, an important consideration in the merger of CSR and CNR was to reduce the vicious competition between SOEs and to enhance the international competitiveness of CRRC as a whole. In the context of economic downturn and serious overcapacity in the iron and steel industry, in order to improve the overall competitiveness and concentration of the steel industry, eliminate backward production capacity, so that shifting the product development to high-end and finishing products, Baosteel and WISCO naturally merged into Baowu. As for the merger of CSSC and CSIC that is actively brewing, it is not difficult to find practical reasons such as how to quickly and better reduce production capacity and accelerate structural upgrading under the deep dip and shock of the global shipbuilding industry, which has become the key to China's shipbuilding industry to achieve corner overtaking. Compared with South Korea and other shipbuilding powerhouses, China's shipbuilding industry still has a lot of room to improve its concentration, and restructuring and integration are the general trend.

The question is, since there are many benefits of M&A, why should we emphasize, as in the title of this section, that mixing is better than merger in SOE reform?

First of all, the high profits brought by the temporary or local monopolistic industrial structure formed by the merger cover up the problems of system transformation that SOEs need to solve. In the long run, it is not conducive to the transformation of the SOE operating system and the improvement of management efficiency.

A typical example comes from Tianjin Bohai Steel Group, which has been exposed frequently in the media recently. Faced with serious overcapacity in the steel industry that emerged after the stimulus policies in response to the international financial crisis, the State Council issued the *Adjustment and Revitalization Plan of the Iron and Steel Industry* in March 2009, hoping to strive to form several mega steel enterprises with a capacity of over 50 million tons and several large steel enterprises with a capacity of 10 to 30 million tons by 2011. Under the guidance of the plan, the Tianjin Municipal Government merged four SOEs in 2010 to form Bohai Steel Group: Tianjin Pipe Corporation (TPCO), Tianjin Iron and Steel Group, Tianjin Tiantie Metallurgical Group and Tianjin Metallurgy Group. In 2014, after the financial statements of the above four companies were consolidated, Tianjin Bohai Steel Group was ranked 327th in the Fortune Global 500. In 2015, its ranking in the above list rose from 327th to 304th.

According to relevant media reports, the four subsidiaries merged into Tianjin Bohai Steel Group are old SOEs. Their problems in production and operation, product sales channels, and especially personnel placement, are troublesome. Each subsidiary operates independently and requires a lot of effort to coordinate. It is obviously not a one-day effort for the four different enterprises to achieve the initially expected M&A synergies and form strong joint forces from merger in form to real integration. However, after its establishment, Bohai Steel Group not only enjoyed the recessive guarantee and financial endorsement provided by the government as a mega SOE, but also has the reputation of Fortune Global 500. Almost all banks in Tianjin have offered loans to Bohai Steel Group at one time, and its credit line once reached 100 billion yuan, according to media statistics. It was both lucky and unfortunate. Backed by a large number of funds with relatively low costs, Bohai Steel Group inevitably embarked on the road of rapid expansion, leaving far behind the more important and fundamental issue of system transformation for SOEs.

It should be noted that the Fortune Global 500 ranking does not necessarily indicate the comprehensive strength and status of the company. In the past two years, there are not only many examples of Fortune Global 500 companies like Bohai Steel Group defaulting on their debts, but also many companies on the list whose operating income significantly exceeds the data in the audit report.

Compared with the time-consuming and laborious process of introducing strategic investors with private capital background to mixed ownership, the M&A of enterprises in the same industry are relatively simple to operate and seem to be able to directly achieve the purpose of expanding SOEs. The case of Tianjin Bohai Steel Group tells us that SOEs cannot be made bigger simply by merging them. They need to be stronger first to be bigger.

Second, the transformation of management system of SOEs covered by merger still needs to be solved by mixing. Because failing to complete the task of SOE reform by merger, Bohai Steel Group had to seek the help of mixing. Since the end of 2015, Bohai Steel Group has fallen into a serious debt crisis after rapid expansion, with 105 banks and financial institutions involved in liabilities amounting to 192 billion yuan. Subsequently, the production and operation of Bohai Steel Group fell into difficulties.

In terms of solving the debt crisis of Bohai Steel Group, the first thought of the Tianjin SASAC was to separate Tianjin Pipe Corporation (TPCO) from Bohai Steel Group in April 2016, which was in relatively good operating condition, to become an enterprise under the direct control of the Tianjin SASAC. After only six years of union, Tianjin Pipe Corporation and the other three companies entered the state of separation again. In the past, many SOEs were divided into different companies to improve competitiveness and operational efficiency. After several years, in order to achieve the purpose of making SOEs bigger, they were merged again in the way of matchmaking. But now, given the serious debt crisis and the failure to achieve institutional transformation, they must be separated again.

From the new measures launched by Tianjin government for Tianjin Pipe Corporation and Bohai Steel Group, on the one hand, at the level of real economy, the total 240 billion yuan liabilities of Bohai Steel Group series enterprises are divided into two batches: the steel industry and the non-steel industry. Among them, the steel industry introduced Delong Steel Limited with a private capital background as a strategic investor to carry out mixed-ownership reform. On the other hand, in terms of the state-owned assets management system, Tianjin SASAC transferred all the shares of Tianjin Pipe Corporation to Tianjin Bohai State-Owned Capital Investment Company, a wholly owned subsidiary of the Tianjin state-owned capital operation platform – Jinlian Investment Holdings – realizing the transformation of the state-owned assets management system from managing enterprises to managing capital.

As we know, the new round of reform of state-owned assets and state-owned enterprises featuring mixing is now mainly carried out at two levels in parallel. The first is to complete the transformation of the regulatory function from managing enterprises to managing capital at the level of state-owned assets management system. The SASAC, which used to manage personnel, affairs and enterprises, participated in the investment and capital operation of entity enterprises through restructuring and newly establishing investment and operating institutions as the interface between the government and enterprises, thus realizing the capitalization of state-owned assets and the effective separation of ownership and operation rights. The second is on the basis of corporate system reform, SOEs as operating entities introduce strategic investors to realize the mixture of ownership, improve corporate governance and establish a modern enterprise system. We can see that after the reform ideas of Tianjin Pipe Corporation and Bohai Steel Group experienced various difficulties brought by the merger, the Tianjin SASAC is now advancing and developing along the idea of mixing.

In a certain sense, the above-mentioned practice in Tianjin provides a good example for the SOE reform that mixing is better than merger, as we have emphasized in this book. In fact, only through mixing can we introduce strategic investors with clear profit motive and private capital background to form competition among major shareholders, thus automatically correcting errors and creating an effective separation of ownership and operation on the one hand, and transforming the management mechanism and establishing a long-term incentive mechanism on the other. Just as reform can be carried forward continuously only by maintaining continuous opening to the outside world and continuously providing external pressure and internal motivation for reform, we believe that only by mixing of different ownership can achieve the reform of management mechanisms, and only mixing can bring real reform. Merger can only temporarily solve the pain of SOE reform. If we want to fundamentally solve the transformation of SOE management mechanism, we can only achieve it through mixing. Therefore, in the choice of the path of SOE reform, we emphasize that it is better to mix rather than merge.

China Unicom, known as the first central enterprise to press ahead with mixed-ownership reform, provides a good example of reform through mixing to achieve a transformation in the management mechanism. After the completion of the mixed-ownership reform, strategic investors such as BATJ and China Life have five of the eight non-independent directors on the board of China Unicom, creating the so-called Unicom model, in which state-owned capital dominates in the equity structure and strategic investors dominate in the board organization. Previously, in state-owned holding listed companies, it was rare for non-state-owned institutional investors to appoint directors, let alone imagine that the directors they appointed accounted for the majority. Wang Xiaochu, chairman of China Unicom, said at the 5G/Innovation Summit held on April 23, 2019, that after the mixed-ownership reform, China Unicom has changed in terms of ideology, ethos and mechanism. Imagine what China Unicom would look like today if it did not implement mixed-ownership reform by introducing BATJ but merged with China Telecom. Of course, history cannot be assumed.

It is important to note that the mergers undertaken by some SOEs today do not appear to be as useless as one might think. The number of SOEs under the direct control of SASAC can be reduced by M&A of SOEs in similar or related industries. This creates positive conditions for the reorganization or reconstruction of state-owned holding group companies into capital investment and operating companies as the interface between government and enterprise, which will eventually facilitate the transformation of the state-owned asset management system from managing enterprises to managing capital. Eventually, this will facilitate the transformation of the state-owned assets management system from managing enterprises to managing capital.

3   SOE Mixed-Ownership Reform: Who to Share Uncertainty With

Since debt financing decisions in the daily operations of enterprises are mainly risk-taking behaviors, today's SOE reforms are more often associated with uncertainty. Therefore, the new round of SOE reform with the theme of mixed ownership needs to solve the problem of who to share the uncertainty with.

Knight, an American economist, distinguished between uncertainty and risk early on. In essence, the difference between the financial attributes of debt financing and equity financing is largely reflected in the difference between risk and uncertainty. To illustrate this point well, before discussing with whom SOEs should share uncertainty in mixed-ownership reform, we first use two stories that happened in the Mongolian steppe during the Ming and Qing dynasties to reveal the risk and uncertainty, and then analyze the difference between the financial attributes of debt financing and equity financing.

The first story is about Chinese merchants in Mongolia conducting a money lending business called the Issuance of Stamped Notes during the Ming and Qing dynasties. It is said that after his death, the Prince Sengge Rinchen, who had been in power in the late Qing dynasty, still owed no less than 100,000 taels of silver to Shanxi trade house Da Sheng Kui.[2] Aside from the usurious nature, from the perspective of business operation, the risk of stamped notes issued by Shanxi merchants in Mongolia was generally within the scope of control. For one thing, a mortgage guarantee makes a herdsman who accepts stamped notes face the possibility of having his yurt torn down and his cattle and sheep taken away if he failed to repay his debts. For another reason, based on business experiences, the Chinese merchants in Mongolia can generally estimate how many of the 100 herdsmen who have been given stamped notes will not be able to repay their debts when they fall due, and can even infer whether the number of such families will increase or decrease in the year based on the lushness of the pasture. In mathematical terms, the probability distribution of the risk of Chinese merchants in Mongolia engaging in stamped notes is measurable. In the language of the modern banking industry, risk management models can be developed to identify and control the risk of stamped notes.

Let's imagine that a Chinese merchant was invited to attend the wedding of a local herdsman and presented a considerable amount of money to his friend as a wedding gift. It would be completely impossible to predict in advance when he would recover the investment. In fact, it was an important custom of Mongolian herdsmen in the Ming and Qing dynasties to raise high betrothal gifts in a short period of time, which most poor herder families could not afford, by giving money to each other among friends and relatives. Even today, we know that marriage is not a matter of one's own discretion. A man needs the consent of not only a woman, but also her family and even her clan. Polygamy was practiced in Mongolia at that time. When the Chinese merchant was thinking about recovery of his investment by marrying a concubine, it was unfortunate for him, the herdsman may have just made the decision to marry a third wife. Therefore, we can see that in contrast to the probability distribution of stamped notes which can be measured and the risks can be controlled within a certain range, the investment of gift cash to a herdsman who marries is obviously unable to measure the probability distribution. Of course, there was no way to establish a risk management model to identify and control risks.

The Chinese merchant presents money to the Mongolian herdsman who marries, or to put it another way, the herdsman raises high betrothal gifts by accepting money. This involves more about what American economist Knight calls uncertainty, rather than the risk of lending stamped notes. As for the Chinese merchant in Mongolia, what is more frightening than the risks faced by issuing stamped notes is the uncertainty of the investment to the herdsman who marries. Therefore, the sharing of uncertainty is considered a more significant attribute of finance.

Before discussing with whom SOEs should share the uncertainty in their mixed-ownership reform, let's first see what uncertainties SOEs will face in the future. One of them is uncertainty about raw materials and markets. The industrial Internet can help use the Internet to solve the information asymmetry problem plaguing raw materials and markets of SOEs, and was once considered the "next flying pig"[3] after the consumer-oriented Internet in the Internet era. However, the imperfect competition and even monopolistic market structure formed by the concentration of raw material supply in a few enterprises makes the enterprises lack the incentive to join the industrial Internet. So where is the industrial Internet, the next flying pig? We still don't know today. The second is the uncertainty that comes from R&D and innovation. As for Internet finance, which is regarded as a good embodiment of financial innovation, we often hear the saying, "If it does well, it is Internet finance. If it does badly, it is financial fraud." It seems that there is only one step from financial innovation to financial fraud. R&D and innovation, including artificial intelligence, not only involves the cost-benefit analysis of R&D itself, but also faces many controversies and challenges, such as social ethics. The ongoing trade friction between China and the United States has undoubtedly brought new uncertainties to R&D and innovation. The third is other uncertainties. For example, how can SOEs strike a balance between improving the enterprise efficiency and keeping the bottom line of avoiding mass unemployment as one or more of housing, health care and education could be the last straw for the middle class at any time.

Given the uncertainties in the above three aspects faced by SOE mixed-ownership reform, we use the financial stories of four iron and steel companies to reveal with whom SOE mixed-ownership reform should share the uncertainties.

The first story comes from Dongbei Special Steel Group, which shares uncertainty with the bank. In 2016, Dongbei Special Steel Group fell into the debt crisis again when it proposed a new debt-to-equity swap plan that was opposed by creditors. Shen Wenrong's holding of Dongbei Special Steel Group was interpreted by the media as an accidental privatization. In fact, it was a desperate move by the local government to solve the debt crisis of Dongbei Special Steel. To a certain extent, the debt crisis of Dongbei Special Steel is a reappearance of what economist Kornai observed decades ago about how bank loans were transformed into bad and doubtful debts due to the softening of budget constraints. Therefore, we tend to see debt-to-equity swaps under the government intervention as a soft budget constraint in the guise of market-oriented operations. As we can see, whether the SOEs in the mixed-ownership reform can share the uncertainty with the banks in the form of debt-to-equity swap largely depends on whether the debt-to-equity swap is a real market-oriented behavior based on the value judgment and investors' willingness.

The second story comes from Tianjin Bohai Steel Group, a company that has shared uncertainty by merging local companies to huddle together for warmth. In 2010, four state-owned enterprises – Tianjin Pipe Corporation, Tianjin Iron and Steel Group, Tianjin Tiantie Metallurgical Group and Tianjin Metallurgical Group – merged to form Tianjin Bohai Steel Group. In 2014, after the financial statements were consolidated, Bohai Steel Group entered the Fortune Global 500 list of the world's largest companies. However, at the end of 2015, less than two years later, Bohai Steel Group fell into a serious debt crisis after rapid expansion, with debts of up to 192 billion yuan, involving 105 banks and financial institutions. In fact, the vast majority of the top 500 giants in the coal, steel and non-ferrous metals industries with state-owned backgrounds are merged enterprises. So how does Bohai Steel Group solve the new debt crisis? On the one hand, separate the companies that were originally merged. In April 2016, Tianjin Pipe Corporation, which had relatively good operating conditions, was stripped from Bohai Steel Group. On the other hand, Delong Steel Limited with a private capital background was introduced into Bohai Steel's iron and steel industry as a strategic investor to carry out mixed-ownership reform, thus returning to the SOE reform idea of mixing. We can see that the uncertainty shared with local enterprises through M&A only makes the transformation problem of institutional mechanism that SOEs facing temporarily covered up by superficial doing bigger, which makes the uncertainty increase rather than decrease.

The third story comes from Ma'anshan Iron & Steel Company, which shares the uncertainty with its excellent peer. On June 2, 2019, Ma'anshan Iron and Steel announced the restructuring of Ma'anshan Iron and Steel by China Baowu, and the SASAC of Anhui Province transferred 51% of Magang Group's equity to China Baowu without compensation. Through this restructuring, China Baowu will directly hold 51% of Magang Group and indirectly control 45.54% of Ma'anshan Iron and Steel through Magang Group, becoming the indirect controlling shareholder of Ma'anshan Iron and Steel. Although through the above restructuring, as the controlling shareholder of China Baowu, the SASAC of the State Council became the actual controller of Ma'anshan Iron and Steel, I believe that the local government has made great determination to transfer 51% equity of Magang Group to China Baowu without compensation. This event has been interpreted by some media as a landmark event of a new round of mixed-ownership reform in recent years, in which local enterprise has introduced central enterprise to carry out mixed-ownership reform, and the actual controller changed from the local SASAC to the SASAC of the State Council through M&A. It is also worth noting that Ma'anshan Iron and Steel and its controlling shareholder, China Baowu, both belong to the iron and steel industry. So they will face the challenge of the basic rules of the capital market, such as that horizontal competition is not allowed between listed companies and their parent companies. Of course, given that China Baowu has just completed the restructuring of Ma'anshan Iron and Steel, whether the uncertainty sharing with excellent peer is really conducive to the expected transformation of SOE system and mechanism remains to be further observed around the specific measures to improve the basic corporate governance system.

The last story comes from Chongqing Iron and Steel Group, which chose to share risks with excellent strategic investors. At the end of 2017, after the completion of the restructuring, the actual controller of Chongqing Iron and Steel was changed to Four Rivers Investment, which is equally held by four companies, including China Baowu, China-US Green Fund, China Merchants Group and WL Ross of the United States. According to Zhou Zhuping, chairman of Chongqing Iron and Steel, Four Rivers Investment as the actual controller "neither sent technicians, nor invested in facilities other than maintenance, nor replaced workers and middle-level staff"; instead, it retained the original outside directors, but only sent "five executives who had no experience in steel making".[4] Chongqing Iron and Steel Group, which had been on the road to bankruptcy for ten years, stopped the bleeding and came back to life in one year.

The restructuring case of Chongqing Iron and Steel proves again that the key issue to be addressed in the SOE mixed-ownership reform may not be the resources or the market, but how to form a motivation to transform the management mechanism. After the restructuring, Chongqing Iron and Steel faces the huge investment return pressure not only from original shareholders, but also from the new shareholders after the debt-to-equity swap, as well as Four Rivers Investment as the actual controller. In addition, realizing profitability as soon as possible has become the basic and the only motivation for the transformation of backward management mechanism, and the long-standing problems of traditional SOEs, such as multi-objective conflict, have been solved.

In summary, driven by the actual controller Four Rivers Investment, the restructured Chongqing Iron and Steel has made adjustments to the corporate governance structure in the following two aspects. First, establish an incentive mechanism for managers and employees based on the principle of marketization. After the restructuring in 2018, the annual salary of Chongqing Iron and Steel's CEO was 5.5391 million yuan, about ten times the general manager's annual salary of 548,900 yuan before the restructuring. Many incentives that SOEs try to implement but often end without success, such as the *Chongqing Iron and Steel Executive Compensation Incentive Plan* and the *2018–2020 Employee Stock Ownership Plan*, were launched after the restructuring of Chongqing Iron and Steel. Second, restore the CEO's role as the decision-making center of operation and management to achieve a rational division of labor between the CEO and the board of directors. We know that one of the main problems facing SOEs is a fuzzy boundary between the controlling shareholders, the board of directors and the managers, and the inability to effectively separate ownership and management rights. After the reorganization, the board of directors of Chongqing Iron and Steel explicitly authorized the CEO to have the power of institutional settings and technological transformation, and even allowed him to report to the board of directors for approval afterwards. On the other hand, the role of the board of directors returned to the basic functions of selecting, appointing and evaluating CEOs. As we can see, in choosing with whom to share the uncertainty, Chongqing Iron and Steel formed the pressure to transform the management mechanism by introducing excellent strategic investors with clear profit motive, and gathered the power to overcome the obstacles of the mechanism and system, and finally converged into the win-win cooperation of all parties, which has become the key point and breakthrough for Chongqing Iron and Steel to gain a new life after the restructuring.

Now let's briefly summarize the story of the four SOEs from the same industry. Faced with the debt crisis, they chose to share the uncertainty with different parties to carry out the mixed-ownership reform. As we have seen, Dongbei Special Steel Group chose to share the uncertainty with banks through debt-to-equity swaps, which became a soft budget constraint in the guise of market-oriented operations. In the end, Dongbei Special Steel had no choice but to take the path of privatization. Tianjin Bohai Steel Group chose to share the uncertainty by merging local companies into one group to huddle together for warmth. However, after a short period of glory, Bohai Steel Group went back to the separation and more fundamentally, introduced strategic investors with a private capital background to implement mixing. Restructured by China Baowu, Ma'anshan Iron and Steel chose an excellent peer from central enterprises to share the uncertainty. The actual effect of this emerging practice of local SOEs sharing uncertainty by introducing central enterprises in the same industry to carry out mixed-ownership reform remains to be further observed. In contrast, Chongqing Iron and Steel Group chose to share the uncertainty with excellent strategic investors, seeing this as the key point and breakthrough of mixed-ownership reform. This move has formed the pressure of transforming the management mechanism, gathered the power for overcoming the obstacles of mechanism and system, converged into the win-win cooperation of all parties, thus winning a new life for Chongqing Iron and Steel Group.

The stories of the four SOEs about with whom to share the uncertainty in the mixed-ownership reform clearly show that: just as only opening-up can promote reform, in the practice of SOE mixed-ownership reform, only mixing can truly achieve reform, and mixing is better than merger.

Notes

1 《郭广昌：国企改革目的是激发活力》. http://www.gaizhi.com.cn/index.php?m=content&c=index&f=show&catid=95&l=1&id=255.
2 Da Sheng Kui was the largest trade house with Mongolia founded by Shanxi people in the Qing dynasty.
3 Flying Pig Theory, also known as Tuyere Theory, refers to the words of Lei Jun, the founder of Xiaomi: entrepreneurship, is to be a pig standing on the tuyere. If the pig stands on the right tuyere, it can fly.
4 Xuefeng, Y. & Y. Xuan. (2019). 公司治理是企业发展最重要的因素 [Corporate governance is the most important factor for enterprise development]. *FX361.com*. https://www.fx361.com/page/2019/0619/5221249.shtml.

Bibliography

Baumol, W. J. (1982). Applied fairness theory and rationing policy. *The American Economic Review*, *72*(4), 639–651.

Bennedsen, M. & D. Wolfenzon (2000). The balance of power in closely held corporations. *Journal of Financial Economics*, *58*(1–2), 113–139.

Bolton, P. & E. L. Von Thadden (1998). Blocks, liquidity, and corporate control. *Journal of Finance*, *53*(1), 1–25.

Butler, N. M. (2009). *Why should we change our form of government?* New York: Charles Scribner's Sons, 1912, p. 82.

Cai, Guilong, Zheng Guojian, Ma Xinxiao, & Lu Rui. (2018). Decentralization and mixed-ownership reform in China. *Economic Research Journal*, *9*.

Cai, Guilong, Liu Jianhua, & Ma Xinxiao (2018). Non-state shareholders' governance and executive compensation incentives of SOEs. *Management World*, *5*.

Claessens, S., S. Djankov, & L. H. P. Lang. (2000). The separation of ownership and control in East Asian corporations. *Journal of Financial Economics*, *58*(1–2), 81–112.

Fang, Mingyue & Sun Kunpeng. (2019). Can mixed ownership reform of SOEs cure zombie firms? A mixed ownership pecking order logic. *Journal of Financial Research*, *1*.

Friedman, Milton. (1970). There is one and only one social responsibility of business—to increase its profits. *The New York Times Magazine*. September 13.

Geng, Yunjiang & Ma Ying. (2020). The influence of non-state-owned blockholders on the excess employees of state-owned enterprises: Cost effect or incentive effect. *Accounting Research*, 154–165.

Gomes, A. R. & W. Novaes. (2001). Sharing of control as a corporate governance mechanism. *Penn Caress Working Papers*, 1–2.

Grossman, S. J. & O. D. Hart. (1986). The costs and benefits of ownership: A theory of vertical and lateral integration. *Journal of Political Economy*, *94*(4), 691–719.

Hao, Yang & Gong Liutang. (2017). State and private non-controlling shareholders in SOEs and private firms, and firm performance. *Economic Research Journal*, *3*.

Hart, O. (1995). *Firms, Contracts, and Financial Structure*. Oxford: Oxford University Press.

Hart, O. & J. Moore. (1990). Property rights and the nature of the firm. *Journal of Political Economy*, *98*(6), 1119–1158.

Holmstrom, B. & P. Milgrom. (1991). Multitask principal-agent analyses: Incentive contracts, asset ownership, and job design. *Journal of Law, Economics, & Organization*, *7*, 24–52.

Jensen, M. C. (2005). Agency costs of overvalued equity. *Financial Management*, *34*(1): 5–19.

Jensen, M. C. & W. H. Meckling. (1976). Theory of the firm: Managerial behavior, agency costs and ownership structure. *Journal of Financial Economics*, *3*(4), 305–360.

Johnson, S., R. La Porta, F. Lopez-de-Silanes, & A. Shleifer. (2000). Tunneling. *American Economic Review*, *90*(2), 22–27.

Kornai, J. (1986). The soft budget constraint. *Kyklos*, *39*(1), 3-30.

Liu, Hanmin, Qi Yu, & Xie Xiaoqing. (2018). The allocation logic of equity Ownership and control rights from equivalence to non-equivalence: An empirical test of listed companies with mixed-ownership under the supervision of SASAC. *Economic Research Journal*, 5.

Lu, Dong, Huang Dan, & Yang Dan. (2019). The board power of non-ultimate-controller and M&A efficiency in state-owned enterprises. *Management World*, 6.

Ma, Lianfu, Wang Lili, & Zhang Qi. (2015). Pecking order of mixed ownership: The logic of market. *China Industrial Economics*, 7.

Ma, Xinxiao, Tang Taijie, & Cai Guilong. (2021). Governance of non-state shareholders and de-zombification of SOEs: Evidence from the "Mixed" board of directors of listed SOEs in China. *Journal of Financial Research*, 3.

Müller, H. M. & K. Wärneryd. (2001). Inside versus outside ownership: A political theory of the firm. *RAND Journal of Economics*, *32*, 527–541.

Qi, Haodong, Guo Junchao, & Zhu Wei. (2017). Mixed ownership reform of SOEs: Driving force, resistance and the implementation path. *Management World*, 10.

Wang, Dongjing. (2019). The path selection and operation ideas of the SOE reform. *Management World*, 2.

Yi, Yang, Jiang Fei, Liu Zhuang, & Xin Qingquan. (2021). Decentralized privatization, mixed-ownership reform and employee efficiency in China. *The Journal of World Economy*, 5.

Zheng, Zhigang. (2019). Shared control and the theoretical foundation of mixed ownership reform of SOEs. *Securities Market Herald*, 1.

Zheng, Zhigang. (2020). Logic, path and realization pattern choice of mixed reform of state-owned enterprises. *China Policy Review*, 1.

Zheng, Zhigang. (2021). Misunderstandings in the practice of mixed reform of state-owned enterprises and key issues for future breakthroughs. *Securities Market Herald*, 3.

Zheng, Zhigang. (2021). Mixed ownership reform of state-owned enterprises: Two modes, two misunderstandings and two Key Problems. *China Policy Review*, 2.

Zheng, Zhigang, & Liu Lanxin. (2022). Absence of owners and breakthroughs directions of mixed-ownership reforms of SOEs. *Economic Research Journal*, 2.

Index

Page numbers in *italics* indicate a figure and page numbers in **bold** indicate a table on the corresponding page. Page numbers followed by "n" indicate a note on the corresponding page.

Printed in the United States
by Baker & Taylor Publisher Services